Praise for
All Ages Becoming

"Valerie Grissom has put together a useful overview of recent work in intergenerational ministry with *All Ages Becoming*. This book includes voices from around the world and across a wide range of Christian expressions to introduce important topics and support those of us who want to invite people of all ages to gather together to learn and worship. Each chapter also contains helpful questions to encourage us to move past programs and to focus on forming the faith of those with whom we work as we apply what we are reading to our own contexts and ministries. This is a great book for a ministry team to study together."

   —**Robert J. Keeley,** PhD, Professor of Education, Emeritus, Calvin University; former visiting Professor of Faith Formation and Discipleship, Calvin Theological Seminary; author of *Helping Our Children Grow in Faith, Bridging Theory and Practice in Children's Spirituality, Shaped by God*, and *Dear Parent*

"I often get asked what books I recommend for ministers or parents/caregivers who are interested in connecting generations in relationship for discipleship. This book will now top the list. Not only do these authors give a wide array of information about intergenerational ministry, spiritual formation, and discipleship at church and at home, they do so in a way that is accessible to everyone who is looking to learn and grow their understanding. Whether someone comes looking for theological foundations or practical application, the answer can be found in one or more of the chapters included in the pages of this book. More than just a collection of articles, *All Ages Becoming* is a handbook for ministers and caregivers; one that will sit on the shelf in an easy-to-grab location for frequent reference and consultation."

   —**Rev. Dr. Christina Embree,** Director/Founder of ReFocus Ministry, Minister of Generational Discipleship, Great Lakes Conference, Brethren In Christ US

"To minimize generational conflicts or accommodate preferences, congregations often divide along age or affinity lines. Except in rare cases, all generations seem to lose. *All Ages Becoming* is a collaboration from an eclectic group of educators, theologians, and practitioners that serves as a model for unity even in our diversity. The convergence of their various cultures, expertise, and experience offers a practical guide any faith community can use to discover biblical and theological foundational principles to help frame their intergenerational practices. This timely resource reminds our congregations how much better we are when every generation is the Church together."

   —**Dr. David Manner,** Executive Director Treasurer, Kansas-Nebraska Convention of Southern Baptists, author of *Better Sundays Begin on Monday: 52 Exercises for Evaluating Weekly Worship*

"The third book in the InterGenerate series, *All Ages Becoming* adds much to the study, conversation, and practice of intentional intergenerational community for the Christian church. Woven throughout is the language and metaphor of 'becoming,' helping us understand that this transformation is always a work-in-progress. All the 'questions to consider' that are included help us ponder and process the content and ideas. I am grateful for these voices—the practitioners and the researchers alike; each one excited and committed to this critical approach to being the body of Christ, together."
   —**Liz Perraud,** Executive Director, GenOn Ministries

"What a gift this book is to the church today as we struggle with effective ways to engage and equip all generations *together*, including the youth and children that desperately need to know they belong with—and are connected to—an embodied community of faithful people who care deeply about their *becoming*! In my sojourn as an official children and family pastor in a large congregation, I would have given anything to get my hands and eyes on a book such as this one that brings together the best thinkers—and doers—for intergenerational formation! Now this gift for the church is yours to read and share, discuss and try out. As Linda Staats says in Chapter One of this meaty book, here is an invitation for all of us to find our place of becoming in the 'beautiful circular pattern of intergenerational blessing.'"
   —**Trevecca Okholm,** MA, former Children and Family Minister (PCUSA) and Professor of Practical Theology, Azusa Pacific University, coeditor of *Children's Ministry and the Spiritual Child: Practical Formation-Focused Ministry*

"*All Ages Becoming* is a fine addition to the growing body of theory and practice in intergenerational ministry and faith formation. The chapters address the needs of the veteran practitioner and those who are just beginning on the journey to an intergenerational future for their church. There is a wide scope of study—theological foundations, faith formation with parents and the family, intergenerational preaching and worship, intergenerational practices and models—all to help pastoral leaders create communities and ministries that are more intentionally intergenerational. Our future is intergenerational and *All Ages Becoming* is a guide to that future."
   —**John Roberto,** Lifelong Faith Associates, author of *Lifelong Faith: Formation for All Ages and Generations*

"What a beautiful picture of the body of Christ! *All Ages Becoming* not only allows you to envision intergenerational ministry but equips you with the theology needed to align your heart and soul to this lens of ministry and offers practices to make it realistic in your faith community and home."
   —**Joy Wendling,** Founder of Created to Play Ministries; Host of *Playfully Faithful Parenting* podcast; Christian Parenting Coach, Speaker, and Writer

"*All Ages Becoming* gives us both the theology and practice—the whys and hows—of intergenerational ministry. These chapters delve into the challenges and opportunities of bringing generations together and explore the life-giving transformations that can occur when we are in intentional relationship with others of different ages and stages as we try to follow Jesus. Whether you are looking for inspiration or ideas your congregation can take and run with, Valerie Grissom and her colleagues offer an increasingly relevant and deeply compelling way of being church in a changing world."

    —**Wendy Claire Barrie,** Canon for Intergenerational Ministries at Saint Mark's Episcopal Cathedral, Seattle, Washington; author of *Faith at Home: A Handbook for Cautiously Christian Parents*

"As the field of intergenerational ministry continues to gain traction, its great strength is the breadth of the voices engaged in research, advocacy, and storytelling. The authors in this compilation represent a wide range of theological and denominational traditions, guaranteeing that every reader will be encouraged and challenged to critically engage with the perspectives taken. Grissom has collated established authors, fresh voices, and emerging researchers into a work that will spark the imagination toward wise and creative intergenerational ministry practice in the local church."

    —**Tim Beilharz,** Children's Ministry Advisor and Intergenerational Ministry Lecturer at Youthworks

"*All Ages Becoming* is a new, rich, and life-giving text that all leaders who seek to engage across all ages need to read. It is like a choir of voices, all with their unique flavours and tones, coming together to bring harmony, strength, and beauty to the growing conversation of what it means for all ages to grow, love, and serve together. This book is filled with a balanced blend of theology and practice. It is easy to read and shares very helpful tools and keys to implement into your own faith communities and leadership."

    —**Tammy Preston,** Team Leader, Intergenerate Australia, and author of *Piece by Piece* and *Collide: Exploring Intergenerational Ministry*

"Imagine faith formation that is alive and engaging and seeks to form disciples of all ages. Intergenerational faith formation seeks to form every person in our faith communities, no matter where they are on the journey. Understanding that faith is not only passed down from those with much life experience but also passed up through the eyes of youth who see the world with fresh insights is at the heart of intergenerational faith formation. *All Ages Becoming* is a great resource to help faith communities move beyond traditional classroom-based programs toward dynamic faith formation that seeks to form disciples for a lifetime of growing in faith."

    —**Catherine Souto,** Pastoral Assistant for Religious Formation, The Catholic Community of St. Charles Borromeo, Skillman, NJ

"*All Ages Becoming* is a worthy addition to the growing intergenerational ministry canon. Featuring a well-judged mix of fresh and familiar voices, it helpfully blends theology, research, and practical ministry application into one very accessible book. Most powerfully, it is an invitation to become who we are meant to be as we reimagine faith practices, discipleship, worship, preaching—and more—with a focus on intergenerationality."

—**Chris Barnett,** Executive General Manager, Intergen, Australia; former Intergenerational Leader, Uniting Church Synod of Victoria and Tasmania

"*All Ages Becoming* is not only a superb read, it will alter the way you think about and practice intergenerational ministry. What sets this book apart is it moves readers from a theology of intergenerational ministry to how to practice it. Learning how to practice it from various voices helps readers imagine what is possible in their context. What I really love about the book is it invites readers to experiment and be open to what the faith communities can 'become' in the future."

—**F. Douglas Powe Jr.,** PhD, Director of Lewis Center for Church Leadership, James C. Logan Professor of Evangelism (E. Stanley Jones Chair), Wesley Theological Seminary

"Though pursuing intergenerational relationships is ingrained in the Chinese church community, employing intergenerational practice is challenging in a trilingual Chinese church setting. However, the authors of this book offer practical tips and strategies for implementing intergenerational practices, which are inspiring for trilingual settings, as well as compelling examples of how these practices can help to build stronger relationships and promote spiritual growth in the church. Whether you are a pastor, a church leader, a parent, or simply someone who cares about the future of the church, this book is a must-read. I highly recommend it!"

—**Rev. Dr. Amy Yu,** Charge Pastor of Next Generation Ministry, Scarborough Chinese Baptist Church

"COVID brought death and disruption, ushering our world into a virtual standstill. Although its devastation produced grief and pain, the pandemic has forced us to search for new paradigms in every arena of life, including communicating and practicing our faith. In *All Ages Becoming*, editor Valerie M. Grissom brings together scholars and practitioners contributing to a study of new models for such a time as this. *All Ages Becoming* introduces questions, suggestions, and options for corporate worship and discipleship that utilize the perspective, gifts, and needs of all ages. The reader is reminded the biblical example for discipleship begins with the home (Deut. 6:1–9), and the church as the Body of Christ is intergenerational."

—**Dr. Randel Everett,** President, 21Wilberforce Global Freedom Center, author of *Pillars: The Ten Commandments Still Standing after Centuries of Change* and *Speak Freedom: Developing Emergent Leaders in the Struggle for Justice*

"Intergenerational ministry is a growing frontier of practice that is being embraced by an increasing number of churches across the globe. In *All Ages Becoming*, Grissom brings together the 'A' team with cutting-edge biblical, theological, theoretical, and practical ideas to help theologians and practitioners move beyond programming toward faith formation for churches and homes. In this book you will find potent, life-changing intergenerational ideas that will transform the whole community."

—**Daron Pratt,** Children and Family Ministries Director for the Greater Sydney Conference of the Seventh-day Adventist Church, founding member of Intergenerate Australia

"Wow! This is one of the most comprehensive and rooted works on intergenerational ministry I have come upon in twenty-five combined years of ministry and research. Whether you are looking to get started in intergenerational ministry, you are teaching a class on intergenerational ministry, or you are a veteran family ministry practitioner, you will find each contribution refreshing and empowering. One feature I think makes this book stand out from other ministry books are the 'Theology in Practice' sections in each chapter that probe readers to think on how to apply the concepts and ideas from each chapter to their individual context through questions and challenges. Kudos to the Intergenerate team for putting together such a valuable resource!"

—**Dr. Henry Zonio,** PhD, Sociologist, Director, Center for Academic Excellence, Asbury University

All Ages
BECOMING

All Ages BECOMING

Intergenerational Practice in the Formation of God's People

Edited by
VALERIE M. GRISSOM

Abilene Christian University Press

ALL AGES BECOMING
Intergenerational Practice in the Formation of God's People

Copyright © 2023 by Valerie M. Grissom

ISBN 978-1-68426-401-8

Printed in the United States of America

ALL RIGHTS RESERVED

No part of this publication may be reproduced, stored in a retrieval system, or transmitted in any form by any means—electronic, mechanical, photocopying, recording, or otherwise—without prior written consent.

Scripture quotations noted ESV are from The ESV® Bible (The Holy Bible, English Standard Version®) copyright © 2001 by Crossway, a publishing ministry of Good News Publishers. ESV® Text Edition: 2016. The ESV® text has been reproduced in cooperation with and by permission of Good News Publishers. Unauthorized reproduction of this publication is prohibited. All rights reserved.

Scripture quotations noted *The Message* are taken from The Message. Copyright © 1993, 1994, 1995, 1996, 2000, 2001, 2002. Used by permission of NavPress Publishing Group.

Scripture quotations noted NIV are from the Holy Bible, New International Version®, NIV®. Copyright © 1973, 1978, 1984, 2011 by Biblica, Inc.™ Used by permission of Zondervan. All rights reserved worldwide.

Scripture quotations noted NKJV are taken from the New King James Version® Copyright © 1982 by Thomas Nelson. Used by permission. All rights reserved.

Scripture quotations noted NRSV are taken from the New Revised Standard Version Bible, copyright © 1989, the Division of Christian Education of the National Council of the Churches of Christ in the United States of America. Used by permission. All rights reserved.

Chapter 6, "The Final Frontier?," adapted and used by permission from David M. Csinos, *A Gospel for All Ages: Teaching and Preaching with the Whole Church* (Minneapolis: Fortress Press, 2022).

Cataloging-in-Publication Data is on file at the Library of Congress, Washington, DC.

Cover design by Greg Jackson, Thinkpen Design | Interior text design by Sandy Armstrong, Strong Design

For information, contact
Abilene Christian University Press
ACU Box 29138
Abilene, Texas 79699

1-877-816-4455
www.leafwoodpublishers.com

23 24 25 26 27 28 29 / 7 6 5 4 3 2 1

*This book is dedicated to my parents,
Jim and Sheila Grissom, who modeled for me
what it looked like to be intergenerational
before it was even a word.*

CONTENTS

Introduction	Practicing Our Becoming...	15
	Valerie M. Grissom	

Section One
FOUNDATIONS OF INTERGENERATIONAL PRACTICE

Chapter 1	Circle of Blessing: Foundation and Fundamentals for Intergenerational Ministry	31
	Linda E. Staats	
Chapter 2	Honoring the Image: Recovering a Creational Theology for Intergenerational Ministry	45
	Wilson McCoy	
Chapter 3	Ludicity and Theology: Exploring Some Theological Foundations of Intergenerational Ministry	57
	Gareth Crispin	

Section Two
REIMAGINING INTERGENERATIONAL PRACTICE

Chapter 4	Apprenticing Faith Together: Helping Adults Understand Discipleship and Their Role in Intergenerational Community...............................	75
	Johannah Myers	
Chapter 5	The Church's Role in Restoring Parents as Central to Discipleship	85
	Rachel Turner	
Chapter 6	The Final Frontier? Theological Insights to Support Imaginative Intergenerational Preaching	99
	David M. Csinos	
Chapter 7	Building Ramps Instead of Stairs: Universal Design in Planning Intergenerational Worship	117
	Robert Pendergraft	

Section Three
IMPLEMENTING FORMATIVE INTERGENERATIONAL PRACTICES

Chapter 8	Faith Practices in Community and at Home...............................	133
	Karen DeBoer	
Chapter 9	Growing Faith in Messy Church..	145
	Johannah Myers and Roberta J. Egli	

| Chapter 10 | Let the Spirit Lead: A Framework for Beginning and Sustaining Intergenerational Faith Formation 157
Breen Marie Sipes |
| Chapter 11 | Story Sharing as a Practice of Intergenerational "Being" 167
Valerie M. Grissom |

Section Four
STORIES OF INTERGENERATIONAL PRACTICE

| Chapter 12 | Reinventing Church with Intergenerational Connections: A Case Study 191
Jim Merhaut |
| Chapter 13 | Creating Space to "Taste and See" the Goodness of Intergenerational Ministry 207
Wes Gallagher |
| Chapter 14 | Intergenerational Worship Experiments at Virginia Seminary 217
Sarah Bentley Allred |
| Chapter 15 | Being *Familia*: Latino Intergenerational Connections—Honoring Our Generational and Cultural Treasures 227
Elizabeth Tamez Méndez |

Section Five
SURVEY OF CURRENT INTERGENERATIONAL PRACTICES

| Chapter 16 | Benefits, Challenges, and Recommendations for Intergenerational Ministry: Findings from Recent Congregational Research 243
Holly Catterton Allen |

| Conclusion | A Challenge and Invitation to Become 265
Valerie M. Grissom |

Selected Bibliography 273
About the Contributors 277
Acknowledgments 283

INTRODUCTION

PRACTICING OUR BECOMING

VALERIE M. GRISSOM

> *"Beware of harking back to what you once were when God wants you to be something you have never been."*
>
> —Oswald Chambers

A Story of Becoming

At eight years old, I discovered a fluttery ping-pang in the mason jar I had hidden away weeks earlier, its lid still full of nail holes. Inside, a brand-new yellow and black swallowtail butterfly, with spots of orange and dusty blue, attempted to flap its new lacy wings, fragile and delicate.

Resembling the crinkly skin on a new baby, the new butterfly's accordion-like wings that had been crumpled up in its cocoon worked to unfold. I scurried to open the jar in which I had previously placed the bulgy, lime-green caterpillar weeks before—the jar I lost interest in when the caterpillar lethargically ate its way to the top leafy branch, snuggling in for a long nap; disappearing into a leaf-induced coma, and overnight, spinning a chrysalis, transforming from colorful to colorless, lifeless, gray. I had given up watching this caterpillar "sleep," wondering if it had even been worth collecting. This caterpillar seemed dead, with no life in sight.

Now the cocoon-turned-butterfly slowly jumped out, taking wobbly baby steps, trying to flap its folded wings. It was trying to teach itself how to fly. I placed this delicate butterfly on my hand. It tickled me with its new black antennae, as it crawled slowly up my arm onto my elbow, then onto my shoulder. By then, my younger siblings had joined me, watching in awe—sharing the wonder of how something that had looked so drab and lifeless before could now look beautiful and new. The transformation enthralled us—what had looked dead now looked alive.

Soon, a new problem put a lump in my throat. What began as wonder now transformed into a sense of trepidation. Would this delicate creature survive? Was she really suited for the harsh realities of this world? How could she make her way when she could barely unfold her wings, let alone fly? We decided to "train" the butterfly. On our front porch steps, we coaxed the beautiful butterfly to fly. Still, it crawled on the ground, unsure of itself. Gradually, its unfolded wings became more comfortable. Newness wore off, and the butterfly flapped its wings with ease, practicing ascent. Still, it did not yet know it was a butterfly. It did not know it could fly. So it dropped ever-so-lightly to the ground. Each time, we thought it would break its delicate wings. But each time, it got braver and more experimental. Soon, it flew a foot above the ground, then a yard. Then it landed again on my arm, and then on my head.

Minutes became hours as we watched this butterfly move from baby steps to preflight checks toward aerial prowess. As this new butterfly practiced what it was to *become*, I had a new lump in my throat—a lump of sadness, this time. I realized this butterfly could never remain in a jar or on my porch; it was destined to fly. With each airborne stride, I realized my fat little caterpillar, turned cocoon, turned butterfly, was now to *become* free—to fly away and *become* the butterfly it was always meant to be. The butterfly flew to our flowery bush, then to our tree, to the neighbors' flowers, and out of sight . . .

What Is the Church Becoming?

As I look toward the future, I see so many similarities between this new butterfly and the unfolding wings of the Church[1]—especially in regard to the intergenerational movement forging ahead in our present time. In the past few years, our churches have experienced massive transformation—some changes for good and some warranting concern.

In March of 2020, the COVID-19 pandemic reshaped not only how we live but how we worship. Churches around the world grappled with these questions: *What in the church is essential? Can we really have community online? Who is being left in the margins when we have online worship? How can we honor and protect our oldest, most vulnerable generations? How do we include our younger generations online?* In addition to a worldwide health crisis, we saw the largest global recession since the Depression, supply shortages, and deep racial and political tension. Due to COVID-19, people of all ages suffered from trauma, death, grief, isolation, depression, and so much more.

Meanwhile, our church leaders have been scrambling to keep up with these new pandemic-shaped realities—worship at home, Zoom worship, hybrid worship, worship with masks, COVID resurgences. All the while, we struggle to help *all* ages and *all* generations feel seen, heard, and loved. Exhaustion of leaders, parents, families, elders, and children lingers, even as we continue to crawl our way out of the COVID cocoon and "back to church."

And reports say burnout in ministry leaders is at an all-time high.[2] In the corporate world, they are calling it the Great Resignation—where people are quitting their jobs in massive numbers. A Barna study reports that 40 percent of pastors considered quitting full-time ministry as of March 2022.[3]

---

[1] Capitalization of "Church" denotes the universal church created by God in Christ Jesus (Gal. 3:26–29); lowercase refers to the local church.

[2] Mara Sassoon and Andrew Thurston, "Why Are So Many Religious Leaders Facing Stress and Burnout?" *The Brink*, March 17, 2022, https://www.bu.edu/articles/2022/why-are-so-many-religious-leaders-facing-stress-and-burnout/.

[3] Scott Thumma, "Is a Great Resignation Brewing for Pastors?," Religion News Service, March 18, 2022, accessed October 29, 2022, https://religionnews.com/2022/03/18/is-a-great-resignation-brewing-for-pastors/.

All the while, in the church, leaders are asking, *Will the people ever come back? Where are all the parents with young children?*

Even though COVID cases and restrictions are waning and we have resumed in-person worship, people are still not "coming back" to church in the way we hoped.[4] Studies released in January of 2023 say that, while attendance is returning closer to pre-pandemic numbers in older generations, the percentage of young adults (18–29) who have completely stopped attending church has increased from 30 percent in 2018 to 43 percent as of April 2022—a trend already evident before the pandemic.[5]

Some generations (especially older ones) ask: "Why are you still talking about the pandemic? It's all but over; let's get back to living our best life!" Younger generations, on the other hand, who have experienced educational upheaval, job loss, parenting crises, and financial stress are indignant, insistent that we do not overlook the trauma they have experienced and the new realities they face post-pandemic. Meanwhile, in the church, we forge a new path forward, together, with all these tensions, realities, polarities, uncertainties, and generational discord.

Did "Intergenerational" Go Away?

During the pandemic, many asked, Did "intergenerational" go away? Surprisingly, we observe "intergenerational" continuing to thrive in new and exciting ways—generations coming together to share faith through small groups in the home and on Zoom, FaceTime, evening prayer, outside, and in the gym. Invention, creativity, persistence, and innovation have

---

[4] Justin Nortey, "More Houses of Worship Are Returning to Normal Operations, but In-Person Attendance Is Unchanged Since Fall," Pew Research Center, March 22, 2022, https://www.pewresearch.org/fact-tank/2022/03/22/more-houses-of-worship-are-returning-to-normal-operations-but-in-person-attendance-is-unchanged-since-fall/.

[5] Lindsey Witt-Swanson, Jennifer Benz, and Daniel A. Cox, "Faith After the Pandemic: How COVID-19 Changed American Religion; Findings from the 2022 American Religious Benchmark Survey," Survey Center on American Life, January 5, 2023, https://www.americansurveycenter.org/research/faith-after-the-pandemic-how-Covid-19-changed-american-religion; Bob Smietana, "More Americans Stay Away from Church as Pandemic Nears Year Three," Religion News Service, January 5, 2023, https://religionnews.com/2023/01/05/more-americans-stay-away-from-church-as-pandemic-nears-year-three/; David Roach, "Church Attendance Dropped Among Young People, Singles, Liberals," *Christianity Today*, January 9, 2023, https://www.christianitytoday.com/news/2023/january/pandemic-church-attendance-drop-aei-survey-young-people-eva.html.

shown us that "intergenerational" continues to flourish. And churches keep *becoming*, unfolding those wings, experimenting with new ways forward.

And this kind of experimentation and innovation is nothing new when it comes to Christian community. Whenever we seek to *be* the body of Christ, practices of intergenerationality emerge. To *be* intergenerational is to live more fully into what it means to *be* the body of Christ. Thus, "intergenerational" cannot go away when we continue to practice *being* the people of God.

Becoming through Intergenerational Christian Practice

In Romans 12:2, we, the people of God, are called to be "transformed" (Greek for "metamorphosis")[6] in a metamorphic-like process of transformation akin to the butterfly. We are God's people, all transforming, practicing in different stages—in the same way the butterfly *becomes* by experiencing metamorphosis: egg, larva, pupa, and butterfly. We recognize that we are all in the midst of *becoming* transformed to be more like Christ.

The whole metamorphic process is miraculous—how God designed a bumbly caterpillar to transform into something completely new as beautiful, delicate, and majestic as the butterfly. In the adult stage, the butterfly is called the Imago (Latin for "image").[7] According to *Encyclopedia Britannica*, a "remarkable process" occurs: "from caterpillar to adult, most of the caterpillar tissue disintegrates and is used as food, thereby providing energy for the next stage of development, which begins when certain small structures (imaginal disks) in the larva start growing into the adult form."[8] The parallels here to Christian transformation are uncanny: we die to self (Gal. 2:20) and take on a new DNA—the image of God (*imago Dei*)—as we are transformed to be more like Christ. This picture of metamorphic,

---

[6] μεταμορφοῦσθε, "metamorphoō," "transformed"—"to change into another form, to transform, to transfigure," in blueletterbible.org, accessed June 21, 2023; also see Dan Story, "What Does Metamorphosis Have to Do with Becoming 'Transformed' in Romans 12:2?" May 22, 2016, http://danstory.net/what-does-metamorphosis-have-to-do-with-becoming-transformed-in-romans-122/.

[7] I must give credit for the correlation between Imago and the *imago Dei* (Image of God) in the process of metamorphosis to Pastor Matt Chambers, Sermon "#4: The Gift of Transformation," The Gifts of Christmas Series, South Whidbey Assembly of God, Langley, Washington, December 18, 2022.

[8] "Life cycles of animals," in *Encyclopedia Britannica*, https://www.britannica.com/science/reproduction-biology/Life-cycles-of-animals#ref607676.

Christian transformation is beautiful and nothing short of the miraculous work of God.

Practices, or spiritual disciplines, according to Dorothy C. Bass, are "shared activities that address fundamental needs of humankind and creation and that, woven together, form a way of life."[9] In *Liturgy of the Ordinary: Sacred Practices in Everyday Life,* Tish Harrison Warren states: "God is forming us into a new people. And the place of that formation is in the small moments of today."[10] For Harrison, the smallest of rhythms and patterns, or practices, in the everyday become sacramental-like moments where God extends grace and forms us to be more like Christ. In the same way, in our ministries and churches, we can choose rhythms and patterns of intergenerational Christian practice that form us to be more like Christ and to *become* the people of God.

Intergenerational Christian practices are *intentionally shared rhythms and patterns of participation in Christian community that foster relationships with God among all ages and help us mutually honor God and one another for the sake of becoming more like Christ.* God's design for the Church, as seen in the pattern of Scripture, was for us to live in intergenerational faith communities in which we practice growing in our faith together. As we participate in intergenerational relationships and spiritual patterns of our God-formed family of faith, we are transformed to be more like Christ; we all *become* God's people by *being* God's people. Thus, intergenerational Christian practice is more than a list of ideas, implementations, aspirations, or an ideal to model; rather, it is a *way of life for all generations, together, to become God's people.*

Intergenerational Christian practice reflects miraculous metamorphic transformation; as we share in intergenerational rhythms that help us participate in the family of God, we take on the new family DNA of God (Gal. 3:26–29)—we *become* who we were created to be, in the image of God, as part of God's intergenerational community of faith. Intergenerational Christian practices, when repeated, continually put on this new DNA,

---

[9] Dorothy C. Bass, *Practicing Our Faith: A Way of Life for a Searching People,* 2nd ed. (San Francisco: Jossey-Bass, 2010), xiii.

[10] Tish Harrison Warren, *Liturgy of the Ordinary: Sacred Practices in Everyday Life* (Downers Grove, IL: InterVarsity Press, 2016), 21.

becoming formational spiritual acts, habits, and patterns that form us while *being* in Christian community.

Unlike caterpillars, which are what scientists call "terminal," or unable to reproduce, the Imago adult butterfly can reproduce. In the same way, when we participate in *becoming* the body of Christ through intergenerational Christian practices, we *become* part of a reproducible, ongoing faith transformation, transmitted and reproduced from one generation to the next.

In metamorphosis, transformation is a *process*. We cannot skip a step, but we can have faith that our practice is taking us forward toward God's intended result. Ephesians 2:10 states, "we [the Church] are God's handiwork, created in Christ Jesus to do good works, which God prepared in advance for us to do" (NIV). We are destined to transform into God's beautiful creation—the "handiwork of God." *All Ages Becoming* offers an overview of what we are learning and experiencing in and through intergenerational Christian practice.

Section One: Foundations of Intergenerational Practice

Just as the butterfly in my opening story was unsure who she was, many of us still work to define what "intergenerational" really is. Here, we invite you to explore theological foundations of intergenerational Christian practice.

As with any movement or practice in the church, we must first attend to our theological underpinnings. We cannot *become* when we do not know what we shall *become*. With that in mind, Linda E. Staats, who represents decades of experience in intergenerational Christian practice, describes the beautiful circular pattern of intergenerational blessing. She uniquely lays down an intergenerational foundation that will help both newcomers and longtime practitioners explore the basis and theological foundations for intergenerational practice.

Next, Wilson McCoy recovers a deeper "why" of intergenerational practice: how creational theology based on the *imago Dei* (image of God) enlarges our understanding of intergenerational ministry. He explores what it means for us to honor God's image in one another and, in turn, helps us bear God's image to one another in community.

In our third chapter, Gareth Crispin challenges readers to reexamine their theology of the Holy Spirit, and how the Spirit's work can lay a fertile ground for a more inclusive, intergenerational community. Drawing on the term ludicity (Latin for "play"), Crispin notes how some churches have successfully created contexts with high levels of participation, informality, freedom, and relational safety among members. Can theological convictions and our experience of God nurture intergenerational Christian practice? This section, as well as future sections, should help you begin thinking intergenerationally and identify many questions you can discuss with others as you personalize and embody the theological foundations of intergenerational practice.

Section Two: Reimagining Intergenerational Practice

As a child, I found it difficult to envision a gray cocoon *becoming* a beautiful butterfly. In the same way, churches often struggle to envision intergenerational services, operating in old paradigms and systems; we lack an intergenerational imagination to see what intergenerational ministry could look like in future practice. Section Two offers four intergenerational reimaginations regarding apprenticeship, family discipleship, preaching, and worship—all key areas in need of new intergenerational imagination. These chapters explore both theology and practice, challenging leaders to reimagine how their community might be more intentionally intergenerational.

Johannah Myers offers a reimagining of adult roles in intergenerational discipleship, giving new advice for apprenticing faith. Here, Myers holds up Jesus's ministry as an apprenticeship model, in direct contrast to current methods that prioritize knowledge-based discipleship—not knowing *about* Jesus, but living and experiencing Jesus in an intergenerational community of faith.

Rachel Turner then casts a new intergenerational reimagining of family discipleship in which the church empowers parents to become primary disciplers in the home. Often, in our current church scenarios, church culture elevates everyone but the parents; rather, she shows us how we, in intergenerational community, might reimagine a new way that empowers and enables parents of all ages to disciple children of all ages and pass down faith to the next generation. Turner offers advice to intergenerational leaders for implementing intergenerational practices that can cultivate this kind of parental discipleship for all ages.

Next, David M. Csinos offers a much-needed new theology for intergenerational preaching that sets aside old presumptions and casts a fresh imagination, allowing for the innovation of intergenerational preaching practices. And finally, Robert Pendergraft, who draws upon the principles of universal design, reimagines worship that is accessible for and engages all ages. He calls us as intergenerational leaders to use the intergenerational Christian practice of building "ramps" instead of "stairs"; all ages with differing levels of ableness are given "ramps" that invite and empower them to participate and respond in worship.

As you engage with this section, our prayer is that you will be inspired to reimagine these key areas of apprenticeship, discipleship, preaching, and worship. In turn, our hope is that you will be challenged to reimagine other intergenerational theologies and practices unique to your context.

Section Three: Implementing Formative Intergenerational Practices

Just as a new butterfly has to "practice" being a butterfly, the church must "practice" *being* intergenerational. But the question here moves past the question of "what" and now becomes "how?" My son's percussion teacher often tells him that he cannot get rid of bad habits; he can only replace them with good habits. Implementing healthy intergenerational Christian practice is key to fostering intergenerational values and helping people live more deeply into what it means to *be* the people of God.

We must also realize that intergenerational Christian practices are part of a transformational *process*. Practices are just that—practice! A mindset bent on perfection or completion is not one of practice. Thus, each intergenerational Christian practice becomes an experiment, constantly open to alteration and revision. As we learn and grow and participate more deeply in our intergenerational Christian practices, we might need to adjust, remove, reimagine, or create. We cannot take ourselves too seriously in this process. We will fail. We will make mistakes. Even in the muddling and mistakes, we are formed. With each step, intergenerational Christian practices teach, advise, enlighten, inspire, and renew us.

Karen DeBoer, an experienced teacher and writer regarding intergenerational faith practices, starts by offering a tutorial on the why and how of faith practices, followed by some very practical ways we can incorporate intergenerational faith practices right now, and throughout the week, in our faith communities and at home. Next, Johannah Myers and Roberta J. Egli of Messy Church explore how intergenerational faith communities, using the model of Jesus, can incorporate intergenerational practices for creating space where faith can grow. Breen Marie Sipes follows with a chapter on intergenerational Christian practices for leaders to incorporate that allow the Spirit to lead, cultivating spiritual formation in both leaders and participants. Finally, my chapter discusses how intergenerational story sharing can become an intergenerational Christian practice that helps faith communities practice being the body of Christ in a deeper, fuller way.

Altogether, these intergenerational practices are a sampling of ideas; but even more, they are a tutorial on how to develop and implement the *process* of intergenerational practices. By thinking through their formative power, we, as the body of Christ, can engage with intergenerational Christian practice in tangible, formative ways.

Section Four: Stories of Intergenerational Practice

If you have not figured it out yet, I am a musician—hence, my emphasis on practice! Good practice involves experimentation and innovation. Part of musical practice is the art of improvisation—taking the fundamentals and the music and making it your own. Just as the butterfly in the opening story started branching out and trying new things, working toward flying, in order to *become*, we must engage in intergenerational experiments of practice.

Section Four includes stories of four intergenerational leaders who have experimented with intergenerational Christian practice in their own faith communities. First, leadership and life coach Jim Merhaut shares how his faith community used reinvention principles to implement change to start a new intergenerational worship gathering; through the process, Merhaut shares principles of reinvention we can apply to our unique contexts.

Next, Wes Gallagher shares how he learned, in his role as a children's pastor, the intergenerational Christian practice of creating subcultures (smaller communities within the larger community) where people might experience the "taste and see" of intergenerational ministry. Many of us intergenerational leaders can identify with Gallagher's plight, where he is not able to make church-wide, systemic decisions; thus, the practice of creating intergenerational subcultures becomes vital for those lacking total authority to make systemic change.

Next, Sarah Bentley Allred shares her rubber-meets-the-road story of learning how to plan intergenerational worship, offering many practical insights she learned along the way. Allred offers many ideas for implementing intergenerational practices, tailoring them to your context. Finally, Elizabeth Tamez Méndez, founder and executive director of a global, intergenerational organization called NG3, shares how she learned to practice *familia* by honoring the generational and cultural treasures in her unique Latin American context—an intergenerational Christian practice we can apply to each and every one of our own faith communities.

Though these stories have their unique particularities, here we see implementation of intergenerational practice in progress and realize that by sharing in each other's stories of intergenerational practice, we are formed and inspired to experiment with and implement new intergenerational Christian practices. As with all the other sections, we provide questions to help you consider how you might apply their learnings to your context.

Section Five: Survey of Current Intergenerational Practices
Although I cannot be sure, the butterfly in my story probably never understood what it was to *become* until it soared in flight, taking an aerial view of all that had been, and what happened, and what was to come. In the last chapter, Holly Catterton Allen provides an aerial view, or survey, of more current intergenerational Christian practice by reviewing doctoral projects, theses, and dissertations focusing on intergenerational ministry from 2010 to 2020. She unpacks the findings from these doctoral projects regarding

intergenerational leadership, worship, learning, and other practices. Allen, whose main area of research for two decades has been intergenerational ministry, also shares her own conclusions regarding intergenerational practice. As we all continue to practice intergenerationally, her insights here inspire us to continue practicing—to facilitate new ideas, new innovations, new research, new study, and new experiments—as we engage in future intergenerational Christian practice.

Become What You Receive

> But you are a chosen race, a royal priesthood, a holy nation, a people for God's own possession, that you may proclaim the excellencies of God who called you out of darkness into God's marvelous light. Once you were not a people, but now you are God's people; once you had not received mercy, but now you have received mercy. (1 Pet. 2:9–10 ESV)[11]

Often, in church liturgy, pastors and priests invite the people of God to Eucharist, or Communion, in thanksgiving, using the words of St. Augustine of Hippo: "Behold what you are, *become* what you receive."[12] As you receive and engage in these stories of transformational *becoming* through intergenerational Christian practice, I invite you to be reminded that you are what you receive; you are a child of God; you are a gift from God; you are God's people. You are that picture of beautiful, divine, metamorphic transformation when you participate in intergenerational Christian practice. I urge you to behold God's goodness and blessing that surround your intergenerational community and to *become* what you receive, as you receive the blessing of engagement and participation in intergenerational Christian practice.

---

[11] Pronouns changed by author to avoid gendered language for God.
[12] St. Augustine of Hippo, quoted in Matthew Peat, "Behold What You Are, Become What You Receive," in St. Mary's Church Whitkirk, June 4, 2015, accessed January 21, 2023, https://whitkirkchurch.org.uk/sermons/2015/06/behold-what-you-are-become-what-you-receive, emphasis mine.

How to Use This Book

As you engage with this book, remember that intergenerational Christian practice is formational and unique to your context—a process that happens in community. With that in mind, we offer "Theology in Practice" sections that help you move from the theoretical to the practical. These questions are designed to help you reflect and reimagine both individually and in community, to consider how these ideas and stories might shape your future intergenerational practice.

> *I'm a butterfly ~ in the making*
> *In a protected, sheltered state*
> *I know you wish to see me fly*
> *I know it's hard for you to wait*
> *I can't be rushed or hurried*
> *I need the struggle to break free*
> *My wings are not yet fully formed*
> *I'm not ready. Can't you see?*
> *I'm a butterfly ~ in the making*
> *The pain and struggle are very real*
> *I wish I could make you understand*
> *I wish you could feel what I feel*
> *Maybe you thought I don't try hard enough*
> *Maybe you thought I wanted to stay*
> *I wish you could see how hard I'm trying*
> *To spread my wings and fly one day*
> *Step inside my chrysalis*
> *Take a look inside my world*
> *Then perhaps you'd understand*
> *Why I'm like a rose, struggling to be unfurled.*

—Gayle McMillan, July 16, 2018

Section One

FOUNDATIONS OF INTERGENERATIONAL PRACTICE

*"It's not necessarily the amount of time you spend at practice that counts; it's **what** you put into the practice."*
—Eric Lindros, Professional Hockey Player

CHAPTER 1

CIRCLE OF BLESSING
Foundation and Fundamentals for Intergenerational Ministry

LINDA E. STAATS

"We are what we repeatedly do. Excellence, then, is not an act but a habit."
—Will Durant

I grew up in rural Iowa, where I was surrounded by eight living grandparents and great-grandparents, all of whom lived within fourteen miles of my home. The adults in my small congregation and community called me by name. I knew I was loved and I belonged. It wasn't until I was an instructor in a metropolitan community college that I realized my childhood experience was not the norm. I was surprised to learn that many of my students had few caring adults in their lives, let alone loving, "meddling" grandparents. Later, as Minister for Faith Formation in a large suburban congregation and then serving in a similar role at a judicatory and national level, I was dismayed to learn that intergenerational relationships and ministry were the exception rather than the normal practice in our communities of faith.

Christian leaders and educators have become so accustomed to age-specific culture, curriculums, and interaction that there is often hesitation and even fear at the idea of bringing all generations together. My hope is that this chapter adds to the reader's desire and confidence in creating a **"Circle of Blessing"**—*a community of faith that includes all generations and ages, in all stages of faith and life, where intergenerational ministry simply becomes the natural approach in all we plan and do.*

What Is Intergenerational Ministry?

Intergenerational ministry nurtures Christ-centered community by bringing together two or more generations in planned and purposeful settings where all are mutually invested.[1] Intergenerational ministry is more than a program; it serves as a lens and a foundation for how we see, think, plan, and evaluate ministry. More importantly, the focus is to be truly the body of Christ! The body of Christ, in the Circle of Blessing, is complete when the perspectives and unique gifts of *all* generations are engaged in the ministry and life of a congregation and its community (Luke 15:3–7).

Intergenerational ministry is purposeful, interactive, and inclusive. Intergenerational ministry values the needs, gifts, and perspectives of each generation, resulting in an entire community of faith, its neighborhood, and its households becoming energized. When people of every age care for one another, share highs and lows, worship, learn, and serve together inside and outside the walls of the church, relationships and ministries across the age span are strengthened, and the presence of the Holy Spirit is undeniably felt.

Intergenerational ministry moves away from age-segregated or age-specific ministry, for which there is still a valid time and place. Intergenerational ministry is distinct from multi-age or multigenerational curriculum and ministry where several ages, grades, or decades of participants are grouped together (e.g., Sunday school, youth group, older-adult ministry). Instead, intergenerational ministry is a congregation's commitment to crisscross the borders of age and stages of life,

---

[1] I adapted my definition of intergenerational ministry from GenOn Ministries, accessed October 29, 2022, https://www.genonministries.org/pages/intergenerational-ministry-all-about-intergenerational-ministry.

to create a sustainable, resilient community of faith that breathes life into households and neighborhoods—and to bring hope and healing to the world.

Why Intergenerational Ministry?

Intergenerational ministry is not new! A quick Internet search reveals more than eighty references to generations in the Bible, both in the Old Testament and throughout the New Testament.[2] Pages of biblical text list the genealogy of families, lifting up stories and connections from generation to generation. Authentic relationships between generations and in the gathered community are embedded in our Christian and Jewish faith traditions and in the rituals and practices of our varied denominations.[3]

In Deuteronomy 6:6-7, parents are encouraged to be the teachers of faith—at home and away from home. In Psalm 78:1-6, the generations are encouraged to share their personal experiences of God in order to nurture and keep faith alive. In the Gospels of Matthew, Mark, and Luke, Jesus welcomes and blesses children in the midst of a gathering of adults (Matt. 18:2-6, 10; 19:13-15; Mark 9:36-37; 10:13-16; Luke 9:47-48; 18:15-17). The interchange between David and Saul (1 Sam. 17:31-40), as David prepares to fight Goliath, is an example of God equipping the younger generation with the tools and resources needed, even in the most challenging of times. Biblical characters followed God's call to lead and serve at every age—such as Mary, Jeremiah, Timothy, Samuel, Moses, Sarah and Abraham, Simeon, and Hannah. No one was, or is, too old or too young to be Christ's disciple.

The gifts and perspectives of every generation are needed to create and sustain our communities of faith. By bringing all ages together to hear, know, and give witness to God's story, we discover God's story in one another's story. *Creating an intentional community of all ages—a Circle*

---

[2] For this search, I used biblegateway.com and searched for the words "generation"/"generations" in several translations. I had the following results: *The Message* (37/88), CEV (23/43), KJV (114/206), NRSVUE (108/196). I give a very rough estimate of over eighty.

[3] Christina Embree, "What the Bible Says about Intergenerational Ministry," Good Faith Media, October 10, 2016, accessed October 29, 2022, https://goodfaithmedia.org/what-the-bible-says-about-intergenerational-ministry-cms-23671/.

***of Blessing**—creates opportunity to celebrate God's presence and ongoing activity in every generation.*

My consistent, persistent rallying cry when working with congregational leaders echoes the words of Peter L. Benson: "As a community of faith, we possess a vast untapped potential to gather ALL the generations around the cross of Christ—to create a robust faith that carries individuals through every age, stage, and milestone of life; and [to] equip them to be active, authentic witnesses to the good news of Jesus Christ, at home and away from home!"[4]

Living into a vision for becoming a vibrant intergenerational community of faith and the body of Christ includes these practices:

- Weaving together the views, skills, perspectives, and unique gifts of children, youth, young adults, adults, and elders into the practical, everyday life and witness of a Christian faith community and its households.
- Nurturing lifelong discipleship where generations equip one another and their households as centers for practicing the Christian faith.
- Naming and encouraging the gifts seen in one another in order to grow, shape, mentor, and develop leaders.
- Bringing together youth and caring adults in service learning that transforms the relationship, creates shared stories, and fosters a common identity as Christ's disciples.[5]
- Creating an intergenerational system of support that provides an anchor for the congregation and the community.
- Helping households remain resilient and hopeful in times of crisis, such as during the worldwide COVID pandemic.[6]
- Providing opportunities to truly see "the other" by creating an essential web of care across generational divides and distance.

---

[4] Peter L. Benson, *All Kids Are Our Kids* (San Francisco: Jossey-Bass, 1997), 44. The book and quote influenced my lifelong work in intergenerational ministry.

[5] "TBCYF Unit 2: Service and Learning, Session 6," Select Learning, Vimeo, Interview with Eugene Roehlkepartain, accessed October 29, 2022, https://vimeo.com/36573576.

[6] Find more resources at Search Institute, https://searchinstitute.org. This organization is known for sixty years of research on Developmental Assets and creating communities that support healthy relationships for youth.

Kara Powell, Jake Mulder, and Brad Griffin in *Growing Young* state: "Fuel a warm community: warm is the new cool."[7]

Relationships formed on the foundation and fundamentals of intergenerational ministry provide a lab for households to crisscross and connect the borders of age, stage, and experiences that separate us—right here, and right now—in one's own faith community and each person's daily life. In doing so, individuals of every age, especially children, become more confident and capable of embracing diversity in the larger community and world.[8] Thus, the Circle of Blessing becomes "glocal"—growing from local to global.

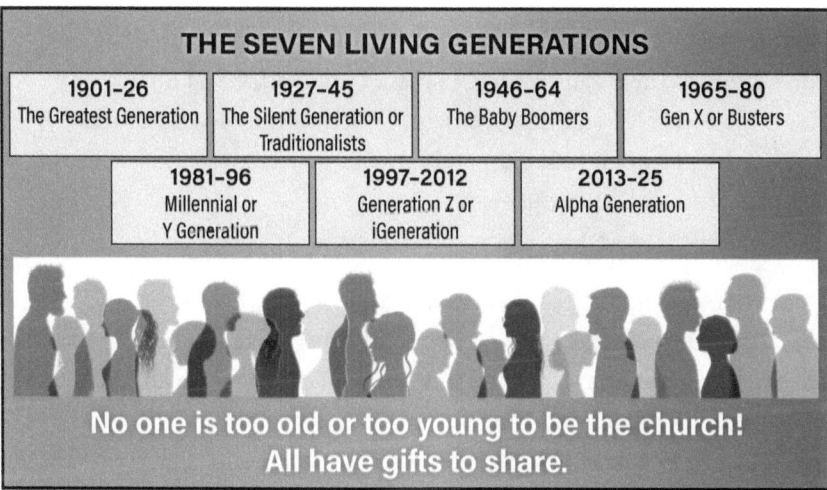

Figure 1.1. The Seven Living Gernerations

Who Are the Generations?

Our news sources are filled with information and opinions about generational characteristics and both the challenges and benefits of working together. Rather than dismissing another generation, relationships across the age spectrum are strengthened when we acknowledge, appreciate,

---

[7] Kara Powell, Jake Mulder, Brad Griffin, *Growing Young: Six Essential Strategies to Help Young People Discover and Love Your Church* (Grand Rapids: Baker Books, 2016), 163–95.

[8] Learn more about the concept of "accompaniment" in the chapter I wrote, "Walking beside Each Other," in *Intergenerate: Transforming Churches through Intergenerational Ministry*, ed. Holly Catterton Allen (Abilene, TX: Abilene Christian University Press, 2018), 221–29.

and celebrate each generation's uniqueness and contributions.[9] The key to breaking down stereotypes and building respect is understanding generational markings that shape and form individuals born within a specific time frame. We must recognize that the beliefs, biases, values, stories, worldview, and faith narratives of individuals are shaped and influenced by each generation's time in history and accompanying life experiences.

Doug Cook, from Cheyenne, Wyoming, and a member of our intergenerational planning team for The Generosity Project,[10] offered this reflection following participation in a mixed-age, multigenerational small-group conversation related to stewardship in his congregation:

> One of the more powerful moments was hearing how a person's life events impacted their faith. I witnessed people sharing stories unique to their age group (i.e., the Depression, Great Society initiatives, civil rights movement, Vietnam War, 9/11, Hurricane Katrina, Haiti earthquake) and how those events affected one's priorities and faith journey.[11]

Generational researchers and specialists typically refer to five or six generations in our society. When we include those who are ninety-five and older, plus the most recently named and youngest generation, then there are seven generations to acknowledge in our communities and in our congregations. The dates and brief descriptions that follow are not universal, but they act as a grid for interpreting key events and experiences commonly cited for generational cohorts.[12] Note that generational allocations

---

[9] See William Strauss and Neil Howe, *Generations: The History of America's Future, 1584–2069* (New York: William Morrow, 1991). Strauss and Howe laid the groundwork for generational theory. Although their work receives mixed reviews, it offers a view that generational values and behaviors are shaped by the historical events a generation encounters and shares by its location in history.

[10] The Generosity Project is an intergenerational approach to stewardship, which I have described more fully in "Connecting Generations to Practice Generosity," *Engage All Generations: A Toolkit for Creating Intergenerational Community*, ed. Cory Seibel (Abilene, TX: Abilene Christian University Press, 2021), 143–50.

[11] Doug Cook, Interview, 2021, The Generosity Project, in "Connecting Generations to Practice Generosity," *Engage All Generations*, 143–50.

[12] Nancy Salamone, "The Events That Formed Each Generation," Medium, July 29, 2016, accessed October 29, 2022, https://medium.com/@nancy_57505/the-events-that-formed-each-generation-cbbd9cd63ab4.

are most specific to people who live in the United States. Certainly other factors such as race and ethnicity, gender, socioeconomic status, and region also influence these generational characteristics.

- **1901–26: The GI Generation/Civic/Greatest Generation.** Impacted by WWI. Served in WWII. Came of age during the Great Depression. Value responsibility, duty, and honor. Sacrifice self for others. Frugal. Loyal to a faith tradition.
- **1927–45: Traditionalist/Silent Generation.** Korean War, Cold War, Industrial Revolution. Value conformity and traditional values. Disciplined, self-sacrificing. Conveyors of generational wealth. Appreciate sermons and traditional music.
- **1946–64: Baby Boomers.** Aftermath of WWII. Assassinations, civil rights, moon landing. Vietnam. Roaring '60s, drugs, yuppies. Challenged traditional institutions. Risk takers. Individualistic. Buy now—pay later. First generation to leave hometowns. Known to "church shop."
- **1965–80: Gen Xers.** AIDS crisis, Challenger disaster, fall of Berlin Wall, Gulf War, 9/11. Personal computers. Latchkey kids. Impacted by divorce. Skeptical. Collaborators. Generation ignored by marketers. Join nondenominational churches.
- **1981–96: Millennials.** Digital natives. 9/11. Iraq/Afghanistan wars. Obama election. Sandy Hook. Risk-averse. Delay marriage. Gay marriage. Social media. Cell phones. Internet. Prefer teamwork. Spiritual, not religious. Religiously nonaffiliated.
- **1997–2012: Gen Z.** Recession, homeland security, school shootings, cyber bullying. Global pandemic. Accept diversity. Connect instantly 24/7. Realistic, private, self-directed. Savers. Reliant on technology. Socially conscious. Disengaged with religious institutions.
- **2013–25: Alpha/Touch Generation.** Global pandemic. A world of iPads, Instagram, apps. Live in a personalized, marketing world. Virtual learners. "Screen" saturated. Reaching age 100 may be the norm. Outer-space exploration. Labeled "Pre-Christian."

Another reason to recognize and celebrate seven generations is found in the Seventh Generation Principle.[13] Many Native American nations and Indigenous people around the world follow this philosophy. The principle is based on an ancient Iroquois belief that the decisions we make today should result in a sustainable world, seven generations into the future. Rev. M. Kalani Souza, a Hawaiian elder, defines seven generations in this manner:

> Each human being is five generations—if you're lucky. If you're lucky, you experience your grandparents, your parents, your generation, your children's generation, and if you're lucky, your grandchildren's generation. You are five generations walking. The sixth generation is everybody who ever came before you. Your ancestry . . . back to the end of time. You should respect that and know it and honor it. The seventh generation—anybody who's ever coming after you. So when we say "make the decision with the seven generations in mind," what decision do you make that is not made for all time? So careful, careful, as you move through the world. So, this should be a lesson for our policy makers and our leadership. No decision that they make is not for all time.[14]

Souza uses the words "five generations walking." All those who came before you, to the beginning of time, represent the sixth generation. All those who come after you represent the seventh generation. Souza passionately states: "No decision should be made that the impact on the seventh generation is not considered!" Similarly, in the church, we too should consider our decisions and the impact we make on the seventh generation. Each choice and each relationship impacts all generations.

---

[13] "What Is the Seventh Generation Principle?," *Working Effectively with Indigenous People* blog, May 30, 2020, https://www.ictinc.ca/blog/seventh-generation-principle. The integration of the Seventh Generation Principle into daily living by many Indigenous people informs and inspires my ministry.

[14] "Seven Generations," from "Pacific Connections: Indigenous Approaches to Climate Change from Tanax Amix to Aotearoa," Bioneers, YouTube, February 20, 2018, https://www.youtube.com/watch?v=IuKmSyCbNk4.

Tips—Where and How to Begin

Where do ministry leaders begin when incorporating an intergenerational approach into their ministry? It does not take a program, a line item in a budget, or a committee's approval to begin. The first step begins with you researching and describing your own lineage and family in generational terms. For example, I am the daughter of Leta, the daughter of Lydia, the daughter of Sophie. As of this writing, my mother is 103 years old and represents the GI Generation. I am a Boomer married to a Traditionalist. Our two sons are Gen Xers. I am the adopted grandmother to two Millennial young adults in Kenya and great-grandmother to their Alpha generation preschoolers. Understanding the generational placement of myself and those around me helps me connect with other generations. The second step toward intergenerational ministry begins by simply naming, claiming, and celebrating the generations already inside the walls of the church and in one's neighborhood. *More than a program, intergenerational ministry is a lens—a language—and a way of being that forms the foundation for the unfolding life and witness, disciple forming, and servant leadership of ministry.*

Often, leaders lament, "Yes, but . . . we don't have any children, teens, or young adults or _____ in our midst." That may be true, but intergenerational ministry offers an opportunity to become a vital community partner. Reach out beyond the church's walls into the neighborhood and connect with the nearest school, after-school or preschool program, senior care center, police or fire station. Equip grandparents, aunts, and uncles for meaningful virtual engagement with grandchildren, nieces, and nephews who live at a distance. Be prepared to meet needs you did not know existed. In return, prepare to be gifted by the Circle of Blessing in unexpected ways.

Intergenerational fundamentals may be translated into any ministry setting. Listed below are ten practices to use as a guide as you begin to create meaningful relationships and facilitate interaction between generations.[15] The time and effort invested in engaging all generations as God's children, ages 2 to 102, are well worth the effort!

---

[15] I have included more tips for facilitating intergenerate ministry in "Connecting Generations to Practice Generosity," *Engage All Generations*, 143–50.

1. **Invite and Celebrate**
   - Invite every age and generation to participate. People often think "intergenerational" does not mean them, assuming it means Sunday school teachers with their students or only parents with children.
   - Welcome, identify, highlight, and celebrate each generation's unique perspectives, values, stories, time, treasure, and talents.

2. **It's All about the Dots**
   - Visually identify the generations when hosting a gathering. (For example, participants add a colored dot to their nametag to indicate their generational cohort. Participants create a centerpiece for their table made up of varied flowers that represent each generation present.)
   - "Three-dot" all teams. (Strive to have at least three generations serve on the altar guild, finance team, property committee, etc.)
   - Proclaim, publish, and post in newsletters, bulletins, and online the number of decades and generations present in worship and ministry-related gatherings.

3. **Create Safe Space**
   - Create a covenant, discuss healthy boundaries, and share guidelines for authentic sharing and safe interaction between generations.
   - Honor and engage all abilities and capabilities across the age span.
   - Offer extraordinary hospitality. (For example, accessibility, signage, greeters, dietary sensitive snacks, activities to engage every age and ability, "shepherds" who are alert to parents and caregivers who need extra hands in caring for children, and helping hands for the vulnerable and elders needing assistance.)
   - Provide wheelchairs, rocking chairs, folding chairs, high chairs, beanbags, and pillows on the floor. Consider a "Pray and Play" space in worship.

4. **Holy Number "5"**
   - The Holy Spirit's best work is accomplished in mixed-age small groups of five—no more! In groups larger than five, it is difficult for people to hear, and it takes too much time to share. Groups smaller than five, such as dyads, can experience moments of uncomfortable silence when sharing.

5. **No Tables**
   - Let the Holy Spirit loose! Turn around in pews, move away from tables, invite people to pull their chairs together, sit knee-to-knee in mixed-age groups of five so people can truly "see" one another and "lean in" to hear one another across generations.
   - Use smaller round tables or create a group of five chairs at each end of a long, oblong table.

6. **Teach and Live God's Story**
   - Use storybook Bibles to create opportunities for everyone, regardless of biblical knowledge, to engage in and embrace God's story.
   - Embody God's story by incorporating all learning styles, the senses, and safe physical movement into the interaction between generations.
   - Utilize digital technology and social media to connect God's story to all generations and connect busy families, the homebound, and those hospitalized, working, retired, volunteering, serving, studying, and traveling.

7. **Create Shared Identity and Story**
   - Create intergenerational community and a shared, common identity by engaging the hearts, hands, and minds of all ages in rituals, traditions, caring conversations, singing, storytelling, meal sharing, playing, praying, blessing, acts of service, and sending.

8. **Generate "Reminders" of God's Story**
   - Connect church and home by creating "reminders" of God's story (instead of a reference to "crafts") for all ages to take home.
   - Encourage households to tell, retell, and live God's story in their daily interactions.

9. **Equip Households**
   - Model a dynamic intergenerational ministry within the walls of the church in order to equip households as Christ's disciples in the domestic church called home (Acts 2:42–47).
   - Engage the gifts of every generation and household in sharing resources. Eric H. F. Law states, "We all have resources—time, place, leadership, relationship, truth, wellness, and money. What makes these resources holy is a dynamic process of exchanging them to empower the cycle of blessings that sustains communities."[16]

10. **A Circle of Blessing**
    - Identify, introduce, and honor the eldest and youngest present each time you gather. Establish them as "bookends" for the sacred circle that is formed as individuals from each generation (or decade) are invited to join, enlarge, and create the Circle of Blessing—always remembering those who came before you and those who will come after.

In constructing a dynamic intergenerational ministry, be prepared to be surprised—by the Holy Spirit's lead and the growing awareness of God's faithfulness from generation to generation. May you be filled with joy and wonder at the intergenerational moments that shine with God's love and grace. May you celebrate the Circle of Blessing that is created when the gifts of every generation are woven into the very fabric of faith and life together as the body of Christ.

---

[16] Eric H. F. Law, *Holy Currencies* (St. Louis: Chalice Press, 2015), xii.

THEOLOGY IN PRACTICE: QUESTIONS TO CONSIDER

1. Stop to consider your own "intergenerational lineage," not only in your family but also in your church, school, community, and more. How might you participate in this intergenerational Circle of Blessing more fully, more deeply?

2. Think about all the decisions you will make this week, this month, this year in your context. Would considering the seven generations affect how you and others might proceed in these decisions?

3. How are you participating in this "intergenerational circle of blessing," and how are you empowering others to participate as well?

4. Review Staats practical list of tips to begin intergenerational practices. What might work well from this list in your context? Make plans with others to begin incorporating a few of these ideas and principles from this list.

CHAPTER 2

HONORING THE IMAGE

Recovering a Creational Theology
for Intergenerational Ministry

WILSON MCCOY

*"When a caterpillar looks in the mirror,
he sees a butterfly."*

—Matshona Dhliwayo

"Yes, Wilson, but why is this a good idea?" I first heard this question a few years ago when I began experimenting with intergenerational ministry in the life of my church. As with any change, I found "early adopters"[1] who loved the idea of bringing generations together and fully supported the changes. Others hesitated to accept these initiatives but warmed up to the concept after hearing positive testimonies from participants. Every age group who shared in these intergenerational experiences expressed gratitude for the *mutual and reciprocal interactions* they were able to have

---

[1] The terms "early adopters," "laggards," and "late adopters" are used in Everett M. Rogers, *Diffusion of Innovations*, 5th ed. (1962; reprint, New York: Free Press, 2003), 267–97. Rogers's seminal work on innovation discusses common trends that occur with change in systems and organizations.

with other generations in our church.[2] Then there was a final group—the "laggards" or "late adopters"—who were resistant and last to embrace these changes. The individual who wanted to know why these initiatives were a good idea represented this group. What might I say to help them understand why I believe intergenerational ministry matters?

I was thankful to be a few months into doctoral research and felt prepared to give a response. I first noted positive observations from my project and the participants involved. I then explained practical benefits of bringing the generations together, while noting the latest research statistics from other church leaders who were years ahead of my efforts in this field. My confidence grew as I made a case for why these changes were a good idea. I knew I had this late adopter on the ropes. He would soon see the error of his ways, repent, and realize that the intergenerational kingdom was near! I was about to deliver my closing remarks when he hit back with an unexpected question. "Yes, Wilson, but why does the Bible say this is a good idea?" "Ah, yes," I thought, as I now felt *myself* backed up against the ropes. "I guess we should bring the Bible into this conversation."

A Biblical Basis for Intergenerational Ministry

A survey of the Bible reveals that faith is often formed through members of different generations sharing with one another about the story of God. The following are some noteworthy examples of the biblical basis for such an intergenerational approach to ministry:

- Moses instructing the people of God to pass along the story of God's deliverance to their children (Deut. 6:4–9).
- The psalmist calling for all generations of a worshiping community to declare the works of God to one another (Ps. 145).
- Jesus instructing his disciples by elevating children as an example of the kingdom of God to adults (Luke 18:15–17).

---

[2] I highlight the words "mutual" and "reciprocal" to draw attention to one of the defining traits of intergenerational ministry. One of the things that makes intergenerational ministry unique is the quality of relationships happening between different age groups. Genuine give-and-take between different generations is a central distinguishing factor of this kind of ministry. We will return to this identifying trait later when discussing practical implications of this creational theology.

- Paul instructing Timothy to create a church where attentiveness and care are offered to all generations (1 Tim. 5:1–4).

The story of Scripture consistently displays a dynamic of faith where all generations are involved in the process of creating, forming, and sustaining faith.[3]

Reciting this brief list of Scripture references appeased the curious member of my congregation. That person walked away satisfied with my response, yet I felt unsettled. I found myself wanting more than just a list of biblical proof-texts for this approach to ministry. Giving intergenerational examples from the Bible is important, but we need deeper, theological rationales for why intergenerational ministry matters.[4] What follows is an attempt to provide a *theological foundation*, grounded in the story of creation, for why members of a church would make intergenerational ministry a core value of their life together and how they might live that value in practical ways.[5]

The Image of God in the Old Testament

A theological foundation for intergenerational ministry begins with the initial claims of Scripture about the nature of God and humanity in the opening chapters of Genesis. Here we are introduced to the Creator God

---

[3] For an extensive list of Scripture references reflecting an intergenerational outlook of faith, see Holly Catterton Allen and Christine Lawton Ross, *Intergenerational Christian Formation: Bringing the Whole Church Together in Ministry, Community, and Worship* (Downers Grove, IL: InterVarsity Press, 2012), 294–307.

[4] Allen and Ross, *Intergenerational*, 109–18. Their work offers a few common theological foundations for intergenerational ministry, such as a trinitarian framework for multigenerational churches and a more robust vision of the body of Christ that includes all ages. These are helpful beginning points, but as the authors admit, there is still a need for additional theological rationales for this growing field of ministry.

[5] The language of "theological foundation" points to a deeper way of reading the Bible that shapes my writing. Instead of a surface-level skimming of relevant texts, I am trying to distill deeper priorities that weave throughout Scripture. To use the metaphor of a story as a way to understand the Bible, there are more prominent themes that hold the plotline of Scripture together. I am making the case that one of those main themes is found in the creation story of Genesis, that it weaves throughout the Bible, and that it has a practical impact on the nature and quality of relationships in our church (i.e., intergenerational).

who forms and fashions the world into a place of structure and stability.[6] The culmination of these divine creative acts happens on day six with the formation of humanity and a description of their fundamental identity and function:

> Then God said, "Let us make humankind in our image, according to our likeness; and let them have dominion over the fish of the sea, and over the birds of the air, and over the cattle, and over all the wild animals of the earth, and over every creeping thing that creeps upon the earth." So God created humankind in his image, in the image of God he created them; male and female he created them. God blessed them, and God said to them, "Be fruitful and multiply, and fill the earth and subdue it; and have dominion over the fish of the sea and over the birds of the air and over every living thing that moves upon the earth." (Gen. 1:26–28 NRSV)

The initial and repeated claim in these opening verses emphasizes that humanity is created in the image of God.[7]

This identity statement is significant for two related reasons. First, this description of humanity as created in the image of God highlights the royal, *representative dynamics* embedded in the ancient context of this passage.[8] In the ancient Near East, to bear the image of a god was to bear the image of the thought-to-be-divine kings. Images of that ruler represented their kingdom reign and served as a kind of presence of that person in places where they could not be physically present. Their image served also to represent them in a given place. The writer of Genesis taps into this ancient worldview in order to make a surprising claim about all of

---

[6] The dominant verb used in relationship with God in the opening chapter of Genesis is the word "create." The primary picture presented is one of God forming and fashioning everything in the cosmos. For more on the dominant theme of God as Creator throughout the Hebrew Scriptures, see Walter Brueggemann, *Theology of the Old Testament: Testimony, Dispute, Advocacy* (Minneapolis: Fortress Press, 1997), 145–56.

[7] For a more extensive discussion of this phrase, see Edward M. Curtis, "Image of God," *The Anchor Yale Bible Dictionary*, 1992, 3:389–91.

[8] Terence E. Fretheim, *The Book of Genesis*, vol. 1, *The New Interpreter's Bible* (Nashville: Abingdon Press, 1994), 345.

humanity. *Humans are created to be image-bearers of the Creator God, who gives them both the identity and function of representing God to the world.*

This theme reappears later in the Hebrew Scriptures in places like Psalm 8. The song begins by celebrating the majesty of God as seen in the creation of the heavens, moon, and stars; yet, the psalmist emphasizes the place of humans in the created order. The song declares, "Yet you have made them [human beings] a little lower than God, and crowned them with glory and honor. You have given them dominion over the works of your hands; you have put all things under their feet" (Ps. 8:5–6 NRSV). Echoing the words of Genesis 1, the psalmist celebrates humans as kind of royal figures, both in the crowning language of "glory and honor" and in their description as "rulers." Psalm 8 reminds the reader of humanity's identity and calling to be representatives of the Creator God.[9]

Another reason the image-of-God statement in Genesis 1 is significant is that this description of humanity highlights the *relational dynamics* embedded in the immediate context of the passage. The God who creates humanity says, "Let *us* make . . . according to *our* likeness" (Gen 1:26). God directly addresses humanity for the first time, saying, "Be fruitful and multiply, and fill the earth" (Gen. 1:28). God, a relational community, creates humanity in "their" image, according to "their likeness."[10] In other words, to be an image-bearer is not just a call to reflect God as an isolated individual, but there is a relational aspect to this foundational identity. Bearing the image of God is about how we relate to God *and* how we relate to others.

---

[9] This one example is not intended to reduce or oversimplify the anthropological testimony in the Old Testament. Complexity and tension develop in such places as the wisdom literature of Job 7, where we hear the cries of a man in the throes of loss. Job cites the words of Psalm 8 in an unexpected way, saying, "What are human beings, that you make so much of them, that you set your mind on them, visit them every morning, test them every moment? Will you not look away from me for a while, let me alone until I swallow my spittle?" (Job 7:17–19 NRSV). Job protests his plight by challenging the claims of Psalm 8 and Genesis 1 by inverting them into an expression of grief. Such texts are important reminders that within the witness of the Old Testament, the people of God are conversing and wrestling with the character of God and the calling of humanity. Nevertheless, as we will see in the New Testament, the image-of-God theme will remain primary and central to the theological plotline of the story of Scripture.

[10] For more regarding the relational, communal nature of the triune God and how that is intentional in the purpose of creation, see Stanley J. Grenz, *Theology for the Community of God* (Grand Rapids: William B. Eerdmans, 2000), 112–15. Grenz finds that the language in the creation accounts of Genesis, along with the whole biblical story, points to "God's intent to establish community with creation" (112).

A final point to be mentioned about this image-of-God identity is noticing the use of this phrase in the larger context of Genesis. Noteworthy to the narrative flow of the book is that this claim is repeated again in Genesis 9, where God enters into a covenant with Noah, demonstrating a priority on human life. God's rationale for this instruction to Noah is a repetition of the Genesis 1 claim, repeating that all humans are created in the image of God and that they are to be fruitful and multiply (Gen. 9:1–6).

This reference in Genesis 9 is important for the purposes of this chapter. The identity statement and function of Genesis 1 is cited *after* the tragic decisions of humanity in Genesis 3. The moment of misdirected love by Adam and Eve to take and eat of the fruit of the knowledge of good and evil does not remove the inherent, God-given identity of humanity. The scene with Noah reveals that even east of Eden, men and women are still celebrated as bearers of the divine image. They are still given their *representative* identity as image-bearers and are still called to a *relational* fulfillment of that identity in their relationships with one another.

The Image of God in the New Testament

This core, creational, theological foundation of the Old Testament is adopted and further developed in the New Testament in light of Jesus Christ. Every Gospel writer allows creation themes to permeate his presentation of the good news of Jesus. In Matthew, the second Greek word of his Gospel reveals that he is giving us a γενέσεως (geneseōs, or genealogy) of the person of Jesus (Matt. 1:1). The Gospel of Mark describes Jesus's temptation with a reminder that he was "with the wild beasts" (Mark 1:13), which echoes back to Adam in the garden. Similarly, the Gospel of Luke tells of the baptism of Jesus as the convergence of water, Spirit, heaven, and God's voice, alluding to the opening scene of Scripture (Luke 3:21–22). Most well-known is that of John, who takes the "in the beginning" language of Genesis to frame our vision of the entrance of Jesus as the creative Word of God (John 1:1). Paul also picks up these creation themes and allows them to shape his theological imagination concerning new creation in God's redemptive purposes.[11] Several examples from his writings illustrate this creational priority (e.g., Rom. 8:18–25; 2 Cor. 5:16–21). For the purposes of this chapter, we will focus on Paul's letter to the Colossians where he uses creational, image-of-God language to describe both his theological belief about the person of Jesus and the implication of that conviction for the church.

Colossians begins with the well-known cosmic Christ hymn, and the claim that the Son "is the image of the invisible God, the firstborn of all creation" (Col. 1:15 NRSV). Layered in this statement are two connected convictions. First, the statement conveys that in Jesus, we fully see the nature of God (cf. 2 Cor. 4:4). Jesus is fully divine, in the flesh.

Second, this statement echoes the image-of-God claims about humanity in Genesis 1. Jesus reveals the intention of humanity. He is the fullness of humanity in the flesh. For Paul, if we want to know what God is like, then we are to look to Jesus. If we want to know what it means to be fully human, as intended from the beginning, then we are to look to Jesus. To use language from our previous reflections on Genesis, the *representative* and *relational* intentions of humanity are *most fully made known in the person of Jesus*.

These convictions inform Paul's guidance for the church. He calls believers to live a different kind of life, and it is worth noting his rationale for this instruction:

> Do not lie to one another, seeing that you have stripped off the old self with its practices and have clothed yourselves with the new self, which is being renewed in knowledge according to the *image of its creator*. In that renewal there is no longer Greek and Jew, circumcised and uncircumcised, barbarian, Scythian, slave and free; but Christ is all and in all!
> (Col. 3:9–11 NRSV—emphasis mine)

---

[11]Richard B. Hays, *The Moral Vision of the New Testament: Community, Cross, New Creation, A Contemporary Introduction to New Testament Ethics* (New York: HarperCollins, 1996), 193–200; for more on the way the story of Israel shapes Paul's vision for the story of the church, see James W. Thompson, *Pastoral Ministry According to Paul: A Biblical Vision* (Grand Rapids: Baker Academic, 2006), 1–60.

Paul's instruction is theologically grounded in his conviction that believers are being renewed into the image of God, which is most fully seen in Christ.

Here, this "new self" to which Paul alludes is less an individual reality and more of a *corporate calling*.[12] The vision of church presented is that of an "in Christ" community where distinctions, which can easily cause division, are reconsidered in light of this new "all-consuming unity in Christ" (cf. Gal. 3:26–28).[13] Paul presents a vision of the church where there is not an *obliteration* of distinctiveness but a *reconsideration* of those various ethnic and social markers. The church is not to view these differences from a "human point of view," which easily leads to dismissing and devaluing each other (2 Cor. 5:16–17 NRSV). *Instead, they are to put on the lenses of new creation where the **image of God is honored** as the primary identity marker of everyone in the community:* "Christ is all and in all" (Col. 3:11 NRSV).

The church is called, then, to live into this new reality—honoring the image of God—through the way they treat each other (Col. 3:12–17). Christians should actively get rid of the things that perpetuate division and disunity, and they are to clothe themselves with the virtues and practices that reflect this new and true self. By doing so, they participate in the transformation reflective of the image of God as seen in Christ Jesus.[14] In other words, *the way the church can more fully become what God has always intended it to be is through its people of faith together honoring that image of God, that new self, in one another.* Paul's theological rationale to the diverse body at Colossae calls them to reconsider their distinctions such as ethnicity, class, and status in light of their new identity in Christ. The image-of-God themes of Genesis are here reinterpreted in light of Christ and for the community that is now in Christ. *The church is given the calling to be representatives of God, in light of the image of God in Jesus, and one of the ways they fulfill that calling is through their relational dynamics as a community of faith.*

---

[12] Scot McKnight, *The Letter to the Colossians* (Grand Rapids: Eerdmans Publishing, 2018), 310.
[13] McKnight, *Letter to the Colossians*, 313.
[14] David J. A. Clines, "Humanity as the Image of God," in *On the Way to Postmodern: Old Testament Essays, 1967–1998*, vol. 2, Journal for the Story of the Old Testament Supplement Series 293 (Sheffield: Sheffield Academic Press, 1998), 447–97.

Honoring the Image of God through Intergenerational Ministry

One of the ways a community of faith can embody this image-of-God identity is through *embracing intergenerational ministry as a way of being the church*. Age distinctions in church, which often serve as identity markers, can also become potential sources for breeding disunity and division. False generational perception, overabundance of age segregation, and an overemphasis on catering to one age group at the loss of another are a few of the ways congregations can break down and break apart. These common, divisive practices need to be put aside and put to death as a part of the old self that no longer guides the baptized community of faith.

Instead, the church needs to embrace the words of one of the shepherds at the church where I serve. After participating in an eight-week intergenerational experiment at our church, he paraphrased the words of Paul in Galatians 3:26–29, which echo the words already mentioned in Colossians, to describe his experience and the possibilities for other churches that do the same:

> What kind of church would be formed if everyone got to experience what we have experienced [intergenerational ministry]? It would be a church that was stronger, more devoted, and a caring church. As we were discussing this, I got to thinking about Paul's statement about neither male nor female, Jew nor Greek, slave nor free, and now we would have to add young nor old, because this has enhanced our experience with God to have all of us here.

This church leader's insight reminds us that *intergenerational expressions in the life of a church are an important way we embrace our new reality as a unified community in Christ*. Bringing the generations together gives witness to our "new self" (Col 3:10 NRSV), which is being transformed more into the image of God in and through Christ Jesus—the image of God— embedded in humanity since the beginning of creation. We, ourselves, participate in and perpetuate the full transformation of that image whenever we, together, honor that renewing image of God in one another. We reflect our identity as representatives of God through the relational dynamics of intergenerational interactions. Thus, these **mutual**

and reciprocal interactions between the generations are one clear way churches can embrace their identity "in Christ."

The How of Intergenerational Ministry

I am not sure if my beloved late adopter would have stood there patiently in that church hallway to hear this theological rationale for why someone would implement intergenerational rhythms into the life of a church. Nevertheless, upon reflection, I realized my main concern should not be his posture toward me but mine toward him. My willingness to clothe myself with compassion, kindness, and patience toward this man from another generation is the real litmus test for my growing theological conviction. *Can I honor the image of God in this older member in the same way I desire him to honor it in other ages within our community?*

This question is a good starting place for anyone who desires for their church to bring the generations together in mutual and reciprocal ways. If we want this change to happen in our congregation, then we should reflect on our willingness to embody this intergenerational way of being as a member of the church. Here are some further questions for reflection:

THEOLOGY IN PRACTICE: QUESTIONS TO CONSIDER

1. Am I being the kind of person who is actively trying to recognize and celebrate the image of God in every age and stage of life within my congregation?

2. In what ways does our church currently try to honor and respect the image of God in all the generations of our congregation? How might we be more intentional about naming these things as intergenerational so our church can see the importance of every age group in our church?

3. What are some additional ways we might try to include and elevate various generations of our church as representatives of God? Are there any areas or arenas within our church that could become more intergenerational?

4. How does our church speak about the different generations within our congregation? Where and when might we find opportunities for various age groups to speak words of gratitude, blessing, and encouragement to and about each other?

5. What would it look like for our church to cultivate relationships between the generations that are filled with compassion, kindness, humility, and patience? Are there any new ministry initiatives we might try that could help us grow into these kinds of relationships?

These questions are far from exhaustive, but they serve as potential beginning points in helping a church consider what it might look like to become more intergenerational in nature.

Ultimately, and as a closing word, my hope is that churches who desire to bring the generations together will remember *why* mutual and reciprocal relationships between the different age groups of a congregation are an important expression of the church. Intergenerational ministry matters because it reflects a core conviction of Scripture about our identity and function as people created in the image of God. All ages of a given congregation are image-bearers of God, and we should strive to become the kind of community that honors that reality in our relationships together.

CHAPTER 3

LUDICITY AND THEOLOGY
Exploring Some Theological Foundations of Intergenerational Ministry

GARETH CRISPIN

"Advice from a Butterfly:
Let your true colors show
Get out of your cocoon
Take yourself lightly
Look for the sweetness in life
Take time to smell the flowers
Catch a breeze
We can't all be monarchs."

—Ilan Shami

Being at St. James was a new experience for me. Unusually, the building had been constructed in the round, so my attention was naturally drawn to everyone in the gathering, not simply those at the front. Then there was the content; it was guided more than led. At times, we all joined in doing the same thing, but equally, there were times when we moved around and selected an activity. Such activities focused on prompting questions, personal response, and reflection, rather than content and answers. Everyone seemed to be included and involved, regardless of age or stage.

This was not what I was used to. I had been reading about intergenerational ministry for a number of years but had never really experienced it firsthand. People at St. James, however, had never heard of intergenerational ministry but had been practicing it for decades! As I mused on what I had experienced, I wondered why some churches are more like cats than ducks when it comes to taking to the waters of intergenerational ministry. Why do some embrace intergenerational ministry, sometimes seemingly naturally (as with St. James), whereas others appear to be averse to it?

Though they did not know it, St. James was embodying intergenerational ministry as defined by Holly Catterton Allen and Christina Ross because they were intentionally bringing "the generations together in mutual serving, sharing, or learning within the core activities of the church in order to live out being the body of Christ to each other and the greater community."[1] They would be equally at home with what Allan Harkness proposes as the four constituent factors of intergenerational ministry, namely mutuality between participants, collaboration, shared experiences, and bidirectional teaching.[2]

The church family at St. James did not use this language; they had never read the books we might think they should have read. Instead, their natural inclination to intergenerational ministry was narrated using these words: informality, participation, freedom, relational safety, joy, and authenticity. Furthermore, as they talked about their church life, it seemed as though the first four of these led to the last two. Joy and authenticity were a result of informality, participation, freedom, and relational safety (see fig. 3.1).

In reflecting on these inclinations, two main ideas came to my mind. First, while there is no one-to-one relationship between the words used at St. James and the ideas found within the definitions of intergenerational ministry, significant overlap and coherence emerges; they are commensurate

---

[1] Holly Catterton Allen and Christina Ross, *Intergenerational Christian Formation: Bringing the Whole Church Together in Ministry, Community and Worship* (Downers Grove, IL: InterVarsity Press, 2012), 17.

[2] Allan Harkness, "Intergenerational Christian Education: Reclaiming a Significant Educational Strategy in Christian Faith Communities" (PhD diss., Murdoch University, 1996), 222–23.

Ludicity and Theology

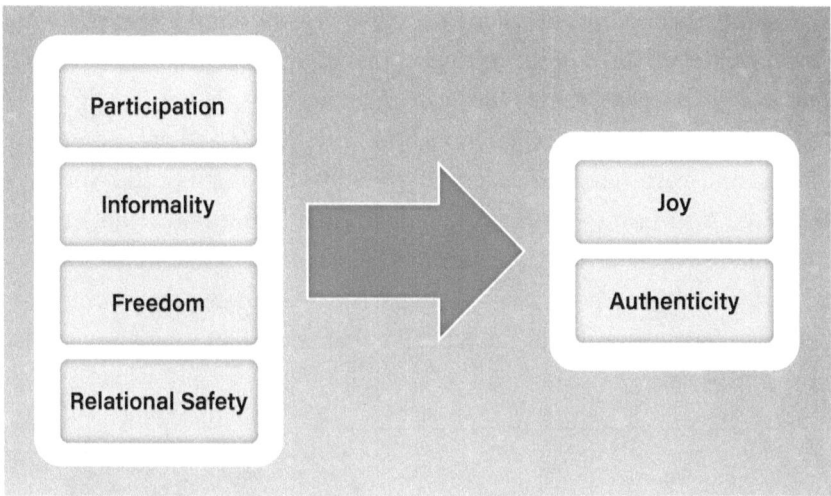

Figure 3.1. St. James' intergenerational church life

concepts. Participation, informality, freedom, and relational safety are highly commensurate with mutuality between participants, collaboration, shared experiences, and bidirectional teaching. Secondly, the words used by those in the church (as well as my observations of their practice) seemed not only to be commensurate with the core parts of intergenerational ministry definitions, but they equally correspond to the idea of *play* and can be helpful when grouped under that higher-level term.

The problem with the word *play* is that as soon as you use the word, images of soft toys and LEGO® sets pervade the mind and can obscure the core truth of what *play* is. The cultural historian Johan Huizinga, in his book *Homo Ludens*, helpfully summarizes his vision of *play* as "a voluntary activity or occupation executed within certain fixed limits of time and place, according to rules freely accepted but absolutely binding, having its aim in itself and accompanied by a feeling of tension, joy, and the consciousness that it is 'different' from 'ordinary life.'"[3] In my theological reflection, I have adopted Huizinga's word *ludens* (Latin for playing) and have altered it into the noun **ludicity** to attempt to get around the issues associated with common images of *play* that people might have.

---

[3] Johan Huizinga, *Homo Ludens: A Study of the Play-Element in Culture* (1949; reprint, Kettering: Angelico Press, 2016), 28.

If ludicity and the central features of intergenerational ministry were so closely linked, then the central question in my mind became: What did and did not promote these four ludic elements at St. James (see fig. 3.2)?

As I reflected on my experiences both with the life and practices of the church and with relevant literature, the wider theology of the churches appeared significant as a major factor in their adoption (or not) of the four ludic elements. While we cannot say categorically that their theology *caused* their intergenerational ministry life, we can certainly say that it provided fertile ground for the ludic life that resembles intergenerational ministry so closely.

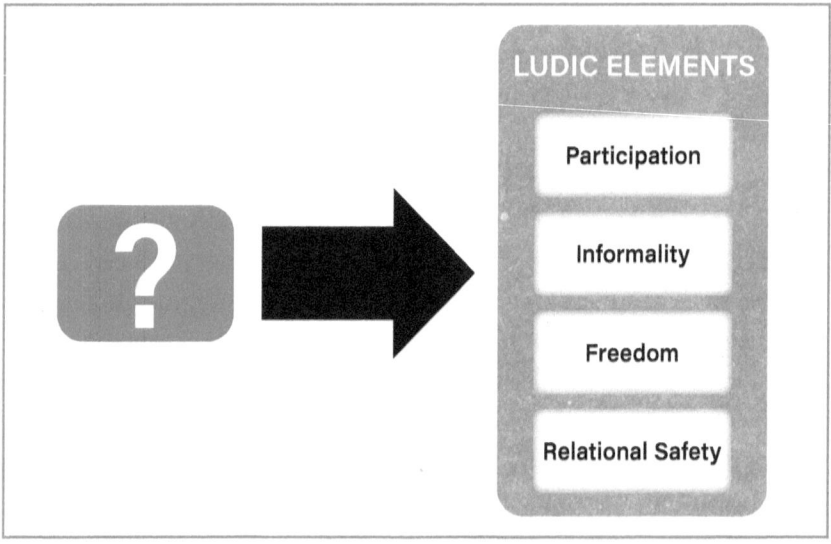

Figure 3.2. What did and did not promote these four ludic elements at St. James?

What then, within the theology of St. James (in theory and practice) might contribute to the foundations of ludicity and intergenerational ministry (see fig. 3.3)?

In order to explore the theological foundations of ludicity further, allow me a brief moment to explain the specific context from which this thinking arises. Knowledge from one context is not necessarily immediately applicable to another, and so, for you to be able to consider how this relates to your context, and the relevance for what is to come, you need to know more about my current context.

Ludicity and Theology

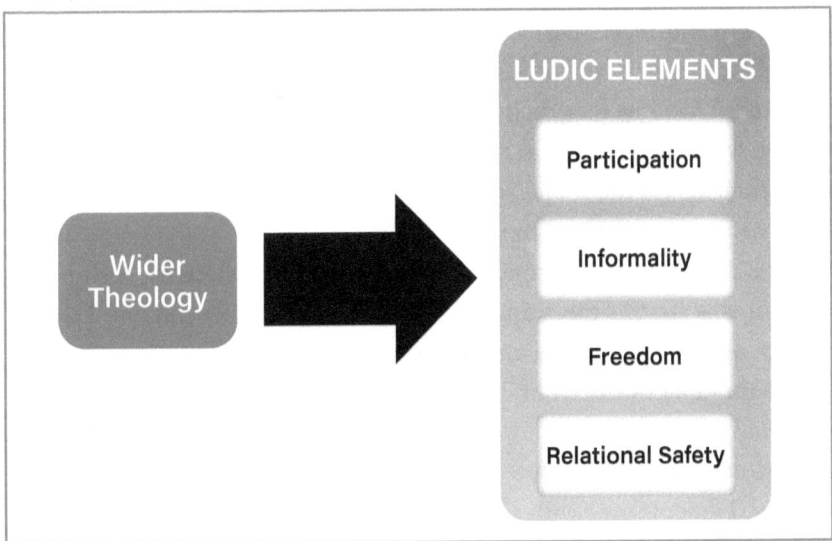

Figure 3.3. How does St. James' theology contribute to ludicity?

St. James is one of three Church of England churches I have been involved in during the last few years; each of these churches shares some common theological commitments that seem to be important in their approach to church life, in particular for intergenerational ministry. As I articulate these theological commitments and explain some of the labels that go with them, it will be important to appreciate the Church of England background; these churches are not United Methodist churches in the United States of America; they are not Pentecostal churches in Kenya, or Orthodox churches in Ukraine. All three churches are *evangelical* churches in the Church of England. The first thing to appreciate is that evangelicalism in England does not mean what it means elsewhere; most importantly, here, evangelicalism is not political. In the UK, evangelicalism is a broad movement that is simply focused on the Bible, the cross of Christ, conversion of individuals, and an active church in the world.[4]

Evangelicalism in the Church of England is normally understood to come in three main forms: open, charismatic, and conservative.[5] The main differences relevant for our purposes are that, when compared to

---

[4] For more about evangelicalism in the UK, see David Bebbington, *Evangelicalism in Modern Britain: A History from the 1730s to the 1980s* (London: Routledge, 1989).
[5] Graham Kings, "Canal, River and Rapids: Contemporary Evangelicalism in the Church of England," *Anvil* 20, no. 3 (Sept. 2003): 167–84.

conservative evangelicalism, open and charismatic evangelicals share a belief in an active doctrine of the Holy Spirit, *and* they are more open and less hierarchical in their beliefs about the Trinity. As Graham Kings pictures it, while conservatives are like canals—in that they are fairly fixed and more focused on the Bible—open and charismatic evangelicals are more like free-flowing rivers or rapids.[6]

The other part of the context is me. I researched these three churches and am writing this piece and so have influence in this content. I would not consider myself to be an open or charismatic evangelical. (I'm not even a member of the Church of England!) I am an advocate of intergenerational ministry, but that does not mean I will let that lead me to change my theology from my more conservative leanings simply for pragmatic reasons. I do not agree with all that open or charismatic evangelicals in the Church of England say, but I have been fascinated to see how their beliefs sit alongside the way in which they view intergenerational ministry. I have been reflecting on this from within my own theological home and, if labels such as charismatic, open, or evangelical do not fit you or even mean the same thing in your context, I hope, nevertheless, that you will feel able to connect my findings to your individual theological context.

Theological Commitments Relevant for Intergenerational Ministry

The first thing of note is the *experiential nature of theology and practice*;[7] charismatic evangelical theology in Britain is "dynamic, seen through the lens of experience,"[8] with an emphasis on encounter rather than knowledge; and open evangelicals share this focus. This stress on experience and encounter is present due to an activist doctrine of the Holy Spirit, which also importantly leads to an openness to change and to risk-taking within mission and ministry; here, the focus is on "observing and experiencing a new work of the Spirit."[9]

---

[6] Kings, "Canal, River and Rapids," 167–84.

[7] Ben Pugh, *Bold Faith: A Closer Look at the Five Key Ideas of Charismatic Christianity* (Eugene, OR: Wipf and Stock, 2017), xvii. Also see Keith Warrington, *Pentecostal Theology: A Theology of Encounter* (London: T&T Clark, 2008).

[8] Warrington, *Pentecostal Theology*, 16.

[9] Warrington, *Pentecostal Theology*, 23.

Corresponding with an emphasis on experiential encounters with the Holy Spirit is the second theological commitment of interest to us; that is, charismatic evangelical theology in Britain views the Bible as "a collection of stories intended to lead a person to God and to be transformed as a result, rather than a database of dogma to be discussed."[10] Thus, *the Bible becomes a place of "encounter with the divine author."*[11] As a result, the historical gap between reader and biblical text becomes small; instead, there is a "present-tenseness" to the Bible.[12] Typically, these charismatic evangelicals see the Bible as something addressing the felt needs and emotions of the contemporary reader;[13] it is about "real" life, in that sense. Perhaps unsurprisingly, more value is placed on the narrative sections of Scripture, especially the Gospels and the book of Acts. In interpreting the Bible, it is the Spirit that leads the reader into the truth of the Bible; the Spirit inspired the Bible, so the Spirit interprets the Bible.[14]

The third theological commitment of open and charismatic theology that is important for our reflections on ludicity and intergenerational ministry is a *social doctrine of the Trinity*. Social trinitarianism focuses less on the hierarchy of the members of the Trinity and their substance and more on the equality of the members and their relationships. Two of the three church ministers in the churches I was involved with named the work of Jürgen Moltmann as influential in their theology and practice. Their wider comments on church life reflected Moltmann's views on the Trinity and the implications of that for church practice. Moltmann has advocated a move away from a hierarchical Trinity toward a social trinitarianism; but associated with this is a move away from the importance of the sixth day of creation in terms of work and toward an eschatological focus on the seventh day in terms of rest (including play), and a move away from the Spirit as tied to the Word and church toward the Spirit as free and at work in creation.[15]

---

[10] Warrington, *Pentecostal Theology*, 188.
[11] Warrington, *Pentecostal Theology*, 189.
[12] Warrington, *Pentecostal Theology*, 190.
[13] Warrington, *Pentecostal Theology*, 189.
[14] Warrington, *Pentecostal Theology*, 199.
[15] Jürgen Moltmann, *The Spirit of Life: A Universal Affirmation* (London: SPCK, 1992), 230–31.

The essence of Moltmann's doctrines of the Trinity and Holy Spirit is *relationship rather than substance*;[16] and it is a relationship that includes the impact of the *freedom of the Spirit in creation* that causes change within the Trinity itself, as the Spirit brings experience of creation back to the Godhead.[17] Moltmann's eschatological perspective on creation is commensurate with and linked to this social trinitarianism. He focuses on the seventh day and the resultant centrality of *being rather than doing*.[18] For Moltmann, the Sabbath is a foretaste of the new creation to come, which has been the point of creation all along.[19] Sabbath celebrates resurrection and anticipates not only the end times but also *the beginning of the new creation in the present*.[20] From this celebration comes an emphasis on *enjoying the presence of God rather than focusing on activity for God*,[21] an enjoyment of rest, feast, and joy in existence that is holistic, embracing body and mind, individuals and communities, and the whole of creation.[22]

Okay, so far, so theological, but how does all this work out in the practice of intergenerational ministry?

Relevance of Ludicity for Intergenerational Ministry

The theological commitments outlined above are *supportive* of the ludic elements of freedom, participation, informality, and relational safety mentioned at the start and so provide a good foundation for intergenerational ministry. Let's look at each one in turn, in theory and practice.

Freedom

Freedom to express yourself is a key component of charismatic and open evangelical worship.[23] In this "grassroots" movement,[24] where communal[25]

---

[16] Jürgen Moltmann, *The Trinity and the Kingdom: The Doctrine of God* (1981; reprint, Minneapolis: Fortress Press, 1993), 19.
[17] Moltmann, *The Trinity and the Kingdom*, 161.
[18] Jürgen Moltmann, *God in Creation: An Ecological Doctrine of Creation* (London: SPCK, 1985), 276–77.
[19] Moltmann, *God in Creation*, 277.
[20] Moltmann, *God in Creation*, 295.
[21] Moltmann, *God in Creation*, 280.
[22] Moltmann, *God in Creation*, 277.
[23] Warrington, *Pentecostal Theology*, 221.
[24] Pugh, *Bold Faith*, 49.
[25] Warrington, *Pentecostal Theology*, 221.

and spontaneous activity is key,[26] pastors tend to discern rather than determine, actively using gifts of the Spirit that are "unlicensed" and uncontrolled by leadership.[27] In striking parallel, Moltmann's doctrine of the Spirit also implies a flattening out of church authority, such that "the church of Christ is a community of free and equal men and women who exist with one another and for one another in the charismatic diversity of their gifts and lifestyles."[28]

I observed this freedom in the worship and wider life of the three churches in view. The minister of St. James often iterated that he did not have "a monopoly of the good things of God." He embodied a Moltmannian view of freedom and authority in the way in which he curated worship, allowing people to speak; he did not crowd out the voices from the church, regardless of age. For him, emphasis in the church was "organic in terms of playing to the passions and gifts of people that are with us."

THEOLOGY IN PRACTICE: QUESTIONS TO CONSIDER

1. In your context, how free are people to express their faith and life in the Spirit?

2. How might the abundance or lack of freedom translate, when encouraging all generations—all ages—to share in their faith together?

3. In your context, do church leaders enact or have the perception of a more free and equal status among parishioners, or do you see hierarchy and top-down leadership, as well as systemic structures, that elevate leaders over others? How might these perceptions hinder or help intergenerational ministry?

Participation

This freedom, when expressed, necessitates ***participation***, with every believer seen as a channel for the Spirit.[29] According to Jean-Jacques

---

[26] Warrington, *Pentecostal Theology*, 223; Jean-Jacques Suurmond, *Word and Spirit at Play: Towards a Charismatic Theology* (London: SCM Press, 1994), 22.
[27] Warrington, *Pentecostal Theology*, 141.
[28] Moltmann, *The Trinity and the Kingdom*, 236.
[29] Warrington, *Pentecostal Theology*, 133.

Suurmond, these participative forms include "applause, laughter, exclamations or laments," while "at other moments the response can be a prayer, praise in glossolalic sounds, a dance, a prophecy, testimony, a song or a text from scripture."[30] Crucially, from the perspective of intergenerational ministry, Suurmond finds that all this participation "encourages personal involvement and interaction between the participants,"[31] regardless of age. Suurmond notes that "it is obvious that where there is more room for a subjective contribution, greater reference is made to the different capacities of the community."[32]

Moltmann's doctrine of the Spirit and his social trinitarianism have similar participative implications. His views on fellowship imply "reciprocal participation and mutual recognition"[33] in all relationships, but, even more importantly, an equality of access to the Spirit. This access to the Spirit is available to all ages; thus, Moltmann finds that older generations, in the Spirit, should "withdraw, in order to give scope to the coming generations," which will "give the new experiences of younger generations a chance."[34] Moltmann's views on authority and church life and relationship between the generations, as well as his view of the Spirit as free from the church and its hierarchy, are all elements of an approach promising significant resources for intergenerational ministry, which Moltmann himself explicitly recognizes and embraces.[35]

This focus on participation was woven into the church life of St. James, as well as the other two churches I surveyed. A consistent narrative of seeking to value contributions and creations of all ages, including youth and children, was woven through everything in which they participated. This intergenerational tapestry ranged from the details of participative activities within worship gatherings to preaching and on to church-wide discussions regarding church life.

---

[30] Suurmond, *Word and Spirit at Play*, 23–24.
[31] Suurmond, *Word and Spirit at Play*, 22.
[32] Suurmond, *Word and Spirit at Play*, 24.
[33] Moltmann, *The Trinity and the Kingdom*, 217–19.
[34] Moltmann, *The Trinity and the Kingdom*, 237.
[35] Moltmann, *The Trinity and the Kingdom*, 237.

> **THEOLOGY IN PRACTICE: QUESTIONS TO CONSIDER**

1. Consider the participation of different generations in your ministry gatherings. Do all generations feel free and invited to participate in their unique ways, with their unique giftings?
2. How might a culture of participation be elevated by valuing contributions and creations of all ages?

Informality

The outworking of the theology delineated above results in a tendency toward **informality**.[36] Formal and rigid structures and practices would work against the democratic, "grassroots," participative nature of charismatic and open evangelical church life. Attention to the work of the Spirit makes room for intuitive communication such as sharing dreams, a practice that requires informality to function.[37] Suurmond focuses on uncodified liturgies, which are "not set down on paper"; here, again, and importantly for this research, these liturgies are "accessible to people who have little or no literary training."[38]

At St. James, people did not stand on ceremony. It was not chaos, but there was little by way of formal liturgy and expectations. Equally, at the other two churches I visited, a relaxed feel pervaded almost everything that happened. People dressed informally; little had to be done in a certain way or order.

> **THEOLOGY IN PRACTICE: QUESTIONS TO CONSIDER**

1. Would you describe your current context as formal or informal? How do you think informality leans toward intergenerational interactions and relationships?
2. Examine the different generations present in your gatherings. Do specific generations prefer formality, while other generations prefer informality? How might informality frighten some while helping

---

[36] Warrington, *Pentecostal Theology*, 223.
[37] Suurmond, *Word and Spirit at Play*, 24.
[38] Suurmond, *Word and Spirit at Play*, 22.

others participate? How is this related to the theological convictions of freedom in the Spirit?

3. Are there places in your current ministry context that could use more informality?

Relational Safety

Lastly, the theological commitments explored above can also be seen as providing a good foundation for **relational safety**. When fewer rules exist where participants might transgress, less fear results when people make mistakes. When it is less about what is known cognitively and more about what is felt subjectively, participants experience less concern about getting answers wrong. When participation is open and fluid and potentially variegated, with everyone seen as a potential "channel of the Spirit," then people experience less worry about "giving it a go." Equally, Moltmann's social Trinity, with its dynamic, changeable nature, leads to conceiving church governance in such a way that "authority and obedience are replaced by dialogue, consensus, and harmony."[39]

This idea of relational safety was expressed by many people across all three churches. Parents did not feel judged by others when their children freely moved around and informally participated in church gatherings and life in general. Youth felt able to express their thoughts freely and ask questions because those around them were "safe." Youth and children felt that relational safety came, in part, because those around them believed similar things, but also because more focus was made on contributing to discussion rather than getting answers right.

THEOLOGY IN PRACTICE: QUESTIONS TO CONSIDER

1. Do all people, from every generation, feel "safe" to not only express their faith but to also experiment and ask questions?

2. How would a theology that sees participation as a potential "channel of the Spirit" be helpful in making all people and all ages feel safe to share and express their faith?

---

[39] Moltmann, *The Trinity and the Kingdom*, 202.

Bringing the Four Together

When talking about these four ludic characteristics, difficulty arises when trying to separate them; hence, the sense in bringing them under the theme of ludicity. Unsurprisingly, Suurmond concludes his consideration of charismatic practices by musing "just how like a game charismatic celebration is" and how all of them "have an element of play in them."[40] Equally unsurprising is how Moltmann views the Trinity, Spirit, and creation as a means in which creation sees "the character of play, which gives God delight and human beings joy."[41] Creation, like play, is meaningful, but not necessary;[42] and this link between the two provides an openness to ludicity that other views of the Trinity, Spirit, creation, and Sabbath would not necessarily provide.

There is something intrinsically ludic about many of the practices born out of charismatic and open evangelical theology (as I encountered it in England), and thus there is much in those traditions that can provide fertile ground for intergenerational ministry. Because ludicity correlates with and is commensurate with the central concerns of intergenerational ministry, we find mutuality between participants, collaboration, shared experiences, and bidirectional teaching.

Implications for Intergenerational Ministry

Several possible implications arise from the list above. We will focus on four:

First, Explore the Theology of Your Church

We cannot simply say, "If a church believes X, then it will do Y." At the same time, we can clearly see some relationship between belief and practice. So, when thinking about intergenerational ministry, consider the theology of your church. What does your church believe about some of these important doctrines such as the Spirit and the Trinity? Are these beliefs held by all? If not, what are the key differences? This is not to say, of course, that "if your church doesn't hold to a social model of the Trinity, it should

---

[40] Suurmond, *Word and Spirit at Play*, 25.
[41] Moltmann, *God in Creation*, 311.
[42] Moltmann, *God in Creation*, 311.

change!" Rather, we should believe things because we think they are true rather than helpful.[43]

Second, Reflect on the Implications of Your Theology

If your church holds to similar theological commitments as set out above, commitments that provide fertile ground for ludicity and intergenerational ministry, then draw attention to that. If not, meet with people to capture their imaginations with a theological vision that will lead naturally to ludicity and also to intergenerational ministry.

Third, Consider How to Embody Ludicity in Your Church Life and Practices

If you have established that your church holds open and/or charismatic theological commitments and have corporately reflected on the implications of these commitments, then you can work on embedding ludicity into the everyday life and practices of your church. Review each area of your church and think about how it embodies freedom, participation, informality, and relational safety. What needs to change regarding how you run activities, teach, worship, do mission, plan, and pray? If instances of inconsistency emerge where theological commitments are not being followed through into practice, then highlight those commitments.

Fourth, Think about the Limits

Free-flowing rivers and rapids have lots of positive aspects, but being in them can be as nerve-racking as it can be fun. In exploring and reflecting on the implications of charismatic and open evangelical theology, churches need to consider how to steer the boat. In the context of ludicity, another way of looking at this is to acknowledge that all play has rules and boundaries; play without rules and boundaries ceases to be play. So, what are the limits and boundaries going to be? And how do you determine these limits and boundaries? No easy answers exist to these questions, but not

---

[43] I, myself, come from a tradition that holds to little of the open and charismatic theology discussed above. A commitment to intergenerational ministry and to a more conservative theology led me to explore the doctrine of accommodation as a resource that helped churches develop intergenerational practices within a more conservative evangelical framework. See Gareth Crispin, "Intergenerational Communities and a Theology of Accommodation," in *InterGenerate: How Churches Can Become More Intentionally Intergenerational in Outlook and Practice*, ed. Holly Catterton Allen (Abilene, TX: Abilene Christian University Press, 2018), 51–61.

addressing them in your context will mean disagreements when you reach certain points. Even at St. James Church, where a number of people were happy with the open evangelical ethos, some, nevertheless, voiced a need for more direction from the top, at times.

This issue of boundaries in play brings C. S. Lewis's *The Lion, the Witch and the Wardrobe* to mind. Narnia is a land in the grip of the rule of the evil White Witch when two boys and two girls arrive seemingly by accident, but according to a prophecy. While seeking to help those opposing the White Witch, these four children hear and finally meet a great lion named Aslan who leads and wins the battle against the witch. In Narnia, the White Witch oversees a hierarchical, tyrannical regime; by contrast, there is a great sense in which life with Aslan is like a game, a fun game, a good game. The children play with Aslan at various points in the story; the story reveals a very ludic life, free and participative—an intergenerational community with children empowered and given voice, with mutuality and reciprocal relationships abounding. However, the game—the play—is not open-ended, and relationships are not symmetrical. Boundaries support the game, making it possible, and a magic provides a framework for what can and cannot be. Perhaps Mr. Beaver captures the tension, a tension we all face, in his famous exclamation. When Susan worries whether or not Aslan is safe, Mr. Beaver replies: "Safe? Who said anything about safe? 'Course he isn't safe. But he's good. He's the King, I tell you."

THEOLOGY IN PRACTICE: QUESTIONS TO CONSIDER

1. What theologies in your church fuel your approach toward ludicity in regard to freedom, participation, informality, and relational safety?

2. How can the theologies of your context enliven your approach toward ludicity and intergenerational ministry?

3. List and evaluate your current practices in your ministry setting. How might you adjust your practices to cultivate ludicity?

4. What boundaries need to be established in your ministry that allow and encourage all generations to flourish by cultivating a fertile ground for ludicity?

Section Two

REIMAGINING INTERGENERATIONAL PRACTICE

"Re-imagination is the birthplace for vision and change. Your imagination is one of the most valuable talents you have and deserves your full attention. Imagining how you want to live your life is one thing, but connecting your imagination to a visual representation will give you exactly the traction you need to make it a reality."

—Susan C. Young

CHAPTER 4

APPRENTICING FAITH TOGETHER
Helping Adults Understand Discipleship and Their Role in Intergenerational Community

JOHANNAH MYERS

> *"Adding wings to caterpillars does not create butterflies. It creates awkward and dysfunctional caterpillars. Butterflies are created through transformation."*
> —Stephanie Pace Marshall

"We didn't have much *adult* discussion . . . I didn't get a lot out of it." This was one man's description of his experience after his participation in a yearlong intergenerational small group. He considered the whole experiment a failure. Meanwhile, in the children's evaluation of their experience in the same small group, they expressed genuine appreciation of their time together and wanted their intergenerational small group to continue meeting long after the year together concluded. Did the intergenerational small group experiment fail? Was the model fruitless as the man suggested? Or was his frustration more about a failure to understand why the intergenerational group was important and *what role* he was supposed to play within it?

Our attempts to make existing ministries more intergenerational are often reduced to what to do with the children, or contemplations regarding what model of intergenerational ministry to use. *Yet even the most successful intergenerational models can lead to frustration and lack of enthusiasm by the adults because they struggle to understand discipleship and their roles within intergenerational communities.* As leadership author and speaker Simon Sinek explains, "Very few people or companies can clearly articulate WHY they do WHAT they do . . . people don't buy WHAT you do, they buy WHY you do it."[1] We, too, often invite adults to participate in intergenerational ministry without laying the "why" foundation. Why do we think intergenerational ministry is important? Why are adult roles critical? Adjusting how we as leaders communicate the reasons behind discipleship and spiritual formation can help lay a foundation for positive experiences and discipleship. This chapter explores how apprenticeship can help church leaders understand why intergenerational ministry is important in the formation of disciples. It also clarifies the role adults play in intergenerational community.

A Vision for Apprenticeship

Adults who grew up attending church were most likely raised in a congregation whose Christian education model mimicked the public school system.[2] The familiar, age-segregated ministry models are what most adults consider comfortable. Our adults have been raised to believe the purpose of Christian education is to teach knowledge and information about the Christian faith with little emphasis toward a hands-on practice of the faith. Paul Moore, one of the pioneers of Messy Church, suggests that "in the church we have tended to assume that it is best to send the children out to age-segregated groups, largely because of the notion that young minds cannot understand more complex concepts."[3] Because many in our

---

[1] Simon Sinek, *Start with Why: How Great Leaders Inspire Everyone to Take Action* (New York: Penguin Group, 2009), 39, 41.

[2] John Drane, "Messy Disciples," in *Messy Church Theology: Exploring the Significance of Messy Church for the Wider Church*, ed. George Lings (Abingdon, UK: Bible Reading Fellowship, 2013), 121.

[3] Paul Moore, *Making Disciples in Messy Church: Growing Faith in an All-Age Community* (Abingdon, UK: Bible Reading Fellowship, 2013), 106.

churches have been conditioned to think of discipleship as something best learned in classroom settings, inviting them into intergenerational settings is at odds with their understanding and experience of learning how to be disciples of Jesus—especially because this setting is more often centered around hands-on, relational learning.

Helping adults understand the *why* of intergenerational ministry starts with asking, *"Is discipleship only about what we know?"* Jesus called his disciples not to go to school but to experience a way of living, the way of living Jesus himself embodied. Holly Catterton Allen and Christine Lawton Ross notice how Jesus called together a group of disciples and "walked with them, talked with them, ate with them, taught them, and modeled prayer, healing and servanthood for them."[4] Jesus formed a community of diverse people who were all learning how to practice his way. *A call to discipleship was a call to learn a way of living and to join a community of others who were also learning about this life.* Therefore, the learning of a disciple, according to theologian Keith Ferdinando, "was not simply a cognitive process, but a reorientation of life, values, and character, through experiencing the life of Christ quite as much as through hearing his words."[5] Jesus called his disciples not to learn rules or concepts but to live his life.

An age-segregated classroom model of discipleship formation can be useful for teaching about Jesus, but this model does little to help people of any age learn how to *live* like Jesus. The way Jesus taught his own disciples more closely mirrors an *apprenticeship model of learning*. Educational theorists Jean Lave and Etienne Wenger offer insights into apprenticeship with an invaluable method of learning they refer to as "situated learning."[6] Students, or newcomers, learn not in a sterile classroom setting but situated in hands-on doing in real-life situations. For example, a newcomer learning to bake best learns how to bake by being allowed in the kitchen alongside a baker with years of experience. The new baker might start by

---

[4] Holly Catterton Allen and Christine Lawton Ross, *Intergenerational Christian Formation: Bringing the Whole Church Together in Ministry, Community, and Worship* (Downers Grove, IL: InterVarsity Press, 2012), 112.

[5] Keith Ferdinando, "Jesus, the Theological Educator," *Themelios* 38, no. 3 (November 2013): 364.

[6] Jean Lave and Etienne Wenger, *Situated Learning: Legitimate Peripheral Participation* (Cambridge, UK: Cambridge University Press, 1991).

observing, and then as she grows in skill, move toward more and more hands-on practice. Lave and Wenger call this "legitimate peripheral participation."[7] Legitimate peripheral participation allows newcomers a place within a community and access to practices that help them grow in skill through observation, learning from those more experienced members of the community and gradually experiencing more hands-on practice themselves.[8] As the newcomers grow in skills, they become more ingrained within the community of practice.

This model of apprenticeship described by Lave and Wenger fits with how Jesus taught his disciples. For his disciples to learn this way of life, Jesus did more than simply sit them down and instruct them as if in a classroom. The disciples' learning was *situated* in day-to-day life. Jesus gave his disciples legitimate access to his practices and allowed them space to learn, beginning from the periphery and then gradually adding more hands-on involvement. First, the disciples learned by observing Jesus at work. His disciples heard him teach (Mark 4:1–34; 6:2–6). They watched him heal, cast out demons, and perform great miracles (Matt. 8:1–17; Mark 4:35–40; 5:1–20). The disciples also learned through active, engaging conversation with Jesus. For example, when Jesus taught the parable of the sower to the crowds, his disciples later asked him for more explanation; then, Jesus engaged with them further, conversing about the meaning of this parable (Matt. 13:3–23; Mark 4:1–9, 10–20). Along the way, Jesus invited his disciples into active, hands-on participation; he invited them to collaborate with him in ministry. After observing Jesus at work, his disciples began to get hands-on with Jesus's ministry. For example, when a great crowd followed Jesus to Bethsaida, the disciples struggled with what to do with all those people (Luke 9:10–17). Jesus put the initiative on the disciples to feed the people, drawing them into his work. Though it was Jesus who blessed, broke, and gave the food, the disciples helped distribute the meal among the crowd. The disciples struggled, but they learned.

As the disciples grew in their kingdom skills, Jesus sent them out on missions without him, inviting them further into his ministry (Mark 6:7–13).

---

[7] Lave and Wenger, *Situated Learning*, 45.
[8] See David Csinos, "Come Follow Me: Apprenticeship in Jesus' Approach to Education," *Religious Education* 105, no. 1 (January–February 2010): 45–62.

Before sending his disciples out, Jesus demonstrated skills they would need through word and action. He taught and explained the parable of the sower, healed, cast out demons, and handled rejection (Mark 4:1–34; 5:1–43; 6:1–6). After a time of instruction and modeling, Jesus instructed his disciples to proclaim the kingdom, cast out demons, and heal the sick, while warning them of their potential rejection by some people. The disciples grew into living Jesus's way of life gradually, through observation, conversation, participation, and gaining responsibility.

For the disciples, learning Jesus's way of life meant learning a new vocation. We hear vocational invitation when Jesus calls to the disciples, "Follow me and I will make you fish for people" (Mark 1:17 NRSV). Before Jesus ascended to heaven, he told his disciples, "Go therefore and make disciples of all nations, baptizing them in the name of the Father and of the Son and of the Holy Spirit, and teaching them to obey everything that I have commanded you" (Matt. 28:19–20 NRSV). With his ascension, the disciples were then tasked to fulfill their original call to fish for people. Ferdinando finds that Jesus's first call to follow "always had the final commissioning in mind."[9] Jesus taught and trained his disciples like apprentices learning a trade, readying them to take over the "business" after the master returned home. Sylvia Wilkey Collinson observes the following about how Jesus apprenticed his disciples: "Like every Jewish male learning a trade they [the disciples] were expected to observe and learn from working with Jesus. They were apprentice-proclaimers of the kingdom, bearing testimony to Jesus."[10]

Apprenticeship and Intergenerational Ministry

When we approach disciple formation akin to learning a trade or vocation, the concept of apprenticeship can then help adults understand *why* churches must shift discipleship away from age-level classroom settings. Learning the vocation of following Jesus necessitates creating a community of practitioners who are apprentices of faith. A community of apprentices must have participants of varying skill levels on how to live Jesus's way of

---

[9] Ferdinando, "Jesus, the Theological Educator," 361.
[10] Sylvia Wilkey Collinson, *Making Disciples: The Significance of Jesus' Educational Methods for Today's Church* (Waynesboro, GA: Paternoster Press, 2004), 70.

life; in other words, *our community of people apprenticing faith needs both newcomers to faith alongside those who have years of experience.*

Lave and Wenger demonstrate how legitimate peripheral participation works with newcomers learning from "old-timers"—those who have more years of hands-on experience.[11] The key to apprenticeship is having someone with more experience working alongside a newcomer. Since learning the way of Jesus looks more like apprenticeship than formal classroom teaching, churches need people who have years of experience living the story and practices of faith walking alongside those who are new to the community. In other words, we need an intergenerational approach to discipleship. As Martyn Payne, Messy Church leader and intergenerational ministry leader, writes in *Messy Togetherness*, "If we want to see our Christian faith caught and nurtured today, those with faith need to be alongside those who are learning faith. . . . The old need to be alongside the young, who can bring the gift of a lively spirituality and an eager sense of adventure when it comes to exploring the wonders of God's creation and what faith in Jesus means."[12]

Using the model and language of apprenticeship helps shift disciple-making from age-segregated classrooms to all-age communities of practice by helping establish the "why" for making this shift. The language of apprenticeship also helps adults understand their roles within intergenerational, apprenticing communities. Adults' roles are two-fold. First, they are to be apprentice-learners themselves, learning from one another and most especially from Jesus. *When we approach discipleship as apprenticing faith, everyone is a practitioner—an apprentice of Jesus.* In this way, Jesus's disciples are different from apprentices in traditional trades because, as Collinson astutely observes, "there was no expectation that they would eventually progress beyond their teacher."[13] In a traditional apprenticeship, students could, in time, surpass the master in skill or artistry and become a master themselves. Jesus's disciples will not. Disciples of Jesus make new disciples while still retaining their own status as disciples and students.

---

[11] Lave and Wenger, *Situated Learning*, 45.

[12] Martyn Payne, *Messy Togetherness: Being Intergenerational in Messy Church* (Abingdon, UK: The Bible Reading Fellowship, 2016), 32.

[13] Collinson, *Making Disciples*, 46–47.

Ferdinando states, "It is significant that in the epistles Jesus's own life and ministry continue to be a focus of discipleship. The teaching of future disciples in new situations and contexts still centred on following Jesus."[14] As the apostle Paul would tell the church at Corinth, "Be imitators of me, as I am of Christ" (1 Cor. 11:1 NRSV). Paul taught others but was always being taught by Christ. Though disciples move from the periphery into full participation within the community of practice, Jesus remains at the center as master and teacher. *In any ministry, at any age, we are all apprentices of Jesus—lifelong learners who are developing the skills and practices necessary to live Jesus's life.*

We are all apprentices, but, within our communities of practice, we need people who have years of experience living the story and practices of faith to walk alongside those who are new to the community. This is the second aspect of adult roles within intergenerational communities. For children, youth, and newcomers to Christian discipleship, having relationships with disciples from other generations provides authentic modeling. These less experienced people are watching more experienced craftspeople at work, and thereby, they begin to learn the craft for themselves. As Christian educator and author Ivy Beckwith says, "When the child brushes up against people of faith through this participation in the life of the community, the child sees models of faith. The child sees adults who struggle, who trust God, who make mistakes and are forgiven, who work for mercy and justice, who model kingdom values."[15] For newcomers of any age, witnessing the struggles and joys of others is essential for faith development. According to Kara E. Powell and Chap Clark, "the greatest gift you can give your children is to let them see you struggle and wrestle with how to live a lifetime of trust in God."[16]

Returning to the example shared at the beginning of this chapter, the older man, who was around eighty years old, was active in both a Sunday school class and an adult Bible study in addition to participating in this yearlong all-age discipleship group. He was accustomed to a model of

---

[14] Ferdinando, "Jesus, the Theological Educator," 364.

[15] Ivy Beckwith, *Postmodern Children's Ministry: Ministry to Children in the 21st Century* (Grand Rapids: Zondervan, 2004), 66.

[16] Kara E. Powell and Chap Clark, *Sticky Faith: Everyday Ideas to Build Lasting Faith in Your Kids* (Grand Rapids: Zondervan, 2011), 46.

disciple formation where adults held one of two roles: *teacher* (one who lectures and leads discussion) or *student* (one who listens and sometimes participates in discussion). In his Bible classes, the man was primarily used to being in the role of student. *However, within a community of practice, there is not as great a need for clearly delineated teacher and student roles.* In the intergenerational small group, Bible study was primarily discussion using open-ended questions that allowed participation from all ages and through hands-on engagement with the Bible story.[17] While people in the group took turns facilitating the gathering, there was *no designated teacher*. The group was designed so all participants of any age had the potential to offer insight as well as the expectation to learn. It was clear from the man's review of his experience that *he never understood his place in the group*. His comments about there not being enough "adult discussion" and not getting a lot out of this time suggested he struggled to learn in an environment that was not his usual formal classroom setting with the expected role of being a passive student. He was not assigned to be the teacher, either. What was he supposed to do? Had we approached this intergenerational group using apprenticeship language, the concept that he was first and foremost to be an apprentice of Jesus would have been more central; and secondly, he would have known he was to serve as an "old-timer" in the community sharing his lifetime experience of faith, as he practiced faith alongside the others in his group.

In his book *The Shape of Living*, theologian David Ford wrote: "Wisdom is best learned face-to-face by apprenticeship to those who have themselves learned it in the same way."[18] We need intergenerational communities of people who are practicing faith together, learning as apprentices together. Inviting adults into this discipleship approach, into these intergenerational communities, can, however, lead to frustration. As intergenerational leaders, we need to be prepared to explain why we need all ages together, why we need generations serving together, and the roles of adults within these all-age communities. Because apprenticeship closely mirrors the way Jesus

---

[17] His specific group, for reference, included an adult couple slightly younger than himself and a family with two adults around forty years old and three kids—a young teen, a middle school student, and a preschooler.

[18] David F. Ford, *The Shape of Living: Spiritual Directions for Everyday Life* (Grand Rapids: Baker Books, 2004), 99.

formed his own disciples, using apprenticeship as a foundational model for building intergenerational communities can help leaders minimize frustration and pushback.

THEOLOGY IN PRACTICE: QUESTIONS TO CONSIDER

1. In your experience, and in your context, what would it mean to reimagine intergenerational discipleship as an all-age apprenticeship in the way of Jesus—as a way of living rather than a knowledge or skill to obtain? How do current paradigms that emphasize teacher/student models in your context hinder Myers's reimagining of intergenerational apprenticeship?

2. Consider the different generations in your context. When it comes to discipleship, which generations feel sidelined or do not wish to be involved?

3. How might you and others in your context begin teaching this reimagined Christian discipleship, utilizing Myers's intergenerational apprenticeship model?

4. How would giving adults in your context a new view of intergenerational discipleship help them embrace and adopt intergenerational ministry

CHAPTER 5

THE CHURCH'S ROLE IN RESTORING PARENTS AS CENTRAL TO DISCIPLESHIP

RACHEL TURNER

> *"Culture does not change because we desire to change it. Culture changes when the organization is transformed—the culture reflects the realities of people working together everyday."*
>
> —Frances Hesselbein

In my first few years of children's ministry, I ran into a problem. While children were flourishing in their faith during my programs, for the rest of the week, very little spiritual formation seemed to happen. My job was to help children meet and know God so they could walk daily with him, but I only saw them once or twice a week. I tried to make my programs more impactful, more significant, more effective, but I quickly came to the conclusion that I needed parents to get on board with what I was doing. I needed them to take the baton from me and keep it going until the next church program.

So I wrote letters to parents letting them know how to take what the children were learning and continue it at home. I gave them activity packs.

I sent home devotional ideas. Most parents did nothing with it. I was so frustrated. I was asking so little from them and was doing all the thinking for them. How could they not manage to do it?

As a church staff member, I was given a few days a year to go on retreat with God to pray and plan. My whole goal for the retreat was this: *How can I get parents to do what I am asking them to do so we can all see children flourish in their faith?*

I went away to a little cabin in the English countryside, surrounded by rolling green hills dotted with sheep. As I was praying, I felt drawn to Deuteronomy 6:4–9 (NIV):

> Hear, O Israel: The LORD our God, the LORD is one. Love the LORD your God with all your heart and with all your soul and with all your strength. These commandments that I give you today are to be on your hearts. Impress them on your children. Talk about them when you sit at home and when you walk along the road, when you lie down and when you get up. Tie them as symbols on your hands and bind them on your foreheads. Write them on the doorframes of your houses and on your gates.

I felt like the rug had been pulled out from under me. I read it again. Phrases began to drill into my heart. *When you sit at home. When you walk along the road. When you lie down. When you get up. Doorframes of your houses.*

It appeared that God's plan for children's discipleship was not centered in my fantastic children's church program. God's first step for children meeting him was not in my after-school club. It was in the ordinary, everyday lives of family. It was when a parent and a kid ate breakfast together, or when a guardian and a new foster child learned how to walk home after school and talk about their day. It happened when Grandma got to read a bedtime story, and when a family was waiting in the bleachers for another child to get out of swimming class. God had designed children's discipleship to happen in the ordinary, everyday boring bits of life because that is where he is. It is where God wants children to learn to live with him.

I even did the math. If children came to every Sunday and every midweek group, I would get 100–150 hours a year with those children. Parents on average get between two- and three-thousand hours a year with their children—hours upon hours of ordinary, boring life where God lives with parents and their children—plenty of time to help their kids meet and know God right where they are.

If my job was to disciple children, then I did not need parents to get on board with my program. I needed to get on board with theirs. I needed to change my whole approach. I had been treating children as separate individuals and ignoring their wider context. But a child is, or should be, daily supported by parents or caretakers.

That little family is rooted within a support circle of extended family and close friends. That wider family unit is often built into a church community, and then the wider family of God. A circle within a circle within a circle. In order for a child to be discipled in the everyday, I could not only work with children. I had to work across every layer of circles that surround them: their parents, their community, their church family—all of it.

If parents could step into their role of discipling children in the everyday, then the church would be free to do what church is designed to do: together draw near to God through teaching, praying, and worshiping, spurring each other on to good works, providing a place to love and be loved, being a community of people being transformed to be more like Christ, with every person playing their part in the body of Christ, no matter what age.

What would my ministry look like if I could truly enable parents, caretakers, and extended families to confidently disciple their children? Children's and teens' faith would significantly deepen, parents would discover the joy and freedom of discipling their children, and the adult congregation would become more confident in playing their role in being an intergenerational body able to learn from each other and value each other.

Three major shifts needed to occur for us to successfully go on this journey:

1. Fight the expert culture
2. Give skills, not resources
3. Empower a church culture of parenting for faith

Vision: Fight the "Expert Culture"

For years, parents and churches have been locked into a mutually agreed-upon belief: young people's spirituality requires specialist expert attention that the church is best experienced and positioned to deliver.

We live in an expert culture. Parents want children to have the best teachers, coaches, and medical care. Of course, they want their children to have the best spiritual input, as well. We, as churches, with our thousands of hours of education, time, and focus, are primed and ready to deliver it. But if parents are truly the God-appointed primary disciplers of their children, then we need to begin to fight this idea of expert culture that so many churches have adopted. *The idea of an expert culture robs parents of the confidence and skills needed to step into their role and limits churches by asking them to do and be more than is fruitful or intended.*

Fight the Expert Culture in Us

The first step in my journey was to take a long hard look at myself and my expert identity. I liked being the expert. In order to serve parents, I had to humble myself. My expertise in children's spirituality and church leadership was a tool for serving. Families did not exist to facilitate my ministry. I existed to facilitate theirs.

In addition, I had to really believe in the power of parents. I had to embrace the fact that a parent—even when doing a mediocre job—will always be more powerful than my best Sunday program. I am not saying what we do within children's ministry or intergenerational church is insignificant or unimportant. I am saying parents cannot fully do what the church does, and the church cannot fully do what parents do.

Once I began to serve parents, the spiritual fruit in young people started to grow. Their faith was more natural and woven into their school life, home life, and hobbies. Children would tell me stories about praying in the car for a friend or having a big family discussion about whether there would be bacon in heaven. They talked about middle-of-the-night conversations with their parents about fear and shared experiences of wondering together about Bible stories on their trips to school. When we release expertise of ministry out of the church, discipleship happens everywhere life happens: while walking down the road, in sleepy bedtimes, and during groggy mornings—in all the places God outlined in Deuteronomy.

Fight the Expert Culture in Parents

When I returned from my retreat, I explained my recent change in understanding to the parents in my church. I boldly explained my mistake and outlined their important role as the primary disciplers of their children. The response was not what I anticipated. Rather than the wholehearted cheer I expected, I was met with a sea of confused and apprehensive parents. Some were angry that I was potentially shirking my responsibility at church. Others were fearful because they did not feel they knew enough about faith to be trusted with their children's spiritual lives. Others were worried about talking about faith too much and pushing their children away from God. Many were nervous about getting it wrong and damaging their children. And still, others just thought the church would do it better with more "fun" and "accessibility." When parents want experts to do the job, they often lack confidence to do the job themselves. And certainly, when church leaders see themselves as experts, we implicitly teach parents they are not qualified.

It takes deliberate strategy to coach parents into confident and effective disciplers of their children. Both parents and caregivers start in radically different places: unconfident or controlling, fearful or overly proactive. Our role is to empower everyone to healthily and effectively walk alongside their children's journey with God.

The starting point for many of our parents is giving them a vision of what that could look like. Modern commercials are great at this. Personally, I am a sucker for Red Lobster commercials. I could be happily sitting on my sofa, not hungry at all, and then my screen changes. I see steaming shrimp falling from the sky into garlic butter, and my mouth starts to water. I see the warm basket of cheese bread, and I am done. I want to go now. My future pathway is open before me.

Parents need church leaders to cast a vision for their role in their children's lives because sometimes they cannot see it themselves. Parents are struggling to juggle all the demands of parenting; they can be laser-focused on the immediate needs that arise: physical transport, discipline, homework, and friendship troubles. When it comes to spiritual parenting, they can easily let its importance slip out of view. Often, that is because the spiritual life of their child, in their mind, can be reduced to the few hours on a Sunday, when they take their child to church. If we, as church leaders, are to shift parents' views of themselves to become main contacts who can support, encourage, and journey with their child's daily faith, then we need to make the case for the immediate need of God in children's lives. Parents need stories of what God looks like in the life of the child, and the impact he makes on their daily lives. We know what a four-year-old genuinely praying looks like. We know the beauty of a seven-year-old finding freedom from shame. We have seen the strength of a nine-year-old who has her feet on Scripture. We know that children need God in their ordinary everyday lives, and we know the difference he makes in their minds and hearts. Arming parents with this information empowers them to see themselves carrying out this work. We can give them the stories they need. We can share stories of what children connected to God look like, so parents can say, "I want that for my child!" Parents need vision. They need stories.

Parents also need to be told the truth. For so long they have believed that the church is the center of children's discipleship because this is what we have communicated. If we want to empower them for their God-given role, they need to hear from us that we believe in them and are here to equip them. Wherever they are in their own faith journey, they can guide their children to meet and know God. Over and over, we need to assure parents that their parenting for faith is not about creating church at home or being a perfect Christian. Rather, it is simply helping their children see and engage with God in ordinary life. Parents and caregivers need to know that the church is here to support and encourage them in parenting for faith in their real, everyday experiences.

IKEA and the Dentist

Fighting the expert culture also requires reshaping how parents and the church interact. In my experience, parents often see the church as they do the dentist. I have the nicest and best dentist in the world, yet I still feel nervous when I go see her. She asks me the standard questions about how often I brush and floss. Inevitably, I lie. I make myself look a bit better than

I actually am. I do not want to admit my failure to an expert. Then she invites me to sit on her chair and inspects my mouth. That moment feels so exposing. She can see all my flaws: where I accidentally miss brushing, plaque buildup, or even cavities. She calls out my failings to her assistant to put in my record. Then she gets to work cleaning up. When she is done, she instructs me how to improve, and I leave the office feeling deeply grateful but oddly vulnerable.

I suspect many parents feel similarly about church leaders whose role is to help them and their kids. Certainly, parents are grateful and come to church to help their family flourish. But at the same time, parents can feel very nervous around church staff. Parenting is a very vulnerable subject, and discussing it with church staff often makes parents feel exposed and judged, no matter how nice the staff is. If we want parents to feel empowered, supported, and flourishing in their role as spiritual disciplers, we need to reshape how parents view church staff, moving away from experts and toward IKEA.

IKEA is a large store that sells everything you could possibly need for your home, whether it's plates or furniture or curtains or outdoor plants. When you enter the showroom, you walk through a vast maze all set up to look like rooms in a home, with each beautifully decorated. Everything says, "Welcome! Come and explore different rooms and see which suits your unique family. Do you like black feather lampshades? Bright red countertops? Are you a more natural bamboo type family? You are the expert of your style, and it is your home you are creating. Teach us how we can help you." IKEA does everything it can to make *you* feel like the expert, not the store.

I love watching people in IKEA. They laugh and tease each other. They try things out. People sit on the couches and lie on the beds. They open the cupboards in the kitchen and rummage around in the closets. They buy things they never imagined as well as pieces that feel familiar. IKEA even provides a restaurant halfway through to give you a rest and shortcuts for people who hate shopping.

I want parents and carers to see the church as IKEA. I want the church to invite families with an experience that says, "Welcome, parents! Helping your kid meet and know God is one of the greatest joys of parenting, and it is as simple as being you. Every family is different. You are the experts for your children. You have been given all the gifts you need to do this well, even if you are exhausted. We are here to help you feel encouraged and supported in whatever way you choose to do this. No matter what. Teach us how we can help you."

When parents see us as IKEA, passionately believing in their parenting and the spiritual power of their home, however it looks, they begin to come to the church freely. The church staff can give them a vision of what their children's lives can be like as they journey with God, and be there to help them know how to guide their children in it.

Give Skills, Not Resources

The second shift to make is to *move away from trying to give parents **activities** to do with their kids and move toward giving parents the **skills** to journey with their children's faith*. If parents are dependent on resources, they will always feel they are not enough. Their ability to disciple their children will only ever be as good as the resource they manage to grab. I believe parents *are* the resource God gave to their children, and it is our job to help them learn how to disciple their children in the ordinary every day. **Five core skills** are needed to empower and equip parents.

Core Skill 1: Create Windows

Many parents feel the pressure to make Christianity look positive to their children, so they try to be a "model" for their kids. Instead, I encourage parents and caregivers to **create windows** into their own authentic lives with God. Children need to know it is okay to worry about Grandma and talk to God about it. They need to know you cry in your car and ask God to give you a hug and how God sent his peace. They can deeply benefit from hearing you wrestle with what the preacher talked about at church or wonder out loud about parts of the Bible that are surprising or confusing you. When parents learn how to create windows through which kids can peer into their quiet times, prayer moments, and the worship music they love to sing in the car, then their kids see real Christians in action. From how they process grief to how they find encouragement to persevere in difficult times, parental ups and downs are vital information for a child looking for authentic faith. Looking through the windows of a parent's faith offers answers as to why parents show up to church socials—why they allow their children to see what life with God looks like. If parents can create a window into situations in their lives, then their children will be able to know what to do when they experience it too.

Core Skill 2: Framing

All parents *frame* life for their children. From why the sky is blue to how to cross the road, parents explain how the world works. Daily, parents have the opportunity to walk alongside their children and explain what they are looking at and how to engage with it. Parents create a framework of understanding about the world around children, so children can know how to operate within it. Parents can do this with the spiritual things of life too. Framing is simply explaining where God is and how to engage with him as part of everyday life—reflecting on where God was during your difficult day at work, or whispering to your child at church to explain what God does when we sing to him. Children need us to frame God in the ordinary bits of life, so they can learn to see God in those times.

Core Skill 3: Unwinding Warped Views of God

Our children are growing in their understanding of God, and sometimes they can get a warped view of him. This can happen even when they are being taught all the right things because they are simultaneously building from other experiences. Children are constantly building their understanding of God from all aspects of their life, including the opinions of their friends, their personal experiences, movies and images, and even their own brain development. Parents get to walk alongside their children's journey of understanding and help to **unravel** warped views of God. We can use a variety of techniques to keep conversations flowing and gently shepherd how our children see God and interact with him.

Core Skill 4: Chat and Catch

Children find their own voice in their **communication with God** and learn how they perceive his communications back to them. Formulas can often hamper children in their genuine voice with God. Parents, who know their children so well, can help their children flourish in the way they enjoy talking back and forth with God. Parents can free their children to know how they like talking to God and where this takes place. Then parents are not the central figures in a child's connection with God.

Core Skill 5: Surf the Waves

Just as in surfing, parents can jump aboard spiritual and emotional waves in their children's lives and ride those waves with them. There will be times when children will be into God and church, and then suddenly be uninterested. A child might love reading the Bible together, and then switch to listening to an audiobook Bible alone. A child may be going through a very specific obsession, like Disney films, or particular games. Whatever wave is happening in a child's life, parents can *surf* along and help their children find God in that wave. When one wave collapses, parents simply wait for a new one.

Teaching the Skills

When a parent begins to gain confidence using these skills in everyday life, spiritual growth is encouraged both in the parent and the child. *When a community of parents begin to gain their footing, church culture begins to shift.* And when children begin picking up these skills, they will disciple their siblings and gain confidence using these skills with other adults in their intergenerational communities.

There are many ways of teaching these skills. Options include gathered teaching, like the Parenting for Faith course developed at my church, or even onetime events focusing on a specific pain point that parents are experiencing. Skills can be taught little by little, enabling whole communities to grow in them together.

However you do it, equip parents with the skills they need to disciple their children in the ordinary days of family life. If parents choose to pick up a resource, they will have all the skills they need to adapt it to their children. And if they do not want a resource, then *every conversation and time together with their kids is an opportunity for discipleship.*

Empower a Church Culture of Parenting for Faith

The process of learning how to parent has always been rooted in community. God designed a child to be within a family unit, and that family unit to be within extended family, and that extended family to be within a local community, and on and on—a circle within a circle of influence and support. If the church is hoping for parents to flourish in their spiritual roles, it needs to seriously consider what parents need from their church community.

Parents and caregivers bring their childhood, emotional and spiritual scars, newness in faith, theological assumptions, and past experiences into figuring out how to parent for faith. When people lived in villages next to their immediate and extended families for their whole lives, they learned how to parent as part of an intergenerational community. Now, our local communities often are not as integrated into each other's lives. The best opportunity for people to learn how to parent as part of an intergenerational loving community is the church.[1] I believe that, as a church, we have the potential to restore to parents this joy of discipling their children and, therefore, teaching their children how to raise future generations, as well.

I firmly believe that it is never too early or too late to start parenting for faith. Parents do not stop becoming parents when their children reach the age of eighteen. Parents are always parents. It just looks different in every phase. My approach is that we always resource parents, no matter what their age. They can still be influential even when they are eighty as parents, grandparents, and great-grandparents. We have seen great spiritual fruit borne when an eighty-year-old decides to start proactively parenting for faith!

Each stage of parenting requires new skills and biblical assurances of their significance in their family's life. Parents of teens and young adults need to know how to equip their children when finding their path with God in a complex world. New grandparents need support and encouragement navigating their new spiritual roles and tools in how to help their children shape a new family. They may need new information and

---

[1] For further reading, see Rachel Turner, *It Takes a Church to Raise a Parent: Creating a Culture Where Parenting for Faith Can Flourish* (Abingdon, UK: Bible Reading Fellowship, 2018).

equipping if their grandchildren are fostered or adopted, or if they are living far from them. Parents of middle generations need us to shout about how influential they are to their teenage grandchildren, and how to be a steadying faith anchor for the big choices their adult children are making. Parents who are retiring can be greatly encouraged as we help them explore their calling in the next season of their lives and how their family fits into what God might be asking them to do.

What might our intergenerational ministries look like if we saw family ministry as coming alongside every stage of parenting, throughout a lifetime? How a parent creates windows for their five-year-old child is the same way they grow to create windows into their spiritual lives for their grandchildren when they visit at Christmas. All the skills can be used throughout a lifetime of parenting; but we, as ministers, rarely seek to continue equipping them in each stage. Parents need us to champion them in their parenting and grandparenting roles, giving them skills and encouraging them as they navigate their ever-changing roles in their families' lives. Their calling to disciple their children does not end at a certain age.

This will be a journey that looks different for every community, every church, and every family. What is common between us all, though, is a desire to see generation upon generation meet and know God for themselves. Whatever your starting point, it is worth the journey. When we can restore parents to their role within the discipleship of their children, I believe we will not only see fruit in children's lives but in the parents' lives, as well.

Let's be a church that fights expert culture and enables parents to be imperfect primary disciplers of their children, while we speak truth, inspire, encourage, and support them. Let's be a church that trains parents how to think, giving them the skills they need to truly disciple their children, not just do activities with them. Let's be a church that decides to be an intergenerational community that wraps around parents of all ages to see their children and grandchildren know God in the everyday. It's a journey worth taking.

THEOLOGY IN PRACTICE: QUESTIONS TO CONSIDER

1. How are the terms "family ministry" and "intergenerational ministry" different but complementary?

2. In an intergenerational context, how can all generations support parents and families of all ages in passing down faith throughout the week?

3. How is intergenerational ministry especially poised to fight what Turner calls the "expert culture"?

4. How might intergenerational relationships and ministry contribute to helping parents of all ages build skills—not resources—for sharing their faith with their children?

5. As an intergenerational leader, what would it look like to reimagine and nurture a culture in your context that empowers parents of all ages to be the primary disciplers of their children?

CHAPTER 6

THE FINAL FRONTIER?

Theological Insights to Support Imaginative Intergenerational Preaching

DAVID M. CSINOS

*"When she transformed into a butterfly
the caterpillars spoke
not of her beauty
but of her weirdness.
They wanted her to change back
into what she always had been.
But she had wings."*

—Dean Jackson

A few years ago, twenty of my friends and colleagues gathered in London for an international roundtable about intergenerational ministry.[1] At one point in this time together, we pored over all the different ways worship can become intergenerational. One member of this group soberly informed us that, despite all the innovative ideas we were tossing around, he had found it

---

[1] This chapter is adapted from David Csinos, *A Gospel for All Ages: Teaching and Preaching with the Whole Church* (Fortress Press, 2022). Used by permission. Copies of the complete book are available at fortresspress.com.

incredibly difficult to adapt preaching to reflect values of intergenerational ministry. We agreed. Try as we might to intergenerate our faith communities—to cultivate environments in which relationships are fostered among people of all ages—we all felt as though the pulpit was the final frontier, a bastion of adult-centeredness within the liturgical landscape.

Central to the tenacity of common approaches to preaching that overlook some people because of their age is the theology one holds about preaching. It is difficult to change a liturgical practice—especially one as central as preaching—without being undergirded by a *theological foundation* that supports and even requires more creative, imaginative, and experimental approaches to that practice. If we want to preach in intergenerational ways, then we need a robust theology for intergenerational preaching to guide us.

Homiletician O. Wesley Allen argues that preaching "is but one method of proclamation, standing alongside (not above) all of the other methods."[2] While gospel proclamation certainly happens beyond the walls of the church, I use the term "preaching" here to refer to *Christian proclamation of the gospel as it happens within the liturgical life of faith communities*. Yes, preaching can happen through *sermons* and *homilies*, two specific and closely related forms of "speaking the gospel"[3] to the faith community as part of its corporate liturgy. But preaching can also happen as the worshiping community wrestles with a text in small groups, listens to stories of faith told by its members, and seeks to learn where and how God is at work within its neighborhood. Preaching can take many forms within the faith community.

As a practical theologian, I value the theological work that can be constructed through the intermingling of practice and theory. And so, in this chapter, I support the concrete practical work of those who wish to experiment with preaching among all-age faith communities by offering ideas that are helpful for *building an intergenerational homiletic; that is, a*

---

[2] O. Wesley Allen, *The Homiletic of All Believers: A Conversational Approach* (Louisville: Westminster John Knox, 2005), 18.

[3] See David Schnasa Jacobsen and Robert Allen Kelly, *Kairos Preaching: Speaking Gospel to the Situation* (Minneapolis: Fortress, 2009), 21.

theology of preaching in intergenerational contexts.[4] I will begin in Scripture by considering how Jesus's preaching ministry was inherently intergenerational. I will then offer four principles about the cultural nature of preaching, Christian identity, meaning-making, and the democratization of preaching—all principles that reinforce concrete practices to form a composite that strengthens preaching within intergenerational faith communities. I will conclude with some practical ideas for all-age preaching that rest upon the theological insights I offer in this chapter.

Biblical Insights about Intergenerational Preaching

Biblical scholar and professor of preaching William Brosend highlights preaching as central to Jesus's mission. Some of the first words of the Gospel of Mark make this clear: "Jesus came to Galilee, proclaiming the good news of God" (Mark 1:14 NRSV).[5] Using parables, one-liners, allegory, object lessons, questions, and countless acts of love, Jesus proclaimed the good news that the kingdom of God is at hand.

Jesus was an intergenerational preacher. He traveled, proclaiming the good news to families and crowds consisting of people of several ages, including children who were too young to walk up to him by themselves (Matt. 19:13–15), teenagers with existential questions (Mark 10:17–27), well-established career-driven adults (Luke 19:1–10), and elders who were nearing the end of their lives (Matt. 8:14–17). Rather than offer a broad sweep of the many instances of Jesus's intergenerational preaching practices, I narrow my gaze to one particular passage:

> People were bringing little children to him in order that he might touch them; and the disciples spoke sternly to them. But when Jesus saw this, he was indignant and said to them, "Let the little children come to me; do not stop them; for it is to such as

---

[4] Holly Allen and Chris Barnett succinctly name intergenerational churches as those that actively nurture spaces in which "there is comprehensive *mutuality, equality,* and *reciprocity* that makes individual or collective transformation more likely." See Holly Catterton Allen and Chris Barnett, "Addressing the Two Intergenerational Questions," in *InterGenerate: Transforming Churches through Intergenerational Ministry,* ed. Holly Catterton Allen (Abilene, TX: Abilene Christian University Press, 2018), 18.

[5] William Brosend, *The Preaching of Jesus: Gospel Proclamation, Then and Now* (Louisville: Westminster John Knox, 2010), Kindle loc. 178.

> these that the kingdom of God belongs. Truly I tell you, whoever does not receive the kingdom of God as a little child will never enter it." And he took them up in his arms, laid his hands on them, and blessed them. (Mark 10:13–16 NRSV)

This passage comes in the middle of a longer narrative in which we find Jesus teaching crowds as he and his disciples travel toward Jerusalem. Jesus had just responded to the disciples' questions about who among them will be greatest (Mark 9:33–34). His answer included giving a child a big hug (Mark 9:36) and stating that the greatest among them is the one who welcomes this young one. We then read that some Pharisees posed a question to Jesus (Mark 10:2) in order to test him among the crowd that gathered around him as he traveled. Then comes the passage above.

There Jesus was, in the midst of a crowd, halfway through his response to the Pharisees' question, when some people interrupt to bring children close to him so he can offer them a blessing. Like the child who "disrupts" the average Sunday morning speech-like sermon, it might have been cute the first couple of times. But eventually, the crowd becomes annoyed, and his disciples try to stop these children from interrupting their teacher and the adults who are trying to listen to him.

For this chain of events to unfold, people of many ages—adults and children alike—had to be present when Jesus was teaching and preaching that day. What if this was not an anomaly? What if each time a crowd is mentioned in the Gospels, we imagine that people of all generations are part of it? This radically alters how we might imagine some of those well-known stories playing out when we picture them in our minds. I can imagine that when Jesus raised Jairus's daughter from the dead (Mark 5:21–43), the house was filled with young teenagers who were her friends from around the block. Or, perhaps the crowds Jesus taught in the twelfth chapter of Luke's Gospel were made up of families with children who wandered over to a neighboring adult and showed them the lily they just picked from the field or struck up a conversation about the ravens flying overhead. And I can picture Zacchaeus looking down from the sycamore fig tree (Luke 19:1–10) and seeing a mass of people consisting of everyone from babes in their parents' arms to elders limping along with the help of kind young strangers.

Let's refocus on the Markan passage at hand. Jesus may not have thrown coins, overturned tables, and flung a whip around like a first-century Indiana Jones, but his response is nothing short of anger.[6] Out of this ire, Jesus uses words and actions to proclaim a message to those around him: that kingdom of God he had been preaching about all along—it is for all generations. In fact, he says older generations have much to learn about that kingdom from the young, the vulnerable, and the humble among them. Jesus preaches a paradigm-shifting reversal of the status quo, instantly flipping the script: the people with the least status are, in fact, the ones everyone else must emulate. Thank God that both children and adults were part of the crowds of people who were learning what it takes to enter God's kingdom that day.

Building a Theology to Support Intergenerational Preaching

The passage from Mark 10 is one instance in which Jesus connected both substance and style in his preaching. Using words *and* actions, he told everyone present that day—adults and children alike—that it is the young, the humble, the most vulnerable among them who are the true heirs of God's reign.

The medium through which the gospel is proclaimed is intimately tied to the substance of the proclamation.[7] Homiletician Paul Scott Wilson has written that "the sermon form we choose influences the theology we preach and so affects everything we say."[8] Style and substance are deeply interconnected. The theological ideas we preach—both those that are featured in our messages and those that undergird our assumptions about preaching—and the homiletical practices we use to preach them affect

---

[6] See, for example, John R. Donahue and Daniel J. Harrington, *The Gospel of Mark* (Collegeville, MN: Michael Glazier, 2002), 299; Robert H. Gundry, *Mark: A Commentary on His Apology for the Cross*, vol. 2 (Grand Rapids: Eerdmans, 1993), 546; M. Eugene Boring, *Mark: A Commentary* (Louisville: Westminster John Knox, 2006), 289.

[7] Marshall McLuhan, *Understanding Media: The Extensions of Man* (New York: McGraw-Hill, 1964). McLuhan famously stated that "the medium is the message" more than half a century ago.

[8] Paul Scott Wilson, *The Four Pages of the Sermon: A Guide to Biblical Preaching*, rev. ed. (Nashville: Abingdon, 2018), 13.

one another. Thus, to help promote creative styles for intergenerational preaching, I offer some theological substance that can support emergent styles among those experimenting with preaching for all ages.

The Culture of Preaching

I have already stated that preaching is just one of many forms of Christian proclamation; likewise, sermons are simply one of many ways that preaching can occur.[9] However, the sheer diversity of possibilities for preaching can easily be overlooked because of a reliance on particular sets of standards and expectations for the proclamation of the gospel. These often-unnamed norms shape our worship practices and are upheld by both explicit doctrines and implicit expectations.

Human beings are cultural creatures who are shaped by and, in turn, shape the norms of the cultures and subcultures in which we live. Sociologist Carl James defines culture as "a dynamic and complex set of values, beliefs, norms, patterns of thinking, styles of communication, linguistic expressions, and ways of interpreting and interacting with the world that help people understand and thus survive their varied circumstances."[10] Church is one of these cultures. In fact, both the church universal and every individual faith community around the world can be understood as cultural groups in their own right, according to James's definition. Everything we do as Christian people is related to the culture(s) of our churches, including our practices of preaching.

Once we name the cultural nature of preaching, we gain the freedom to move beyond norms and standards that place parameters around what we assume makes a sermon. Faith communities wishing to foster intergenerational approaches to worship help unveil common assumptions and norms for preaching, and they forge new cultural values and patterns by experimenting with ways of proclaiming the gospel that are appropriate for all-age communities. To practice intergenerational preaching, preachers and parishioners alike must let go of adult-centric methods of

---

[9] See O. Wesley Allen, *The Homiletic of All Believers: A Conversational Approach to Proclamation and Preaching* (Louisville: Westminster John Knox, 2005).

[10] Carl E. James, *Seeing Ourselves: Exploring Race, Ethnicity, and Culture*, 4th ed. (Toronto: Thompson Educational, 2010), 26.

"speaching" (a term coined by Doug Pagitt[11]) that overlook younger people. As an alternative to "speaching," we can reimagine a time of questions and discussion in worship. In turn, we must also let go of an array of simplistic approaches to children's messages that sideline adults. Perhaps, instead, we might present an experiential and interactive message that includes the participation of all the people. Together, faith communities can create new approaches for offering the gospel that *bring people of every age together*. The resulting forms of preaching might not end up looking like sermons as our faith communities know them. But they are certainly counted as preaching nonetheless.

> **THEOLOGY IN PRACTICE: QUESTIONS TO CONSIDER**

1. What cultural norms and expectations shape the preaching in your context?
2. Which of these cultural norms and expectations for preaching contribute to intergenerational faith formation and which do not?

Identity Matters

As cultural creatures, we human beings exist in multiple cultures and subcultures. The apostle Paul was aware of this reality. He names several cultural groups among the church in Galatia: Jewish and Greek, slave and free, male and female (Gal. 3:28). Regardless of the boxes people would tick from this list, they were part of Christ's body. Even more, Paul claims our identity as Christian people is to be our *primary* identity, superseding any other identities we bring to the community. When Paul wrote "you are one in Christ Jesus" (Gal. 3:28 NRSV), he was not indicating that these other identity markers cease to exist once one is grafted onto the body of Christ. However, our faith in Jesus provides a new identity that stands above all others, the one that Christians are called to hold in common, regardless of the differences that might distinguish one disciple from another.

---

[11] Doug Pagitt defines "speaching" as a style of preaching that is "hardly distinguishable from a one-way speech." Doug Pagitt, *Preaching in the Inventive Age* (Nashville: Abingdon, 2014), 10.

Our identity as siblings in Christ has important implications for intergenerational preaching. When an adjective like *intergenerational* is placed before nouns like *worship, formation,* or *preaching,* the adjective captures our attention. Naming something as *intergenerational* underscores the importance of age as a marker of identity. Paradoxically, describing an aspect of ministry as intergenerational reinforces the normativity of age segregation. Age becomes the primary identity marker.

Paul calls us to look beyond our age-based identity markers and see each person as a member of the body of Christ. Greek or Jewish, man or woman, adolescent or adult—Paul wishes for all of us to be one in Christ Jesus. When we do so, our differences become relativized—yet not erased!—and secondary to the discipleship that unifies us all.

Psychologist Lina Ponder noted this unifying dynamic in her research among first- and second-generation Chinese American Christians. Each generation expressed differences in worldviews and values. Yet those with a shared Christian identity built a stronger sense of connection among members of the two groups.[12] Similarly, when members of the church see one another as disciples, as co-pilgrims along the path of following Jesus,[13] our distinctions become secondary to our shared identity as disciples. This is part of the witness of the church: whoever we are, wherever we come from, and whenever we were born, we are all one in Christ Jesus.

Imagine what would happen if the generational identities that separate people in churches became less important than the identity as disciples of Christ they hold in common! Preaching, as a core practice of the church, is vital for the formation of *all disciples*. In affirming a theological stance in which common discipleship supersedes generational diversity, preachers can consider how their preaching practices help form the disciples in their faith community, whether they are six years old, sixteen years old, or sixty years old.

---

[12] Lina S. Ponder, "Intergenerational and Personal Connectedness: Held Together in Christian Faith," *Journal of Psychology and Theology* 46, no. 2 (2018): 133–39.

[13] The ideal of being co-pilgrims with one another across age groups is certainly not new. John Westerhoff addresses it in *Will Our Children Have Faith?* (New York: Morehouse Publishing, 1976) and commissioned it to leaders at the second Children's Spirituality Conference: Christian Perspectives, River Forest, IL, June 4–7, 2006.

> **THEOLOGY IN PRACTICE: QUESTIONS TO CONSIDER**

1. Consider primary and secondary identities that affect your context (i.e., culture, family, gender, region, education, neurodiversity, history, etc.). How might the practice of preaching in your context move past our primary and secondary identities, enabling us all to participate more fully in a shared identity in Christ?

2. What identities seem most important to the members of your church and how can the ways you preach remind them of their core common identity as disciples of Jesus?

3. How could naming something "intergenerational" actually prohibit us from living into a shared identity in Christ?

Making Sense

Preaching the gospel is not meant to be a unidirectional method for transmitting information from speaker to hearers. Yet too often, the preaching moment is conceived in a way that is similar to what Paulo Freire referred to as a banking model for learning.[14] In this line of thinking, preachers possess nuggets of information they wish everyone in the congregation to know, and the sermon is a medium through which those pieces of knowledge are passed from speaker to hearer. For example, if a preacher wishes for congregants to be aware that God calls imperfect people to join in the work of God, then one could use Moses's self-identified public speaking issues or Peter's denial of Jesus to prove this point. By the end of the message, it would be assumed that congregants would have acquired knowledge about God's reliance on imperfect people.

The problem with this line of thinking is that theology (which we might define broadly as our ideas about God and the ways we live out those ideas) is not transmitted or passed on from one person to another, like the example I just offered. *Theology is created.* We constantly take new information and fresh experiences and connect them with what we

---

[14] Paulo Freire, *Pedagogy of the Oppressed*, trans. Myra Bergman Ramos (New York: Continuum, 2007).

already know and what we have already experienced in order to generate *new* insights and practices.

This became vividly clear to me as I conducted research to learn about the theological thinking of children.[15] As I interviewed children, I noticed they were actively creating new meaning right then and there through our conversations, rather than simply laying out for me the ideas they already held before walking into the room that day. And I was wrapped up in this creative process too, making theological meaning through my conversations with the children.

Marianne Gaarden's research into how listeners engage with sermons draws a similar conclusion. People actively make meaning as they connect the message they hear from the pulpit with their existing knowledge and ideas.[16] Gaarden asserts that preaching is more than what we know as the sermon offered from the pulpit. Preaching consists of the meanings and ideas that arise through the engagement of the listeners, and the support offered by the preacher through the words he or she offers.[17]

Theology happens in the preaching moment, sometimes bursting forth in an explosion of insight and sometimes emerging slowly as the Spirit stirs in a person over a long period of time.[18] Every person present in worship is actively making meaning about what preachers say and do during their message. This is why members of a church might tell a preacher they liked what she said about a particular idea even though the preacher knows she did not even hint at that idea. Just because she did not *say* it does not mean the listeners did not *hear* it and generate their own insight. In recognizing that theology is created rather than transmitted, preaching becomes not a method for providing particular morsels of theology but a

---

[15] See David M. Csinos, *Little Theologians: Children, Culture, and the Generation of Theological Meaning* (Montréal: McGill-Queen's University Press, 2020).

[16] Marianne Gaarden, *The Third Room of Preaching: The Sermon, the Listener, and the Creation of Meaning* (Louisville: Westminster John Knox, 2017).

[17] Marianne Gaarden and Marlene Ringgaard Lorensen, "Listeners as Authors in Preaching: Empirical and Theoretical Perspectives," *Homiletic* 38, no. 1 (2013): 45.

[18] David Schnasa Jacobsen, through his spearheading of the Homiletical Theology Project, has done much to draw attention to how preaching is a particular method for doing theology, rather than only a method for communicating theology. In preparing, delivering, and reflecting on messages, preachers are engaging in acts that are generative of theology. See, for example, David Schnasa Jacobsen, ed., *Homiletical Theology: Preaching as Doing Theology* (Eugene, OR: Cascade, 2015).

means for helping all people as they actively generate theological insight for themselves. This invites (dare we say *mandates*?) preachers to imagine new possibilities for allowing everyone present to engage with theological ideas and create their own along the way.

> **THEOLOGY IN PRACTICE: QUESTIONS TO CONSIDER**

1. Evaluate all the forms of preaching in your worship gatherings. Identify which methods are unidirectional and which methods encourage people to participate in generating theological insight for themselves. Which methods help you most in your own faith formation? Which methods seem to help different ages interact and generate theological insights?

2. What are some small and simple ways you can begin to change traditional, unidirectional paradigms for preaching in your context? (Hint: If you are not the pastor or lead preacher in your church, consider other areas where the gospel is proclaimed, such as Scripture presentation, music, testimony, prayer, and so on.)

Hearing and Speaking the Gospel

Freire's concept of a banking approach to education rests on a dichotomous nature of the teacher and the student:

> The teacher teaches and the students are taught . . .
> The teacher talks and the students listen—meekly . . .
> The teacher chooses and enforces his [*sic*] choice, and the students comply . . .
> The teacher acts and the students have the illusion of acting through the action of the teacher . . .
> The teacher is the subject of the learning process, while the pupils are mere objects.[19]

His alternative to this banking model rests on an understanding that all people are both teachers and learners. He advocates for a democratic

---

[19] Freire, *Pedagogy of the Oppressed*, 72–73.

approach to learning in which every party has something to offer and something to gain from one another.

These arguments have deep implications for the field of homiletics. If the problematic nature of a banking approach to education resembles that of a banking approach to preaching, might the solution that Freire offers likewise be appropriated for this field? If so, we could begin to imagine what a democratic approach to preaching might look like.

In considering Freire's proposal in light of the preacher-hearer dichotomy, it becomes prudent to acknowledge that all members of the body of Christ—from a newborn baby to a centenarian—have been called by Jesus to both *hear* the gospel and *proclaim* the gospel. Not everyone has the gift, desire, or calling to offer sermons or homilies during worship services. But these are just a few of many ways to proclaim the gospel. Since we all are in relationship with God, we are all called to follow Jesus, and we are all empowered by the Spirit; everyone has something to contribute as we join one another in offering the gospel in our world.

With this view in mind, all people—all ages—have ears to hear *and* voices to speak truth together. In the words of Kate Bruce, "it is important that [preaching] is seen as a communal calling, calling for response to God from preacher and congregation, openness, a desire to hear together and a willingness to engage."[20] By democratizing our understanding of and our practices for preaching, we can transform the preacher-hearer dichotomy and affirm that both preachers and listeners have active roles to play in the preaching moment. This theological stance can empower us to reimagine preaching as a practice for the whole community, transforming how we preach and how we might invite others, regardless of age, to join us in the task of preaching.

THEOLOGY IN PRACTICE: QUESTIONS TO CONSIDER

1. As an intergenerational leader, how might you change your posture in preaching to be both a teacher and a learner?

---

[20] Kate Bruce, *Igniting the Heart: Preaching and Imagination* (London: SCM, 2015), 101.

2. How do congregants in your church make sense of your preaching, and how can you invite them to develop and share their ideas about the messages they hear?
3. How might you enable unlikely people of different ages to proclaim the gospel in your worship gatherings—especially during the preaching moment?
4. In Jesus's day, the "unlikely" people to participate were children, women, the vulnerable, the sick, the poor. In your context, identify those in your midst who would be considered the "unlikely." How might you begin inviting those people to participate in proclamation of the gospel?
5. Identify the generations missing in proclaiming the gospel in your context. How might you begin empowering these people to participate more fully in both hearing and preaching?
6. How might you invite and equip people of every age to both hear and speak the gospel to one another?

Practicing Intergenerational Preaching

Informed by these ideas, practitioners seeking to intergenerate their preaching can be better equipped to do so. I cannot tell you exactly what intergenerational preaching looks like in your faith community or how you should go about trying it out for yourself. It is an emergent, experimental, and highly contextual endeavor that upsets the homiletical status quo. What I can do, however, is offer some concrete advice for those who wish to use these theological ideas as fodder for cultivating practices of intergenerational preaching in their faith communities.[21]

Simplify the Language, Not the Concept

First, when teaching and preaching among intergenerational contexts, we should consider the language we are using. If we want *everyone* present to understand what we are saying, then we need to use simple language.

---

[21] These insights are drawn from six practitioners who contributed to my book *A Gospel for All Ages*: Talashia Keim Yoder, Murray Wilkinson, Karen DeBoer, Amy Casteel, Tammy Preston, and Jim Keat.

However, as Sandy Sasso has pointed out, simple language can be used to convey complex and profound concepts.[22] Talashia Keim Yoder is an intergenerational preacher who knows how important this principle can be: "We do not 'water down' theology or Scripture. On the contrary, we do the difficult work of 'distilling' it and boiling it down to its essence, all the while using language that is accessible to everyone."[23] Jesus knew the power of using simple language that was understandable and relevant to the context in which he ministered. He spoke of sheep (Luke 15:1–7) and lilies (Luke 12:27) and foxes (Matt. 8:20) and seeds (Mark 4:1–20).

THEOLOGY IN PRACTICE: NEXT STEPS

1. **Intergenerational language.** As you prepare your next message, think about the language you are using to convey your ideas. Does it require knowledge that not all ages in the congregation might have? If so, how might you swap out some words for others that are more commonly understood?

2. **Intergenerational explanation.** Do you take the time to explain more complex language, even words that might seem commonplace in church? If not, then add a sentence or two that unpacks what you mean when you say words like hermeneutic, salvation, justification, redemption, and so on.

3. **Intergenerational imagery.** Are the analogies, metaphors, and similes you include relevant for all ages? If not, change them; instead of talking about the importance of a cornerstone through architecture and design, try explaining it through LEGO (you may even build something out of LEGO as you speak).

It helps no one if the powerful ideas you wish to convey in your message are not understandable to everyone simply because of how you say them. So, whatever you do, ensure that you preach with language that

---

[22] Sandy Eisenberg Sasso, "Tell Me a Story: Narrative and the Religious Imagination of Children," in *Faith Forward*, vol. 2, *Re-imagining Children's and Youth Ministry*, ed. David M. Csinos and Melvin Bray (Kelowna, BC: CopperHouse, 2015).

[23] Csinos, *A Gospel for All Ages*, 99.

makes sense to all ages. If the children in your church can comprehend your message, chances are everyone else can too.

Encourage Conversation

Intergenerational preachers know the power of questions and conversation for helping people grow and learn, even if they are unfamiliar with the research and theories that I discussed above. Messages that are monologues proclaimed from the pulpit by one person have a place in the preaching practices of congregations, but their effectiveness can be enhanced when blended with approaches for helping people discuss and wonder about Scripture for themselves. Preachers can invite conversation in many ways.

THEOLOGY IN PRACTICE: NEXT STEPS

1. **Intergenerational conversation.** Consider offering a short sermon and then allowing the preaching moment to continue by asking a question and inviting everyone to turn to a few people around them and respond to it in conversation with one another.

2. **Reflection time.** At one church that I attended, we included a time after the message where everyone in this small, intergenerational community could ask the minister questions or share their reflections on the message they had just heard.

These seem like simple ideas. And in a way, they are no-brainers. And yet messages that are monologues remain the order of the day. As you experiment with intergenerational preaching, consider how you might ask questions and invite discussion as part of your message so everyone present, from a young child to a senior citizen, might dig into Scripture and preach the gospel to one another.

Share the Pulpit

When Jesus lifted up and blessed that child—a child too young to be able to approach Jesus on their own—he was moving over and sharing space with that infant. No longer was Jesus preaching and teaching the crowds by himself; now that child was preaching alongside Jesus, not with words, but by presence alone. Preaching among all-age communities can mean we share the pulpit with people of diverse ages. If the common identity we hold as followers of Jesus surpasses the identity we hold by virtue of our age, education, or ordination status, then we can rest assured, knowing that we all have something to teach one another about the gospel. Intergenerational preachers can make space for other people to preach to the faith community, regardless of age.

THEOLOGY IN PRACTICE: NEXT STEPS

1. **Events with many preachers.** One way to share the pulpit is to ask children, adolescents, and adults of varying ages to prepare a short reflection on a text, on a celebration or feast in the church calendar (like Easter, Christmas, or All Souls' Day), or on a common theme. Instead of having one person preach, the "sermon" could be made up of four or five mini-messages offered by this diverse group of congregants.

2. **Intergenerational testimonies.** Another idea is to ask people of different ages to tell stories of how God has been working in their lives lately and then listen to what these experiences might teach us about who God is and how God works in our everyday lives. Some preachers have shared the pulpit by interviewing a family about a monumental moment in their common faith life, such as when they welcomed a new family member, lost a loved one to an illness, or celebrated the union of two people in marriage. Instead of announcing these events in a bulletin or even mentioning them in a sermon, preachers can (with the family's permission, of course) invite the family to talk about their experience and God's presence therein in front of the whole congregation.

As you can see, when we expand our culturally conditioned views about what counts as preaching, we can make room for all sorts of people to preach in all sorts of ways.

Take It Step by Step

However you experiment with intergenerational preaching, keep in mind that not everything we do as preachers needs to be intergenerational. Jesus was an intergenerational preacher, but that does not mean he *only* preached intergenerationally. At times, Jesus preached only to his closest disciples, and other times, he shared the gospel one-on-one. We must remember that our newfound passion for all-age preaching does not prevent us from also making use of other approaches, even approaches that are not (gasp!) intergenerational. After all, in a gradual step-by-step transformation, one-person preaching need not be thrown out completely.

Some pastors have found that the best way to begin intergenerating their preaching practices is to prepare for a sermon or homily by inviting congregants of diverse ages to reflect on a biblical passage together over a meal a week or two before the pastor plans to preach on it; the ideas sparked by this group can then be incorporated into a message offered by the pastor. This sort of savvy way of adapting preaching practices allows those who want to engage with all-age ministry to self-select and be part of the intergenerational group, while helping those who might be wary of new approaches to preaching. Instead of completely overhauling Sunday morning preaching, preachers might begin facilitating intergenerational preaching during special events (like an anniversary gathering), a one-off gathering (such as World Communion Sunday), or a midweek worship gathering (Maundy Thursday comes to mind). Regardless of when and how you join the adventure of intergenerational preaching, it's vital to begin by knowing your context and finding the best ways to implement small, sustainable changes in your faith community's preaching practices.

But Wait ... There's More!

This discussion on intergenerational preaching is far from exhaustive. Here, I have offered only a few of several ideas that can work together to build an intergenerational homiletic—a theology of preaching among all-age faith communities—on which we can experiment with concrete practices of intergenerational preaching.

As we continue to experiment—to boldly go where we have never gone before in this new frontier of intergenerational preaching—our ideas will grow and expand alongside the concrete theological practices we forge by imagining ways to preach that make room for young and old and everyone in between. And as our theories and practices develop together, they reinforce one another in laying sure foundations upon which we who preach a gospel for all ages can build.

Make it so.

CHAPTER 7

BUILDING RAMPS INSTEAD OF STAIRS
Universal Design in Planning Intergenerational Worship

ROBERT PENDERGRAFT

"The secret of change is to focus all your energy not on fighting the old but on building the new."

—Dan Millman

When we approach the entrance of a public facility, we are presented with a choice—take the ramp or take the stairs. Thomas J. Tobin and Kristen T. Behling describe Ron Mace's invaluable contribution of "ramps" to the world of Universal Design:

> Mace had polio as a child and used a wheelchair to get around. He recognized in the 1950s that the U.S. population was aging. He foresaw that people who were no longer able to navigate stairs or small bathrooms would have to move out of their unusable homes and into nursing facilities or the homes of relatives. Mace believed that if architects designed homes to be "usable by everyone to the greatest extent possible" from the beginning, then more people could continue to stay at home as they aged.[1]

---

[1] Thomas J. Tobin and Kristen T. Behling, *Reach Everyone, Teach Everyone: Universal Design for Learning in Higher Education* (Morgantown: West Virginia University Press, 2018), 21.

Similar to how ramps make architecture more accessible for all, **Universal Design for Learning (UDL)** has provided ramps in the field of education that make learning more accessible to *all* learners. David Rose and his colleagues at the Center for Applied Special Technology (CAST) argue that UDL "puts the tag 'disabled' where it belongs—on the curriculum, not the learner"; rather, Rose calls curriculum "disabled when it does not meet the needs of diverse learners."[2] Consequently, UDL specialist Elizabeth Berquist finds that UDL focuses on intentional curricular design as a means to "improve and optimize teaching and learning for *all* people, based on scientific insights into how humans learn."[3]

At its foundation, UDL promotes intentionality to accommodate diverse populations. Kendra Grant and Luis Perez explain how "UDL is based on the belief that we must proactively and intentionally remove barriers to the access to information and, more importantly, to learning."[4] Just as UDL contributes to the field of education, universal design for worship serves as a means to acknowledge the diversity of people—including the diversity of age—by removing barriers, or "stairs," by building "ramps." UDL is inherently intergenerational because it allows us to make accommodations that are helpful for some and provide them for the whole body so that *all* people and *all* ages can benefit; thus, UDL promotes intergenerational worship, engaging every age in worship.

According to David H. Rose and Anne Meyer, UDL addresses "the divergent needs of special populations" and "increases usability for everyone."[5] Similar to the intentions of UDL, intergenerational worship seeks to improve and optimize participation and engagement of *all* generations in corporate worship gatherings. When it comes to designing worship, intergenerational leaders must learn to provide "ramps" that enable *all* generations to participate. This chapter examines eight intergenerational worship "ramps" that incorporate UDL to include all ages in worship. At

---

[2] David Rose, in Tobin and Behling, *Reach Everyone*, 24.
[3] Elizabeth Berquist, ed., *UDL: Moving from Exploration to Integration* (Wakefield, MA: CAST Professional Publishing, 2017), x, emphasis mine.
[4] Kendra Grant and Luis Perez, *Dive Into UDL: Immersive Practices to Develop Expert Learners* (International Society for Technology in Education, 2018), 55.
[5] David H. Rose and Anne Meyer, *Teaching Every Student in the Digital Age: Universal Design for Learning* (Alexandria, VA: Association for Supervision and Curriculum Development, 2002), 71.

the end of each ramp discussed, I offer questions to help you **identify possible stairs** in your context that impede all generations from worshiping together and also initial questions that help in **designing ramps** for future intergenerational worship to include *all ages* in your context.

Ramp #1: Participation—Empowering All Ages to Participate Fully

According to Grant and Perez, "the ultimate goal of engagement is purposeful, motivated learners."[6] Similarly, the ultimate goal of engagement in worship is purposeful, motivated worshipers. Worship leaders hold a critical role in designing equal opportunities for intentional engagement that attend to each person's age *and* ableness. In *Accessible Gospel, Inclusive Worship,* Barbara J. Newman and Betty Grit say, "Designing environments for worship where we can each tell God 'I love you' and we can each say the prayer words 'Help me' will undoubtedly add a richness not yet imagined by some congregations."[7] When worship is crafted in such a way as to give all ages opportunities to respond to God, worship becomes richer and fuller, and members of the intergenerational worshiping body—all ages—find themselves more attuned to the liturgy.

One UDL strategy for encouraging *full participation* resides in how we plan worship. In UDL, Grant and Perez emphasize the importance of providing autonomy for the learner's choice, including encouraging "them to actively participate in the design of those choices."[8] Here, UDL for worship is applied when the worship designer engages the congregants of varied ages and ableness in the process of crafting worship. When it comes to worship planning, simply including multiple generations and diverse abilities in the participation of planning worship creates this sort of autonomy, where people are participating even in the planning of how they will participate in worship.

Part of the formative power of worship is that participation in the service shapes how the congregation will continue to participate in worship

---

[6] Grant and Perez, *Dive Into UDL,* 81.
[7] Barbara J. Newman and Betty Grit, *Accessible Gospel, Inclusive Worship* (Wyoming, MI: All Belong, 2014), 9.
[8] Grant and Perez, *Dive Into UDL,* 87.

throughout the week. Rose and Meyer emphasize UDL when helping people "learn how to learn."[9] As an example, in my context, our church seeks to provide the ramp of full, intergenerational participation by extending worship past Sunday—encouraging *all* ages to engage daily in the worship of God both individually and in households. Worship designers successfully empower worshipers by providing multiple means and opportunities for every age and ableness to engage fully, both in corporate worship and throughout the week.

> **Identifying stairs:** Think through the generations that are not participating fully in your context now. What stairs might be impeding specific generations from participating fully? Think through current systems and structures that have become stairs, rather than ramps, for full participation of all generations. Similarly, what systems outside your ministry context (family, school, etc.) have become stairs, rather than ramps, to formational worship throughout the week? Could any of these stairs be turned into ramps?
>
> **Building ramps:** What ramps might you begin building to empower all generations to participate fully in worship? Further, what ramps might you begin building so that all generations can participate in worship formation (both individually and in households) throughout the week?

Ramp #2: Intentionality—Providing Meaningful, Valuable Worship Experiences for All Ages

Intentionality precedes meaningful and valuable experiences. According to Grant and Perez, Universal Design is characterized by "proactive planning and design, rather than [being] left to chance or approached with retrofits."[10] Meaningful and valuable worship experiences depend on a connection among those gathered in an intergenerational context. In the

---

[9] Rose and Meyer, *Teaching Every Student in the Digital Age*, 69.
[10] Grant and Perez, *Dive Into UDL*, 75.

classroom, Grant and Perez believe teachers "provide students with tasks, questions, and problems that tackle big ideas and essential questions that are personally important and bring the relevance, value, and authenticity to learning [that] students crave."[11] In worship, the liturgy and those leading can find connections to everyone gathered, attending to the learning needs of each generation, not only a subset of the worship community. This does not mean worship has to be familiar or comfortable to be meaningful and valuable but rather that intentionality in design builds connections among congregants and provides opportunities for meaningful engagement.

> **Identifying stairs:** What unintentional stairs exist in your worship context? Consider what it means for worship planning to be intentional. How does intentionality connect with individuals and generations? Conversely, how can a lack of intentionality in planning cause disconnect in worship?
>
> **Building ramps:** Consider each generation in your worship gatherings. Schedule intentional conversations with people of different ages and abilities in your congregations, seeking to know how to address their unique needs. What ramps of intentionality need to be built when planning worship for each generation in your context? (Note: This will look different in each context.)

Ramp #3: Safe Learning Environment—Creating a Culture Where All Ages Can Learn and Take Risks

When it comes to UDL, Grant and Perez find it vital to "create a physically and emotionally safe space in which learners themselves can discover their preferred levels of novelty and sensory stimulus."[12] In the same way, meaningful engagement in corporate worship requires a supportive environment where congregants of differing ages can safely role-play the act of worshiper. Every worshiper should find a ***safe environment***, free of

---

[11] Grant and Perez, *Dive Into UDL*, 87.
[12] Grant and Perez, *Dive Into UDL*, 87.

judgment and criticism, where he or she can engage with God and others. In my context, we see this when a family sits with young children, continually guiding them through the acts of worship. In the same way, we see families of older saints struggling with Alzheimer's or dementia that use the worship guide to refocus their loved one in the acts of worship amid wandering thoughts and fleeting recognition. All people, regardless of age, ability, or experience, need the "ramp" of a safe environment, allowing them to respond to the revelation of God's redemptive acts.

> **Identifying stairs:** Consider the worship culture of your context, in relation to safety and freedom to experiment and expression of worship to God. How can a culture of performance or perfection in worship become a "stair" for different generations and abilities to respond in worship to God?
>
> **Building ramps:** What ramps might you begin building that allow people of all ages, young and old, to build a culture together where they can express their worship to God in diverse ways?

Ramp #4: Repetition—Providing Deeper Formational Worship through Pattern and Ritual

Worship is a formational act. Thus, as worship designers, we must recognize that formative acts need *repetition* to deepen and reinforce our expressions of faith. The repetition of a liturgy each week—both in form and in individual acts—shapes worshipers. Using UDL, Rose and Meyer explain this concept in educational terms, showing that a learner must "*automatize*, or over-learn, the individual steps in the process until each is automatic."[13] As God reveals, we respond in worship.[14] The shape and form of worship depends on our repeated engagement with the liturgy. Repetition can be experienced in the actual format, or liturgy, of worship.

---

[13] Rose and Meyer, *Teaching Every Student in the Digital Age*, 120, emphasis mine.

[14] For a deeper study about revelation and response and the dialogical nature of worship, see Constance M. Cherry, *The Worship Architect: A Blueprint for Designing Culturally Relevant and Biblically Faithful Services,* 2nd ed. (Grand Rapids: Baker Academic, 2021), 19–20.

This is explicitly seen in the simple four-fold pattern of worship: Gathering, Word, Response, and Sending.[15] In my context, we divide worship into consistent sections every week that are set apart with color and icons so each person, be it a pre-literate child or a senior adult who has been in church for his or her entire life, can easily see what role the worship element is intended to play in that service. This chunking of worship elements into groups communicates consistency in the worship narrative while allowing multiple means of representation from week to week. When our worship elements are organized into these four large headings, directions in worship become clearer. God calls us together for worship and then speaks to us through his Word; we respond to the Word, and then we are sent out in response. Though the content of each section changes from week to week, the order of worship is constant for the sake of formation. This is a simple way we allow repetition to help shape us in our worship.

> **Identifying stairs:** What stairs prevent you from the use of repetition, in both form and practice, in your worship context? Even further, what generations find comfort in repetition, and what generations balk at the use of repetition? Consider how each generation benefits uniquely from repetition in worship. How might repetition in worship continue to form us more deeply throughout the week?
>
> **Building ramps:** What ramps of repetition (start small!) might you begin incorporating into weekly corporate worship that could be seen as formational acts of worship for all ages—both in form (i.e., Gathering, Word, Response, Sending) and through specific acts of worship (weekly repetition of a song, creed, prayer of confession, worship action, etc.)?

---

[15] For further explanation of the Christian four-fold pattern of worship developed and practiced throughout history, see "Four-Fold Pattern of Worship," Calvin Institute of Christian Worship, September 17, 2014, accessed October 24, 2022, https://worship.calvin.edu/resources/resource-library/four-fold-pattern-of-worship/.

Ramp #5: Community—Cultivating Relationships of Collaboration in Worship

According to Grant and Perez, learning in a *community* "can deepen and extend your Zone of Proximal Development... which is the space between what is known and unknown, the space between what you can and cannot do, and, most importantly, the space where learning occurs."[16] Accordingly, they find that these goals are often accomplished through the creation of "collaborative learning groups with clear goals, roles, and responsibilities."[17] In worship, such groups already exist with people of all ages in the gathered congregation and smaller connective groups comprised of those same congregants. Consequently, we recognize that Christian worship is not an individual event; rather, we engage fully with God when we engage together—all ages, all people, all abilities—worshiping in community. In UDL, we learn better through design that empowers community; in Christian worship, we worship more fully in community.

> **Identifying stairs:** In your context, identify stairs of individuality that prevent collaborative worship of all ages taking place. Where do you see stairs in your community that leave out certain generations or prevent intergenerational community?
>
> **Building ramps:** How can you begin building ramps of community—relationships within your corporate worship context (e.g., encouraging multiple generations to present Scripture together, offering an intergenerational choir, having multiple generations take the offering together, etc.)? What communal ramps can you focus on outside of worship (e.g., intergenerational dinners, etc.) that will facilitate deeper communal worship in your context?

Ramp #6: Variation—Tell God's Story in Multiple Modalities

A student in higher education from Sheryl Burgstahler's study in UDL reflects on the need for *multiple modalities* in teaching and learning: "For

---

[16] Grant and Perez, *Dive Into UDL*, 18.
[17] Grant and Perez, *Dive Into UDL*, 87.

those who do not catch the concept the first time, a second mode of presentation can enhance the understanding of that concept."[18] Unfortunately, worship gatherings often do not present multiple modalities. Most frequently, leaders prioritize words over other mediums of learning. In contrast, UDL reminds us that we should accommodate *all* present, including those who learn using other means, such as images, music, diagrams, experiences—all to help people engage with the gospel more fully. Similarly, Newman and Grit explain how people of varying ages and abilities can benefit greatly from a communication of the gospel that moves beyond words alone: "So often 'word learners' are drawn to positions such as pastors and teachers. Presenters assume that others take information in the same way. That group of ear learners, however, is dwindling."[19] Using UDL in worship means telling the gospel story through multiple means and modalities.

Although words might be a more comfortable, preferred way of learning for those in leadership, UDL compels intergenerational leaders to expand modes of learning and engagement. One simple way we offer multiple modalities of learning in my context is by having worship designers provide items related to the sermon in the pews for our congregants. For example, one Sunday, we left two leaves (one freshly cut and the other dried) that were to be held when talking about the withered tree (Mark 11:20–25). In another worship gathering, we used the children's message—complete with sound effects and pictures—to introduce a new sermon series to the entire congregation. Additionally, we often project or have printed in the worship guide icons that help everyone understand what is being discussed in worship.

> **Identifying stairs:** Identify which methods or modalities of learning are currently preferred in your worship gatherings. Consider how prioritizing words might become a stair for those worshiping—especially for certain generations.
>
> **Building ramps:** Consider how your worship planning might incorporate all the senses (sight, sound, taste, touch, smell),

---

[18] Student, in Sheryl Burgstahler, *Universal Design in Higher Education: From Principles to Practice* (Cambridge, MA: Harvard Education Press, 2015), 124.

[19] Newman and Grit, *Accessible Gospel, Inclusive Worship*, 12.

> along with more experiential learning methods, to build new ramps for all generations to participate in worship.

Ramp #7: Scaffolding—Enhancing Complex Concepts for Intergenerational Comprehension

In the classroom, Grant and Perez describe how educators of UDL often *scaffold* concepts when they "pre-teach new vocabulary and special symbols that may be unfamiliar to learners," and "embed" this "vocabulary" in "hyperlinked definitions and explanations that are available to learners on demand."[20] These same scaffolding techniques can be embedded in worship by defining words, explaining with images or video, or even placing physical objects in the midst of the congregation for worshipers to see and feel. When the congregation, composed of all ages, gathers for corporate worship, not everyone present will understand each liturgical action. On these occasions, the worship designer can proactively anticipate possible confusion by scaffolding the idea or concept so that those of different ages and ableness can understand.

Another means of scaffolding for worship is provided when worship leaders give outlines or other tangible means to assist in comprehension to those gathered. Here, Grant and Perez suggest the use of "advance organizers as well as personal reflection to help learners identify what they already know about a new topic, then use analogies and metaphors to relate new information to that which is already familiar."[21] In the same way, intentional scaffolding, planned by the pastor and worship designer, allows a congregation to engage more thoughtfully and creatively with the liturgy and instruction.

> **Identifying stairs:** List difficult concepts and expressions (even weekly terminology we use in worship like "confession," "redemption," "justification," "baptism," "passing of the peace," etc.) that might be embedded in worship or coming up in

---

[20] Grant and Perez, *Dive Into UDL*, 91.
[21] Grant and Perez, *Dive Into UDL*, 92–93.

> future sermons in your context. How might these difficult concepts act like stairs, excluding certain generations from full understanding and participation? (Hint: If you are unsure what needs scaffolding, pull aside people outside your worship planning context, including different ages and different levels of church experience. Ask them what words in your sermon or in overall worship are confusing. Or, try preaching to your own children. Or ask for help from your church youth. You might be surprised how they might help you scaffold difficult ideas and concepts!)
>
> **Building ramps:** How might you turn these stairs you have identified above into ramps by using scaffolding?

Ramp #8: Response—Enabling All Ages to Respond to God's Revelation

Just as revelation presented through multiple modalities tells the story to worshipers with diverse learning styles, providing a variety of *response* opportunities for those of various inclinations is also critical. Classroom teachers, according to Grant and Perez, often "allow learners to have a choice in the media they use to communicate their understanding: text, speech, video, artwork, a re-enactment of a historical event, and so on."[22] In worship, enabling and encouraging diverse responses to God's revelation allows worshipers of *all* ages to find a means of response. For some, words and music are an inadequate or unattainable means of response. Rather than focusing on those who do not seem to respond in the way response has "always been done," Newman and Grit state: "it seems important to ask the right question—what CAN the person do?"[23] This question is at the heart of UDL for worship. Perhaps someone is unable to physically stand or unable to sing; rather than focus on limitations, seek out opportunities for expressive response for those of varied abilities. A pre-literate child may be unable to articulate a response with words, but drawing may allow that

---

[22] Grant and Perez, *Dive Into UDL*, 96.
[23] Newman and Grit, *Accessible Gospel, Inclusive Worship*, 11.

child to offer a response. Often, I find that my inclusion of varied responses benefits not only the ones that led me to craft it, but all worshipers. In some traditions, the standard response time involves the opportunity to walk to the front of the church to communicate a decision. Decisions, however, need not only be made in one way. One could be allowed to draw a picture as a means of response, while another may benefit from printed reflection questions in the worship guide.

Additionally, worship designers must model these varied opportunities of response for the congregation. They can provide worshipers with what Grant and Perez describe as "a variety of examples that show them how the same goal can be accomplished," modeling for the congregation "a variety of approaches," while supplying "ample opportunities for learners to practice and refine their new skills with varying levels of support."[24] The aim is not always to respond in a way that is familiar or preferred, but within the context of universal design to provide multiple options for worshipers of all generations.

> **Identifying stairs:** Identify any stairs that prevent certain ages and abilities from responding to God in worship in your context. How might these stairs be converted into ramps?
>
> **Building ramps:** When planning your next worship gathering, build new ramps by including worship responses that do not use words or music. Over the next several weeks, consider multiple points of response for each worship gathering. Picture specific people from different age groups, imagining how they might feel free to respond to God. Consider asking different generations to help you plan worship, asking them for new ways and ideas to add for varied worship responses.

Conclusion

We value the engagement of *all* generations in the corporate worship of God just as we value the presence of those of varied ableness in our

---

[24] Grant and Perez, *Dive Into UDL*, 97.

sanctuaries. We build ramps on the exterior of our worship centers so that individuals in wheelchairs, families with strollers, and young children can more easily access the space for corporate worship. When we take those same principles and apply them to our corporate worship gatherings, we not only make spaces for wheelchairs and strollers but we also provide connection points—intergenerational "ramps"—for increased engagement. When we, as intergenerational worship leaders, work with our congregations to design accessible worship, we meet each person, each age, each ability, each generation in the present moment, providing all with ways to respond to God in worship. As we continue to plan and lead intergenerational worship, let's work together to build ramps instead of stairs.

THEOLOGY IN PRACTICE: QUESTIONS FOR CONSIDERATION

1. In the intergenerational practice of worship, what priority should be placed on participation of all ages in your gathering? Why?

2. Can full participation happen when certain age groups are hindered in their ability to respond to God in worship? Why or why not?

3. In your context, what priority is given to participation of all ages? How might the idea of building ramps help encourage full participation of all ages?

THEOLOGY IN PRACTICE: POSSIBLE NEXT STEPS

1. Either by yourself or preferably together with your worship planning team, make a list with two columns: STAIRS and RAMPS. List any stairs you have identified while reading this chapter that inhibit all ages from worshiping. Then, begin brainstorming about possible ramps you might build, and list these ramp ideas in the other column, next to the corresponding stair you have identified.

2. By yourself or with a worship planning team, make a second list, including all the possible age categories and generations, as well as any other possible diversities (ability, culture, ethnicity, gender, neurodiversity, etc.) in your worship gatherings. Consider identifying

one or two people who represent each age category or diversity. As a team, make a goal to have one-on-one conversations where you can ask these representatives to help you identify stairs, perhaps ones that you are completely unaware of, when it comes to planning worship. Have these representatives collaborate and help build new worship ramps with you and your worship planning team for future intergenerational worship gatherings.

Section Three

IMPLEMENTING FORMATIVE INTERGENERATIONAL PRACTICES

"Perfect practice makes perfect.
Perfect practice makes progress.
Practice doesn't make perfect; perfect practice makes perfect.
Practice doesn't make perfect, practice makes progress.
Practice makes improvement. No one is perfect.
Practice makes permanent."

—Favorite Quotes about Practice—Band Directors Talk Shop

CHAPTER 8

FAITH PRACTICES IN COMMUNITY AND AT HOME

KAREN DEBOER

"It's not about perfect, it's about effort, and when you bring that effort every single day, that's where transformation happens, that's how change occurs."

—Julián Michaels

After leading a workshop on family faith formation, I was packing up my supplies when one of the participants asked if she could speak with me.

> "You talked about the importance of reading the Bible and praying with our kids," she said. "I didn't grow up in a home where the Bible was read or where anyone prayed. We're trying to teach our son about God, but we don't even know where to begin. We figured out Christmas—we made a nativity scene and read a Bible story—but we stumbled through Easter. And what are we supposed to do on all the other days? I have no idea how to do this."

That mom is part of my church family. I will never forget the personal faith story she shared during worship on the week she and her husband adopted their baby. I was there the Sunday her son was baptized, and he is part of the small group of children I lead on Sunday mornings. As her brave question showed me, I had been operating under a false assumption that the tools and resources I had been sharing were building on a foundational familiarity with faith practices. During the workshop, I had shown the group my top choices for children's storybook Bibles and had discussed the importance of family prayers, presuming a baseline of familiarity with the faith practices of engaging Scripture and prayer. I never considered the possibility that the people with whom I had been worshiping each Sunday for years had never experienced those faith formation practices.

I wonder how often we as a church make similar assumptions about the people we serve. I suspect that our congregations are filled with people who share that mom's *"I have no idea how to do this"* anxiety, whether or not they grew up in a family that went to church on Sunday. I am realizing that singing the chorus "Read your Bible, pray every day, and you'll grow, grow, grow!"[1] without spending time exploring and experiencing how to practice faith is the equivalent of saying, "Eat fruits and vegetables every day and you'll stay healthy," without providing opportunities to explore and experience their deliciousness.

Teaching people how faith is formed and equipping them with tools to practice their faith at home is important, but it is just one part of the faith formation equation. If the desired outcome is for people to grow in faith as they use the information and engage with the tools, it is critical that we weave adaptable faith practice experiences into times we are gathered in community, doing so in ways that can be woven into daily life as intentionally and as naturally as breathing. Providing firsthand experiences as part of learning is seen as a best practice in other areas of life. For example, before obtaining a driver's license, students need to experience driving themselves—steering, stopping, and turning—until doing so becomes second nature. Similarly, learning to swim requires spending time in the

---

[1] "Read your Bible, pray every day, and you'll grow, grow, grow!" is the chorus of a traditional children's song that the author was taught at church as a child and that, judging by its proliferation on the Internet, is still commonly used today.

water until breathing, bobbing, and treading skills become instinctive. And parents will teach young children to pray by gently folding their hands and inviting them to repeat "Amen!" We learn best by doing. If we want to encourage and equip all ages to engage with faith practices in ways that are both intentional and natural, we must provide opportunities for people to experience faith practices. Before I share ideas for doing so, I will discuss what faith practices are and why they are vital to faith formation.

What Are Faith Practices?

Faith practices, also known as spiritual disciplines or spiritual practices, are *repeated ways of connecting with God that help shape us to become more like Jesus*. And the Christian tradition provides us with an abundance of faith practices! In the revised and expanded edition of *Spiritual Disciplines Handbook*, author Adele Ahlberg Calhoun provides guidance for seventy-five faith practices, including practices such as journaling, rest, truth-telling, and waiting.[2] In the fall of 2020, Faith Formation Ministries (for whom I work) launched the Faith Practices Project, a curated website filled with faith practice resources for ministry leaders, congregations, and households.[3] The Faith Practices Project explores twelve faith practices; here, I will discuss four of these practices: ***engaging Scripture, listening, gratitude, and celebration.***

Why Should We Engage in Faith Practices?

As Chris Schoon explains in the post "Cultivate: What Is a Spiritual Discipline?," faith practices

- enrich our attentiveness to the Holy Spirit,
- cultivate the life and character of Jesus Christ,
- strengthen our love for God and others.[4]

---

[2] Adele Ahlberg Calhoun, *Spiritual Disciplines Handbook*, rev. and expanded ed. (Downers Grove, IL: InterVarsity Press, 2015).

[3] For more resources, see "Faith Practices Project," Christian Reformed Church, www.crcna.org/FaithPracticesProject.

[4] Listed verbatim from Chris Schoon, "Cultivate: What Is a Spiritual Discipline?" *The Network*, accessed August 10, 2021, https://network.crcna.org/faith-practices/cultivate-what-spiritual-discipline.

"Faith practices," says Schoon, "integrate our capacity to experience and respond to God's love by moving us to love our neighbors, which in turn deepens and expands our love for God."[5] Faith practices are not an "all about me" activity. On the contrary, faith practices are missional and life-giving to the faith community. Faith Formation Ministries states: "Spiritual disciplines are not designed to reassure us of our own goodness. Rather, they send us out to love our neighbors with the love that God has for us, which in turn deepens and expands our love for God."[6] In other words, *faith practices help God's people of all ages be the people we are called by God to be.*

Ideas for Experiencing Faith Practices in Community and at Home

How do we begin to incorporate faith practices in our own faith communities and in our homes? Begin by looking around at the ways you are already practicing faith when gathered in community. You are probably already weaving Bible reading and prayer into intergenerational small group gatherings when you begin meetings or head out on a service project. Weddings, funerals, church dinners, and, of course, weekly worship are also places where faith practices are woven into each occasion. You might ask yourself: *How might we deepen our faith practice experiences in ways that encourage people to try what they have experienced in community when they are also at home?* Start small and build on what you are already doing. Each idea below is simply that; use your imagination to reshape each idea into an experience that fits your context.[7]

Engaging Scripture

The practice of **engaging Scripture** immerses us in the true story of God's faithful love so that we grow in recognizing God, ourselves, and the world around us.[8]

---

[5] Schoon, "Cultivate."

[6] Faith Formation Ministries, *Faith Practices: Holy Habits That Help Us Love God and Our Neighbor, Listen to the Spirit, and Become More Like Jesus* (Grand Rapids: Faith Alive Christian Resources, 2022), 6.

[7] Descriptions of each practice are used by permission from Faith Formation Ministries.

[8] "Engaging Scripture," Faith Practices Project, www.crcna.org/FaithPracticesProject/engaging-scripture.

- **Preparation.** Prior to reading Scripture, invite everyone to prepare their whole selves to enter into the passage. You might say something like, *"As you are able, set your feet flat on the floor, take in a deep breath, perhaps placing your hands on your heart as you do, and slowly let that breath out."*[9]
    - ▸ *Taking It Home*: Suggest that people try this practice of preparing their bodies before reading Scripture at home, too.
- **Taking Notes/Drawing.** Provide all ages with paper (on a small clipboard, a notepad to keep, a page tucked into the order of worship, etc.) and a writing tool. Encourage everyone to use these tools during Bible reading—imagining what is being described, drawing pictures, or jotting down any words that come to mind. Read the passage twice, if possible.
- **Reflection.** Invite further reflection by asking: *"As you look at what you've drawn or written, what do you see? What did you notice as you were listening?"* Encourage adults with children to lean in and share their responses with each other.
    - ▸ *Taking It Home*: Point out that having paper and colored pencils nearby when you are reading the Bible or listening to a Bible story being read can be a wonderful way to spend time in God's story. Encourage everyone to try this practice at home the following week.
- **Marking Scripture.** Give each person a printed copy of the Bible passage. You can give young children a smaller portion of the passage and a colored pencil (or two!). Invite worshipers to listen for and then mark any words or phrases that catch their attention as the passage is read aloud twice. Encourage young readers to mark the words they recognize or to make word pictures as they listen.
- **Further Reflection.** Use reflection questions like these: *"What might the words or phrases you marked have to do with you or your life? What might God be saying to you and to God's family? What might God be calling you to do or to be?"*

---

[9] This idea was inspired by the weekly worship practice of Michael Rudenza, pastor at Good Shepherd New York, whose worship services I attended digitally from January to June 2021, https://goodshepherdnewyork.com/.

- ▸ ***Taking It Home*:** Encourage people to continue this practice of marking Scripture at home by providing them with a printed copy of another passage to take with them. Give them some colored pencils to take home.
- **Wonder Questions.** Weave wondering questions into Bible readings. Here's an example of how to do this using the story of Jesus calming the sea (Luke 8:22–25):
  - *Prior* to reading the Bible passage, use connection-building questions to invite people into the story. With this story you might say, *"Think for a moment about the last big rainstorm you were in. If you were indoors, remember the sound of the rain against the windows. If you were outside, did you get wet? What did that feel like? Were you surprised by the flash of lightning and the sound of thunder?"* Follow that with words like these: *"Today's Scripture passage includes a furious storm. As I read it, imagine that you are there."*
  - *During* the reading of a passage, pause and wonder about what you've just read or what might be coming next. For example, after verse 24 you might ask, "I wonder how Jesus rebuked the wind and waves?"
  - *Following* a Bible reading during which you have paused to wonder, provide people with a few moments to reflect to themselves or with someone nearby, asking: *"What do you wonder about the story?"*
- Be clear that those with children nearby are always welcome to lean in and wonder aloud together throughout a Scripture reading. Let them know those whispered conversations are not just okay, but that they are encouraged!

Listening

Listening involves training our attention to recognize God's voice in the midst of all the other voices calling for our attention. It involves learning to be fully present with God and with our neighbor.[10]

---

[10] "Listening," Faith Practices Project, www.crcna.org/FaithPracticesProject/listening.

- **Intentional Space for Listening.** Be intentional about providing time for people to quietly pause and reflect as they look at art, photographs, or other visuals shown during your gathering. Do the same prior to playing music, singing a song, reciting a poem, or reading a passage. Invite all ages to still their minds and bodies (perhaps by taking a deep breath in and out together) as a way to practice being fully present. You might follow up with a moment of silence, asking people to consider, "What might God be saying to you through this music (that song, those words)?"
- **Journal.** Invite someone (of any age) to share how they have used a journal as part of their listening practice (perhaps bringing their journal along to illustrate their story) and how journaling has nurtured their faith.
  - ▶ *Taking It Home*: Encourage all ages to try this practice at home by purchasing in advance a variety of journals and inviting each person to select one to take with them.
- **Read-Aloud Book.** Look for an opportunity to read aloud the picture book *The Rabbit Listened* by Cori Doerrfeld as a way to explore the practice of listening.[11] Make space for conversation afterward, inviting people to share stories of ways they have experienced listening. Encourage them to look for opportunities to be listeners at home.

Gratitude

Gratitude is our response of thankfulness for God's goodness, love, provision, and grace. It flows from an awareness that, regardless of our circumstances, God loves us and is with us.[12]

- **Gratitude Wall.** During the pandemic in 2020, my colleague Dr. Mimi Larson and her husband Keith created a gratitude wall in her office, filling the space behind her office door with sticky notes on which they had written things for which they were

---

[11] Cori Doerrfeld, *The Rabbit Listened* (New York: Dial Books, 2018).
[12] "Gratitude," Faith Practices Project, www.crcna.org/FaithPracticesProject/gratitude.

grateful.[13] Weave this wonderful idea into your own gathering by providing each person with a pad of sticky notes, a writing tool, and time to draw or write things for which they are grateful. You might preface the activity with a broad question: *"What are you grateful for today?"* Or, help people focus by providing categorical questions: *"What are you grateful for personally? At home? At school? In your daily work? In your neighborhood?"* Designate a wall space on which people can stick their answers; conclude your practice with a prayer of thanksgiving.

- ▶ *Taking It Home*: Invite people to think individually for a moment about a space in their own households. Where might they create their own gratitude walls in their homes? Make it easier for them to do so by inviting them to keep the notepad and writing tool you gave them to take home.

- **Noticing God.** Provide people with a writing tool and a page that has been divided into three sections with the following headings:
  - Me
  - My Family
  - My Neighborhood

Guide them through the activity by asking a specific question for each heading, leaving time after each one for them to reflect and to respond:

- *"In what ways do you see God providing and showing care for you? Draw or list them under <u>Me</u>."*
- *"In what ways do you see God providing and showing care for your family? Draw or list them under <u>My Family</u>."*
- *"In what ways are you seeing God providing and showing care in your neighborhood? Draw or list them under <u>My Neighborhood</u>."*

Depending on your context, you might invite those who wish to do so to share their responses with the group or with someone sitting nearby.

---

[13] Mimi Larson, "I Wonder if God Is Here?" *The Network*, Faith Formation Ministries, April 8, 2020, network.crcna.org/childrens-ministry/i-wonder-if-god-here.

▶ *Taking It Home*: Encourage people to continue the practice above at home by sending them home with additional copies of the printed page.

Celebration

Celebration is delighting in circumstances, relationships, and occasions that help us remember God's abundant goodness, creativity, faithfulness, beauty, and love.[14]

- **Day-to Day Celebration.** We often think of celebration in terms of milestone moments in our lives, which are important! But it is also important to encourage households to look for and to celebrate what God is doing in our day-to-day lives. Liz Bewley's family does this each week by incorporating celebration in their Friday night suppers. In her home video about their practice, she shares that their celebration suppers might include worship, music, dance, or simply being still as they remember and share with each other stories of God's faithfulness.[15] As I and my colleagues at Faith Formation Ministries were curating ideas for intergenerational gatherings (including worship) on the faith practice of celebration, we were struck by how few we could find. After all, as Christ followers we have so much to celebrate, don't we?
- **Communal Celebration.** Be intentional about making space for celebrations—both big and small—when gathered in community, by dedicating time for sharing stories of "God's abundant goodness, creativity, faithfulness, beauty, and love." Here are some ideas: offer a round of applause to God following a story of God's faithfulness; serve cake on Sundays when someone is baptized; add a bouquet of colorful helium balloons to your sanctuary; provide opportunities for people to share (in small groups or with the whole congregation) that for which they are thankful to God today.

---

[14] "Celebrating," Faith Practices Project, www.crcna.org/FaithPracticesProject/celebration.
[15] See https://www.youtube.com/watch?v=sImHU6Vb_1Y, home video of Liz Bewley's family as they prepare for their weekly Friday night supper.

- ▸ *Taking It Home*: The Faith Practices Project prompts people to practice celebration at home by providing each household with a bell to ring (a few jingle bells tied on a string work) at home each time there is something to celebrate. Those who live alone might hang their bell in a place where they will see it frequently and be reminded to celebrate God at work in their lives and in the world.
- **Celebration Jar.** Provide every household with some Celebration Notes (a sticky note pad or colored strips of paper) and a fun pen or marker, and a simple container (a jam jar works well); encourage them to jot down descriptions of the things they are celebrating and thanking God for, and fill the jar with their notes.
- **Marking the Church Calendar.** Provide people with replicas of the special objects used during worship to mark church seasons or holy days (an Advent wreath, a purple-colored tablecloth or fabric runner for Lent, a fire-colored cloth for Pentecost, etc.) as a way to prompt them to celebrate that event at home as well.

Conclusion

One Sunday morning at my church, the person leading worship wove a *lectio divina* (prayer, reflection, and listening through Scripture) experience into his message. Each person received a sheet of paper on which the passage had been printed in a large-sized font along with their choice of coloring pencils or crayons. The leader used simple language to explain the practice of *lectio divina* before we tried it together, inviting everyone to listen carefully as the passage was read aloud several times, and then pausing between each reading to provide time for each person to mark, in a way of their own choosing, the words or phrases they sensed God might be bringing to their attention. After a time of reflection, we were invited to share what stuck out to us with those seated nearby.

Adults of all ages from households of all sizes and families with children—including that of the young mom from my workshop—learned and experienced a *faith practice together* at church that day; one which they were probably more likely to try again at home. So did I. Faith practices help people "grow, grow, grow" into the people they are called by God to be. My hope in curating and creating these ideas is that, as you read them, your mind might wander to the times, places, and ways you might build upon and weave them into gatherings in your context—doing so with wide arms and open hands to meet people where they are at (making no assumptions!), while extending an invitation to explore faith practices together in ways that they may become part of the fabric of their daily lives.

Recommended Resources

For additional ideas, here is a list of resources I have found helpful:

- **The Faith Practices Project** is a curated collection of outstanding resources and ideas designed for individuals, groups, and families with children. For each practice you will find creative ideas for individual and communal practices, Scripture passages to read, a helpful intro article, thought or discussion questions, and a list of resources for going deeper. Explore the collection at www.crcna.org/FaithPracticesProject.
- *Faith Practices: Holy Habits That Help Us Love God and Our Neighbor, Listen to the Spirit, and Become More Like Jesus* provides individuals and small groups with an entry-level introduction to twelve of the faith practices. Available from www.faithaliveresources.org.
- *Spiritual Disciplines Handbook: Practices That Transform Us* by Adele Ahlberg Calhoun provides information about spiritual practices along with practical, accessible guidance to assist readers in actually doing them.
- In the "Practices" section of the *Lifelong Faith* **website**, you'll find tools for designing a Christian practices curriculum in your church. Go to www.lifelongfaith.com/christian-practices.html.
- Provide families with free, downloadable **"5 Ways" tools** on faith practices (and more) from **Dwell at Home**. Access at www.dwell.faithaliveresources.org/home.html.
- The pocket-sized *Everyday Family Faith* and palm-sized *God's Big Story Cards* are engaging, easy-to-use faith practice resources for families with children. Find both at www.faithaliveresources.org.

THEOLOGY IN PRACTICE: QUESTIONS TO CONSIDER

1. What are faith practices in your context that are already happening? Do these practices only happen in church or do they extend to home?

2. How might faith practices build intergenerational relationships, in ministry contexts as well as in the home and community?

3. How does building rhythms of intergenerational faith practices form us to be the people of God?

4. Consider the four faith practices DeBoer discussed: engaging in Scripture, listening, celebration, gratitude. Which of these four faith practices occur intergenerationally in your context? Which of these four faith practices (or others) are ones you might incorporate in your context?

5. What specific idea or intergenerational faith practice are you inspired to facilitate next in your context? Make plans now for implementation.

CHAPTER 9

GROWING FAITH IN MESSY CHURCH

JOHANNAH MYERS AND ROBERTA J. EGLI

*"I embrace emerging experience.
I participate in discovery. I am a butterfly.
I am not a butterfly collector.
I want the experience of the butterfly."*
—William Stafford

Where have all the families gone? This is a question many churches are asking after pandemic lockdowns. Since March of 2020, church life, by necessity, has moved into new spaces, worshiping outdoors, at home, online, or through a combination of these modalities. As families adjust to and sometimes even thrive in these creative spaces, church leaders are wondering if families will ever be willing to come back into traditional church worship spaces. A model of intergenerational worship that can be enacted in almost any space, from playgrounds to beaches, church courtyards to traditional sanctuaries, might be an intriguing possibility through Messy Church. Messy Church, a model for intergenerational worship and faith formation, has been likened to a giant picnic, one where everyone is welcome into the story of faith each month. Beginning in 2004, in England,

Messy Church grew around the world, forming intergenerational worship communities. Messy Church invites all ages to gather for hands-on activities and celebration centered around one Bible story or theme each month. Messy Church also includes a meal together, where families of all sizes, shapes, and faith backgrounds can enjoy messy community and Christ-centered love. Extravagant hospitality provides a framework as all ages commingle and relationships are both started and strengthened.

The Gospels tell the story of a big picnic where Jesus is the host. How might this story of Jesus feeding more than five thousand people help us envision what it might look like for churches to grow disciples today in this messy post-pandemic world? Can a model of intergenerational worship that is as messy and extravagant as Jesus's picnic be a helpful model for today's families?

The Story

Jesus sat down one day with his closest followers, those who were learning how to live his Way (John 6:1–14). They were not alone. Large crowds who had experienced teaching and healing from Jesus also gathered around. Jesus's disciples felt overwhelmed by the crowd. Jesus, however, was not fazed. As usual, he used a picnic as a teaching experience, inviting the twelve to stretch their faith. While Philip scratched his head, wondering how Jesus expected to feed all these people, Andrew found a boy with five loaves of bread and two fish. That small offering was all it took. More than five thousand people ate that day from one boy's meal. People ate as much as they wanted, with food to spare.

The crowd at Jesus's picnic was diverse, ranging from the mildly curious to those who had already experienced the healing power of Jesus to those who were deeply committed to following Jesus wherever he led. Scripture offers few details regarding what happened to the crowd after this picnic. Does Scripture offer any evidence that the people in the crowd were committed to following Jesus?[1] We can imagine what happened to the large crowd as they dispersed from that big picnic. Surely some walked away, pleased with a lovely day. Others probably grumbled about the lack

---

[1] Lucy Moore and Jane Leadbetter, *Messy Church: Fresh Ideas for Building a Christ-Centered Community* (Downers Grove, IL: InterVarsity Press, 2017), 9.

of dessert to go with bread and fish. Perhaps some people left their families to follow Jesus and learn more about his ways. As we read further in John 6, we discover that plenty left the hillside with lingering questions about Jesus.

Here, we stop to imagine and ask important questions: *Who are the disciples in this picnic story? Is the young child who offered his food a disciple? Are those who are questioning what happened disciples? The people on the edge of the crowd, who left the picnic pondering what just happened—are they disciples?* This picnic story, where Jesus fed five thousand people, provides a framework for how disciples are formed in Messy Church.

Who Is a Disciple?

At Messy Church, we follow Claire Dalpa's definition of a disciple: anyone who is on "a journey of following Jesus throughout the whole of life."[2] Those at our "Get Started in Messy Church" training want to know if Messy Church really "works": *Can Messy Church grow disciples of Jesus when it is chaotic and fun? Is Messy Church simply a step to guide people into "regular" church?* We also hear denominational leaders ask the question in much the same way that Nathanael once asked: "Can anything good come out of Nazareth?" (John 1:46 ESV). They sometimes ask: *Is this really church when you only meet once a month and there is no sermon to instruct people? How does a gathering where people wander from place to place teach people about the Way of Christ? What are the steps of forming disciples in Messy Church?* To all these questions, our answer is the same as Philip's response to Nathanael: "Come and see."

Come and see how Messy Church, like the crowded picnic in John 6, suggests a diversity of people along their faith journey. Come and see how hospitality in Messy Church creates space for people to explore their own faith. Come and see how the value of creativity in Messy Church brings Scripture to life. Come and see how faith is formed through celebrating how Jesus walks with us in ALL of life's moments, both the joy-filled and pain-filled. Come and see how children learn about faith from adults, and perhaps more importantly, how adults learn about following Jesus through

---

[2] Claire Dalpa, "A Researcher's Journey," in *Messy Discipleship: Messy Church Perspectives on Growing Faith*, ed. Lucy Moore (Abingdon, UK: Bible Reading Fellowship, 2021), 24.

younger generations. Come and see how Christ is at the very center of who we are and what we do in Messy Church.

One of our Messy Church leaders reflected on the walk to Emmaus in her description of discipleship: "It was only at the very end when (Jesus) said he was going to go that they recognized him for who he was . . . and that's what we're doing at Messy Church, we're on that walk to Emmaus."[3] *Disciples are those who are on the Way of Jesus, moving closer to Jesus as they embrace loving God and loving neighbor.* This Way includes, then, the Philips (John 6:5–7) with their questions and doubts as well as the kids who are willing to share their gifts with the community. The Way also includes those who come because they are hungry or curious, who show up *prior* to discovering their invitation to walk in faith with Jesus.

When we begin to see all who show up for Messy Church as disciples—those who are on the Way—the focal point in forming disciples in Messy Church is *creating space for people to encounter Jesus.* Messy Church is a space for everyone gathered to meet Jesus through relationships, exploration, questioning, and sitting at the table breaking bread.

Foundational Values for Growing Faith in Messy Church

Five foundational values of Messy Church create space for disciples to flourish around the globe. While our structure and design may vary from context to context or culture to culture, we hold to five core values. Messy Church creates a **welcoming** space where we **create** and **celebrate**, with **all ages together, centered around the love of Christ**. Lucy Moore, a Messy Church pioneer, believes our five values "either reflect something of who God is, or show something of what it means to have 'life in all its fullness' . . . or demonstrate what the church is all about."[4] Messy Church provides space for the Spirit of God to move among us through interactive worship that begins with exploring the Bible through hands-on activities and ends with all ages sitting around a table sharing food and life experiences.

---

[3] Leader's comments recorded by Claire Dalpa, "A Leadership Team's Journey," in *Messy Discipleship*, 44.

[4] Lucy Moore, "Training Presentation on Messy Church," Getting Started in Messy Church Conference, October 2017.

Growing Faith through Hospitality

Providing **hospitality** is one of the core values of Messy Church. Henri Nouwen describes hospitality as "the creation of free space where the stranger can enter and become a friend instead of an enemy."[5] At Messy Church, we prioritize welcoming everyone—those church "regulars" alongside those who have never set foot in church. Increasingly, we find that we must be aware of those taking tentative steps back into church, despite previous hurts and exclusion. Sometimes, hospitality at Messy Church seems obvious—like the meal we share each time we gather or the welcoming smiles from volunteers. Other times, hospitality is more subtle and more challenging. For example, in one Messy Church, a single dad and his two children had been invited to Messy Church by another family and began to attend regularly. Dad usually sat at one of the tables drinking coffee while the two young children ran around the various tables. The team prayed about how to approach the father. At the next Messy Church, a team member sat and shared a cup of coffee with this dad. Unbeknownst to those in Messy Church, this "dad" was actually the children's grandfather, who had custody due to his daughter's addiction. This grandfather shared that the youngest child required multiple surgeries and trips to the hospital. After that conversation, the grandfather moved from an observer to a participant. From this experience, the Messy Church team learned that hospitality also meant being present with a cup of coffee to listen to one another's story. The team became more compassionate as they created space to be with the grandfather.

Growing Faith through Creativity

Because everyone is welcome at Messy Church, they are invited to engage creatively with Scripture and with one another. Some confuse Messy Church with a craft club, not seeing past the colorful paper and scissors, group games, or glitter. In the midst of what looks like chaos, one can experience the core value of *creativity*. At Messy Church, folks interact in hands-on, creative ways with a creative and hands-on God. We meet our Creator in the act of creating. Scissors, glue sticks, and markers become

---

[5] Henri J. M. Nouwen, *Reaching Out: The Three Movements of the Spiritual Life* (New York: Bantam Doubleday Dell, 2000), 71.

tools for worship of no less importance than brass candlesticks or hymnals. Through creative play, our faith comes to life as we interact with the story of God's interaction with us. When we bake our own bread, decorate placemats, or weave baskets for those leftover loaves and fishes, suddenly, the story of Jesus feeding the five thousand comes alive. As we create, we see ourselves in the story much as preschool children play "house" or play "school" and imagine themselves and how they interact with the world.

Creativity can also lead us to ask deeper questions, inviting us to wonder and think beyond. For theologian Rowan Williams, his "aim" in reading a biblical text is not "to find instructions," but rather "to open myself to 'God's world'—to the landscape of God's action and the rhythms of life lived in God's presence."[6] Similarly, Sandy Brodine of Messy Church in Australia finds that "being open to the text involves bringing all of the creative and wondering powers of one's mind to the text—being open to the possibility that we might discover something new and surprising, or indeed that the text might change us into something new."[7] The creative, hands-on aspect of Messy Church is not a distraction from or an alternative to deep theology; it is a pathway for imagining ourselves as part of God's world, as people on the way with Jesus.

Growing Faith through Celebration

Along with making space for hospitality and creativity, we believe that making space for growing faith brings forth ***celebration***. At Messy Church, we celebrate. We celebrate each other and we celebrate God. Celebration is a specific element of Messy Church. After a welcome and table games and activities exploring the biblical theme, everyone comes together in one space to experience Scripture, sing, and engage in communal prayer. During this time, people who have more traditional experiences and views of worship can engage, while those who are less familiar with church can also participate without feeling alienated or unwelcome during a completely foreign experience. Through celebration, those new or returning

---

[6] Rowan Williams, "Christian Theology and Other Faiths," in *Scriptures in Dialogue: Christians and Muslims Studying the Bible and the Quran Together*, ed. Michael Ipgrave (London: Church House Publishing, 2004), 21.

[7] Sandy Brodine, "Creativity," in *Messy Discipleship*, 84.

to a community of faith are introduced to a God who celebrates. Martyn Payne, a Messy Church pioneer, writes:

> Celebration captures the truth that, as Christians, we worship a party-throwing God: a God who is like a shepherd rejoicing over finding [a] wayward sheep; like the woman gathering with her friends to rejoice over the lost coin she has found. . . . In itself [celebration] is both life-giving and life-affirming, particularly in an age when many of us feel reduced to being a mere statistic and a number.[8]

Here, creativity and hospitality join together with celebration to draw folks to God.

Recently, research regarding the importance of creating space for reflective practice inspired Messy Church to provide such spaces for both our leadership teams and monthly church participants.[9] Rather than add one more activity to our overscheduled lives, teams prioritize creating space in the routines we already have in our planning and implementing of Messy Church. Intentionally taking time to notice how God is already working in our lives, we deepen relationships with each other and with God. Together, we celebrate where God's Spirit is moving among us. By recognizing where our tasks, busyness, or ambition block God's work in our individual and community lives, we confess and celebrate God's grace. Faith grows and deepens in Messy Church through our individual and communal celebration—celebrating that God is actively present in our everyday lives.

Growing Faith through All Ages Together

If Messy Church gets taken for a craft club some of the time, it has a tendency to be confused with children's ministry most of the time. Even within local Messy Churches, some volunteers speak of how Messy Church helps connect with kids with a vague hope that parents will be brought along for the ride. From its earliest days, Messy Church has held *"all ages*

---

[8] Martyn Payne, "Celebration," in *Messy Discipleship*, 106.
[9] See "A Voyage of Discovery: Deepening Discipleship in Messy Churches and Beyond," Messy Church, April 2021, www.messychurch.org.uk/deepening-discipleship.

together" as a core value. Messy Church is passionately intergenerational, seeking to grow faith in both young and old, curious and committed, joining together to explore and engage with faith practices of Scripture, participatory prayer practices, creative activities, and authentic conversation. Faith grows through deepening relationships we experience with each other and with Christ.

Going back to John 6, Jesus does not separate the crowd into age-specific groups. Rather, Jesus uses each experience encountered to teach others about discipleship. He welcomes the gifts of the young child who offers his lunch. He uses questions that allow adults such as Andrew and Philip to stretch their faith. He invites everyone together into a relationship, whether they are near the front or at the margins of the crowd. Martyn Payne writes about this kind of growing faith through relational experiences:

> If we want to see our Christian faith caught and nurtured today, those with faith need to be alongside those who are learning faith. The young need to be alongside the old so that they can hear and learn from those with experience of trusting God in all the ups and downs of life. The old need to be alongside the young, who can bring the gift of a lively spirituality and an eager sense of adventure.[10]

Messy Church values this kind of space, where generations grow their faith together, in relationships, where faith can truly grow deep.

Growing faith intergenerationally is not neat and tidy. It takes space, intentionality, prayer, and a belief that the Spirit of God is already working in the lives of people. Within the space of Messy Church, older adults volunteer alongside youth, sharing a common purpose of helping others. Younger children interact with people their grandparents' age, and single adults, who have no biological children, can make friends with youth, all while working on a building project together. These are the interactions that cannot happen when all ages are separated into their own spaces on Sunday mornings.

---

[10] Martyn Payne, *Messy Togetherness: Being Intergenerational in Messy Church* (Abingdon, UK: Bible Reading Fellowship, 2016), 32.

Our task is to create opportunities for people of all ages to encounter the living Christ through story, song, activity, prayer. The activities are not planned only for kids; everyone is invited to join in the creativity and celebration. Through conversations and activity, young and old engage in exploring faith together. Often, Messy Church is the only space where older adults have the opportunity to interact with young children; similarly, children are able to sit with older adults as equals.

Growing Faith through Keeping Focus on Christ

Finally, but certainly not least, seeds of faith are planted, nurtured, and grown to maturity in Messy Church when we keep all we do **centered on the good news of Jesus Christ.** Initially an effort to reach out to neighbors who were not involved in a faith community, Messy Church has grown into a global movement, as others have passionately joined the party to share the joy of following in the way of Jesus Christ.

In the example of the picnic with Jesus from John 6, Jesus gathered and engaged with a great variety of people, meeting them where they were in their faith journeys. The goal of Messy Church is to invite people to engage with the living Christ, wherever they are in their faith journey. Doubters and seekers, inquisitive and discouraged lifelong followers, and those who are hearing the call of Christ for the first time—all come together as a beloved community to focus on the Way of Christ.

Christ is at the center in the entirety of Messy Church. We begin with an extravagant welcome just as Christ welcomes all into an abundant life. We move into a chaotic time where all ages engage in creative activities exploring the life of Christ through a biblical story. We then transition into a gathered community, encountering Christ through Scripture, singing, and prayer. We conclude with the example of Christ at table, with strangers and committed followers sharing a meal together.

Experiences from Messy Church participants highlight the Christ-centered value in forming disciples:

- "We were talking about God, and it made it feel as if God was listening to us." (child participant)

- "We have been made more aware of what we are doing. We think we have raised awareness of WHY we are doing a particular task. We have put Jesus into the middle so that rather than craft with a little bit of Jesus, it has become more about Jesus with a little bit of craft." (adult leader)[11]

In John 10:10 (NIV), Jesus shares his mission, saying "I have come that they may have life, and have it to the full." From planning to implementation, from the welcome to the meal, from the babe in a parent's arms to the grandmother, Messy Church is about showing how Christ brings life in its fullness to all.

Growing Faith in Messy Church

We have explored how the story from John 6 about a picnic on the hillside created space for people to encounter abundance offered through life with Jesus. At Messy Church, the values of **hospitality, creativity, celebration, all ages together**, and being **centered in Christ** complement one another, creating space for those at the center of the action as well as those on the margins of faith to follow Jesus. At Messy Church, we understand that discipleship includes those on the margins as well as those who have made a commitment to follow in the way of Christ.

We have explored how the five foundational values of Messy Church—hospitality, creativity, celebration, all ages together, and the Christ-centered focus—build upon one another to create space for faith to grow and mature. Growing faith in our own lives and in the lives of those we encounter in Messy Church is not a linear process. It can be messy and chaotic and beautiful all at the same time. Growing faith is not a task that practitioners of Messy Church "do" but rather a gift of grace from our messy experience together. Faith grows as we share our stories of faith with one another. At Messy Church, our task is to create space for God's Spirit to move so that all who gather can experience the good news that it is in Christ that "we live and move and have our being" (Acts 17:28 NIV).

The pandemic has greatly accelerated the rate of change occurring within the church. Local churches, along with larger denominational

---

[11] "A Voyage of Discovery," 7, 20.

structures, have all experienced a fast roller coaster ride of adapting all aspects of traditional church life. These changes were coming but have now burst into reality. For many people, attending church on a Sunday morning conflicts with a need for rest, recreation, family time of exploration, sports, or work. Messy Church offers the local church a model for intergenerational worship that can occur in a variety of spaces and times. It offers a model that has been adapted in multiple contexts and cultures around the world and brings with it a community of Messy Church practitioners ready to encourage one another. Messy Church is one of many ways God's Spirit continues to move among us. We pray that in these times of change, our trust in Christ grows as we experience the abundance that is created in the example of a picnic with Jesus—a picnic in which a small child's lunch provided a feast for all.

THEOLOGY IN PRACTICE: QUESTIONS TO CONSIDER

1. How might other intergenerational ministries emulate Messy Church's practices that create space for faith to grow organically through hospitality, creativity, and celebration, while focusing on bringing all ages together and centering all practices in Christ?

2. Consider your context. In what ways are you as an intergenerational leader inspired to engage in these five fundamental practices, or core values—hospitality, creativity, celebration, all ages, focus on Christ—that guide the Messy Church worship experience?

3. Identify a specific ministry in your context where the Messy Church practice of creating space for faith to grow might be utilized. Discuss next steps for making that a reality.

CHAPTER 10

LET THE SPIRIT LEAD

A Framework for Beginning and Sustaining Intergenerational Faith Formation

BREEN MARIE SIPES

> "We take what we think are the tools of spiritual transformation into our own hands and try to sculpt ourselves into robust Christlike specimens. But spiritual transformation is primarily the work of the Holy Spirit."
>
> —Jerry Bridges

In the Evangelical Lutheran Church in America (ELCA), we pray this prayer from Isaiah 11 over those who are being baptized, as well as those who are affirming their baptism:

> We give you thanks, O God,
> that through water and the Holy Spirit you give us new birth,
> cleanse us from sin, and raise us to eternal life.
> Stir up in us the gift of your Holy Spirit:
> the spirit of wisdom and understanding,
> the spirit of counsel and might,

> *the spirit of knowledge and the fear of the Lord,*
> *the spirit of joy in your presence, now and always. Amen.*

We call on the Holy Spirit to be present in our life of faith, to walk with us as we seek to follow in the footsteps of Jesus, and to guide us as we live out our calling to be disciples in the world. Following this same practice of being Spirit-led, along with extensive experience leading cross generational faith formation in small congregations, I offer **six "spirits"** that guide faith-filled, engaging cross generational formation: *experimentation, vibrancy, teamwork, curiosity, invitation, and tenacity.*

A Spirit of Experimentation: Let's Try an Experiment

All good ***experiments*** begin with a problem to be solved, a burning question to be answered, or something people wonder about. At the smallest congregation of a three-church cooperative ministry in rural Nebraska, where I served as solo pastor (twenty total in worship on a Sunday morning), the problem became two-fold. At that time, we had no faith formation for children and youth at all, and we only had six children and youth total. Both the members of the congregation and the parents of the children and youth expressed to me several times that they felt the loss of Sunday school and longed for it to be revived. We were also all aware that six children and youth, spanning an age difference of over eight years, would create challenges in a traditional classroom setting. Our question became this: *How could we craft a faith formation experience for multiple age levels where everyone would feel welcome and engaged?*

Once we had our question, we needed to form our hypothesis—how we would try to solve the problem. I knew we did not have a lot of children and youth, but I also knew we had oodles of adults who cared deeply about these same children and youth. Our new hypothesis thus became this: *if we paired those adults with the children and youth in faith formation in a meaningful, cross generational way, we could get everyone engaged.*

With that hypothesis in mind, we crafted an experiment to test our hypothesis. I began with the two families who would be involved. We chose to try our experiment once a month after worship and after fellowship time, because that worked best in our schedules (and absolutely no one was willing to give up "cookie time," least of all our children and youth!). We also decided to limit this time to twenty minutes, since three of the six children were under three years old, and short attention spans were a factor. Third, we decided to be very intentional about inviting other caring adults, in addition to the parents, especially since those parents were already consistently cultivating their children's faith lives in the home; here, we aimed to expand that circle of care, involving our congregation. Our experiment would be called "Children of God Devotion Time" (CDT) and would run for one program year, with an option to renew and change as needed, based on what we learned. Now that we had the "why" and the "when," we began working on our "what" by seeking the vibrancy the Spirit was supplying.

A Spirit of Vibrancy: We Do Not Need to Reinvent the Wheel

When it comes to the spirit of *vibrancy*, we must remember that we do not need to reinvent the wheel. *What, within our context, is already working?* Because both families already practiced weekly devotions that were going well, including prayers, Bible stories, and questions, we found it natural to start with what was already working and to invite more adults of multiple generations to participate in this devotional format. For the first couple of years, we used the Revised Common Lectionary Gospel texts, which worked well because it was what we had just experienced in worship; in this way, the adults also felt like they had something familiar with which to begin. As CDT began to take shape, we realized we needed to begin building a team with which to carry out our experiment.

A Spirit of Teamwork: When We Work Together, the Work Is Sustainable

Building a *team* might look different in small churches where you are not big enough to have a committee for everything. As a ministry leader, you might do most of the planning, legwork, and prep on your own or with only a few helpers. But you will still need a team to work with as you engage in the experiment itself. This is different than issuing a broad invitation in the bulletin for help. Rather, recruiting team members involves seeking out the specific people with the gifts needed to pull it off. Team recruitment involves praying for the right, sometimes unexpected, person to appear.

Some questions to ask when seeking teammates include: *Who is ready for a new thing?* Our families were ready because, in their minds, anything was better than nothing. *Who has an open mind and willing hands?* We had lots of helpers in the congregation as long as we were willing to ask. We issued an invitation to several of these helpers, asking them to be "Faith Grandparents" to our children and youth. Soon, we had enough Faith Grandparents to match the adults with the children and youth in pairs. *Who keeps showing up to participate?* I was also surprised by a few adults who did not formally sign up but kept showing up early and staying late to set up and clean up. They soon became integral members of our team. At that point, we had fourteen of our twenty members involved in faith formation. Now that we had our team, it was time to begin practicing the twin spirits of curiosity and invitation.

A Spirit of Curiosity: Every Generation Is Still Learning

The spirit of **curiosity** is a practice I believe we must first cultivate within ourselves. *What do you still have to learn? What do you want to learn more about? What about what you are doing in ministry right now makes you want to learn more?* Even more, building a spirit of curiosity involves being curious about the people we serve. *What is God doing right now in, with, and among the people around you? Where are you surprised in a way that brings you life? How can you share the wisdom that comes from your curiosity in such a way that it sparks curiosity in others about the wisdom of other generations?* For this experiment, I needed to learn how to craft curriculum that could easily be accessed by all ages when I myself was not present to lead.

We know that those in every generation, in order to live out vibrant faith, are always changing, moving, and growing in their faith. Sometimes, within the church, we act as if all the learning is done when youth are in eighth or ninth grade, ready to be confirmed; yet, in many places, we still have adult or women's and men's Bible studies, where I hope people are coming to hear the old, old story with new ears for each new moment, within each new age and stage in life. As ministry leaders, perhaps one of our roles in fostering curiosity is to reflect on all we are continuing to learn in those already-established, age-specific gatherings. During these studies, we have great opportunities to share what we are learning from other ages and stages in our midst. We can tell the story of what God is doing in a different age group right in our own congregation. For our congregation, getting the buy-in of the women's Bible study served as a key starting point in our successful experiment. These women felt the need to revive faith formation for their children and youth, so giving them a direct opportunity to participate in solving this problem served to empower them as a group. In turn, they were less intimidated by their role as co-learners with our youth and children rather than up-in-the-front teachers.

After spending some time cultivating curiosity, both individually and in community, we moved to curiosity during our actual cross generational experiences. Sometimes when multiple generations come together, we operate with an unspoken expectation that those who are chronologically older are also wiser. In my experience, this expectation can become a barrier to learning and participation by older generations because they are afraid they will look foolish if they do not already know something. *How can we lower the stakes for those who are afraid to admit they do not know something or have not tried something before? How can we provide experiences that help us to be surprised by the Spirit?* Consequently, we reminded pairs of learners that no one, regardless of age, was expected to know everything; instead, we focused on asking good questions and wondering together about God and God's message for us. All participants also had the option to stop and say *"Let's ask the pastor"* when they had questions they did not know how to begin to answer. I knew, as the pastor, that I wanted to always be available to wonder with them when they got stuck.

Because the spirit of curiosity is unfamiliar to adult learners, we must emphasize and reemphasize this spirit of curiosity again and again. We each still have something to learn. The Holy Spirit always has something more to teach us. In addition to this spirit of curiosity, we must learn to add the spirit of ***invitation***; these two spirits working in tandem really make our experiments in cross generational faith formation sing.

A Spirit of Invitation: Each of Us Has Something to Teach

When crafting an experiment in cross generational faith formation in a small congregation (or any congregation), we must tailor our experiment to the gifts, talents, and energies of those who will be participating. Each experiment is not a one-size-fits-all proposition. For instance, if you plan to have music, you need to find someone who likes music and is willing to lead it. In addition, you might have to let go of "traditional" categories of gifts and talents and instead explore what talents God has already provided your team, and figure out ways to pair those talents with the needs of the experiment. For example, in our experiment with our children and youth, I made time to find out what the children and youth themselves really liked and began there. They liked having a job to do, so we made sure they each had a way to participate. They liked praying and reading out loud, so that also needed to be included. Tapping into their gifts and talents from the beginning gave our experiment energy and excitement instead of a spirit of dread fueled by the unfamiliarity and uncertainty of trying a new thing.

As CDT progressed, we discovered more gifts and talents. When two of the youth attended summer camp for the first time, they brought back songs they wanted to teach, and so songs became part of our time together. When one of our youth entered confirmation, she became really excited about the creative prayer practices she was learning there and asked if she could share these practices as a leader. In turn, she shared these prayers as gifts with us. When children and youth asked for a craft to go with each session, I asked one of the parents, who was very artsy-craftsy, to lead that session. In turn, this parent recruited five more helpers (especially since the first adults who agreed to participate DID NOT enjoy crafting), and then eighteen of the twenty people in worship on an average Sunday were participating in monthly cross generational faith formation. The Spirit was at work indeed!

In case you are good at math and are wondering about the two people who did not participate in the experiment, I wanted to let you know that they did participate in their own way. They were two older, retired farmers who were best friends, and they only got to see each other once a week during coffee and cookie time at church. Cookie time was their favorite time of the week, and we were not interested in interrupting their life-giving tradition. During CDT, they lingered over their coffee and conversation, but when it was over, they always made a point of calling the children and youth over to share what they had learned. Their curiosity connected them to the experiment and to the children and youth involved in new and Spirit-filled ways.

A Spirit of Tenacity: Culture Shift Requires Consistent Support

In the adventure that cross generational faith formation has been for me in my years of ministry, I present one final spirit I find essential: the spirit of tenacity. Unfortunately, at the beginning of each new experiment, the spirit of **tenacity** is the spirit I seem to forget about with astounding regularity.

No matter what size congregation we serve, institutional memory is strong, and sometimes, even though we know better, we find it easier to slip back into old habits. Tod Bolsinger's book *Canoeing the Mountains: Christian Leadership in Uncharted Territory* becomes especially helpful, providing a framework for sticking with it, for staying the course, and for continuing to experiment until a true culture shift actually occurs, and the church can no longer imagine itself as anything but cross generational.[1]

On the ground, the spirit of tenacity looks a lot like cheerleading and advocacy. Tenacity means texts and handwritten notes expressing encouragement and thanks to your teammates. Tenacity means continuing to cast the vision, to invite more people to discover and share, and to train and retrain them in a cross generational mindset. Tenacity means never assuming an experiment that has begun will run on its own without your leadership and guidance until those who are involved tell you (and can show you) they can do it on their own.

The CDT experiment hit this pull of "institutional memory" snag about five months into their first year. All of a sudden, I noticed that only one or two adults were joining the children and youth. Instead of the shared leadership model we had set up, adults were the ones holding the resources for the day in their hands. I learned that CDT had reverted back to the way they had always done Sunday school: one teacher, one helper, six children and youth learners. This return to a previous model made me curious. *What has happened to make this experiment revert to its previous shape, even though all involved knew the old model wasn't working?* It was

---

[1] Tod Bolsinger, *Canoeing the Mountains: Christian Leadership in Uncharted Territory* (Downers Grove, IL: InterVarsity Press, 2015).

time to apply the spirit of tenacity. I talked with the children and youth involved. I talked with the adults who were sticking with it. We agreed that having everyone involved was much more fulfilling, but that they had just fallen back into their old patterns out of habit.

In response, I sat down with a few key adults to review our plan and remind them why we had been doing what we were doing. After our discussions, these leaders came back excited to try again. We re-recruited the adults into learning alongside the children and youth, and we took the step of actually assigning each person—child, youth, or adult—to the leadership role of their choice so all knew that their part was welcome and necessary to make the whole thing happen for everyone. Because we were committed to the spirit of tenacity, we were willing to discover the snags, retool the experiment, and begin again.

Let the Spirit Lead: We Do Not Have to Go It Alone

Guided by the Spirit, I pray you may be upheld by the spirits of *experimentation, vibrancy, teamwork, curiosity, invitation, and tenacity* as you engage in your own adventures in faith formation. This framework is not a list to be checked off as each step is accomplished but rather a cycle that repeats again and again as your context grows, moves, and deepens in faith. As we practice cross generational faith formation within the framework of these spirits, we become more experienced in seeking the Spirit at every turn, both inviting and partnering with the Spirit's work, in and among us; it becomes not just what we are practicing but indeed who we really are. My final bit of advice to you is to find someone outside your context to be your partner in this fruitful, but often challenging, work. I was able to find this within the Nebraska territory of my denomination, but do not be afraid to connect with someone beyond your neighborhood, denomination, or even country if you find another pilgrim on a parallel path. Together, we can share ideas and solve problems. Together, we can expand our view of God and what God is doing. Together, we can make cross generational connections that exceed our wildest hopes and dreams. Please know that I am in prayer for you:

> *May God, who has a heart for all generations,*
> *stir up in you the gifts of the Holy Spirit:*
> *The spirit of experimentation and vibrancy,*
> *The spirit of teamwork, of curiosity and invitation,*
> *The spirit of fierce tenacity,*
> *and the spirit of joy in God's presence,*
> *now and always. Amen.*

THEOLOGY IN PRACTICE: QUESTIONS TO CONSIDER

1. As an intergenerational leader, consider your own rhythms of practice. Which leadership practices are formative for you and your people, and which ones are not?

2. As you consider your current context, which of Sipes's "spirits" (experimentation, vibrancy, teamwork, curiosity, invitation, tenacity) resonate with you? As you reflect on these spirits, write down a few next possible leadership practices you might begin incorporating.

3. How might these intergenerational leadership practices of experimentation, vibrancy, teamwork, curiosity, invitation, and tenacity enable leaders to be more open to letting the Spirit lead?

4. Consider a current difficulty in your context. How might the spirits of experimentation, vibrancy, teamwork, curiosity, invitation, and tenacity speak into that situation?

CHAPTER 11

STORY SHARING AS A PRACTICE OF INTERGENERATIONAL "BEING"

VALERIE M. GRISSOM

"It is in being the caterpillar that you become the butterfly."

—John Harricharan

Recently, my fourteen-year-old son astutely said: "Mom, I think the problem with the intergenerational movement right now is that people can *talk* about intergenerational, but they aren't *being* intergenerational." As an intergenerational leader, what does it mean for me to go past *knowing* or *doing* intergenerational to actually *being* intergenerational (see the Knowing–Being–Doing Model of learning in fig. 11.1)? Consequently, I have been considering what it means to cultivate a sense of intergenerational *being* and discovered that certain practices can foster intergenerationality in the spiritual life of my congregation, as well as in my own spiritual formation. In *Teaching and Christian Practices*, David I. Smith and James K. A. Smith explore, as teachers, allowing themselves to be formed spiritually as participants in their educational "communities of practice."[1] I would contend that the church is also a living community of practice, where leaders and participants alike are shaped and formed by rhythms of practice in which we participate. Together, we are practicing *being* the body of Christ.

One of these core intergenerational practices *of being* is *intergenerational story sharing*. Unfortunately, the word "story" is often a buzzword in ministry circles, minimized as the next great trend rather than a spiritually formative practice. Often, we share stories, but I wonder if we realize *why* story is so important? Even further, do we understand that the *how* of story sharing is almost more important than what stories are shared? Here, I wish to share the *why* and the *how* of intergenerational story sharing, along with simple, practical steps toward a practice of intergenerational *being* in Christian community.

The Why: Valuing God's Gift of Community through Participation in God's Story

When contemplating what constitutes intergenerational *being*, I realized that underneath all intergenerational practices is a fundamental value that sees each person and all that each person is as a unique gift from God[2]—regardless of age or culture. Brenda Salter McNeil likens diversity in the body of Christ to a beautiful puzzle picture.[3] This metaphor came alive for me when I found a little puzzle piece in my backpack, which we had given up searching for weeks ago. Unfortunately, all I remember from

---

[1] See David I. Smith and James K. A. Smith, eds., *Teaching and Christian Practices: Reshaping Faith & Learning* (Grand Rapids: William B. Eerdmans, 2011). Also see Carolyne Call, "The Rough Trail to Authentic Pedagogy: Incorporating Hospitality, Fellowship, and Testimony into the Classroom," in *Teaching and Christian Practices*, 61–79. Call makes efforts to embody hospitality in the classroom and realizes that "genuine hospitality" originates as a "movement within the interior life of the host." Call's work challenged me to evaluate what originates from my "interior," and how I, as an intergenerational leader, might implement practices in my life and ministry that cultivate my own practice of intergenerational *being*.

[2] Holly Catterton Allen, personal conversation, April 21, 2021. When I asked Allen what practices an intergenerational leader might cultivate for a way of intergenerational "being," the first thing Allen recommended was learning to see each person in his or her community as a gift—especially when thinking about the different generations.

[3] See Brenda Salter McNeil, *A Credible Witness: Reflections on Power, Evangelism and Race* (Downers Grove, IL: InterVarsity Press, 2008), 84–90. McNeil also uses the metaphor of a puzzle in regard to racial reconciliation and calls Christians to seek a fuller picture of God's community by valuing each person and the diversity he or she contributes to God's community.

that beautiful puzzle was that the picture was *almost* complete. When we exclude stories from members of Christ's body, we, too, are almost complete. Through Christ, we are all made children of God and are all equally valuable members of Christ's body (Eph. 2:8–22; 1 Cor. 12). Each person is like a uniquely crafted puzzle piece, bringing individual colors, textures, and variety to the picture of the living body of Christ. We share in the body of Christ through the power of God's Spirit (Eph. 4:4; 1 Cor. 12:4), who joins each puzzle piece together. The church is a living reality of God's intention for us to be in community with the triune God. God, throughout history, has formed us into this living reality as the children of God (Eph. 2, 4), and we, who are in Christ, are a picture of God's new creation *being* formed—God's intention for the redemption of all of creation. When even one piece, or person, of this puzzle is missing, we have an "almost complete" picture of God's redemption, and even further, we have an incomplete view of the triune God! Sharing stories allows us to honor and value each person and experience for a more complete, living picture of Christ's body.

Of course, story itself is a universally shared, powerful practice. Research by scientists and educators points to the power of story to not only communicate elaborate chains of information and humanly connect in ways that mere information falls short, but also to build bridges and break down walls, making connections in the middle of difference.[4] Through God's story, we find that intergenerational storytelling is nothing new. God's story is continually passed down from generation to generation, as revealed in Scripture, and each week, in Christian worship. In "The Power of Telling a Story," Jeff Barker states:

> Great stories cut across the boundaries of age, and if we tell them when the church family gathers, they will bind us. They will bind us in common experience when the characters and events creep into our conversations. They will bind us in common values as we laugh and gasp at the follies and victories in these stories. They

---

[4] To read more about the science and power of story, see Kendall Haven, *Story Proof: The Science Behind the Startling Power of Story* (Westport, CT: Libraries Unlimited, 2007). Also, see my doctoral dissertation for claims about the formative power of story in "Cultivating Intercultural Dialogue Through Story as a Spiritually Formative Practice for Worship at Calvin Presbyterian Church, Shoreline, Washington" (PhD diss., The Robert Webber Institute of Worship, 2018).

> will bind us in love and respect as we sit together, seeing with each other's eyes and hearing with each other's ears.... The intergenerational church should be a storytelling church.[5]

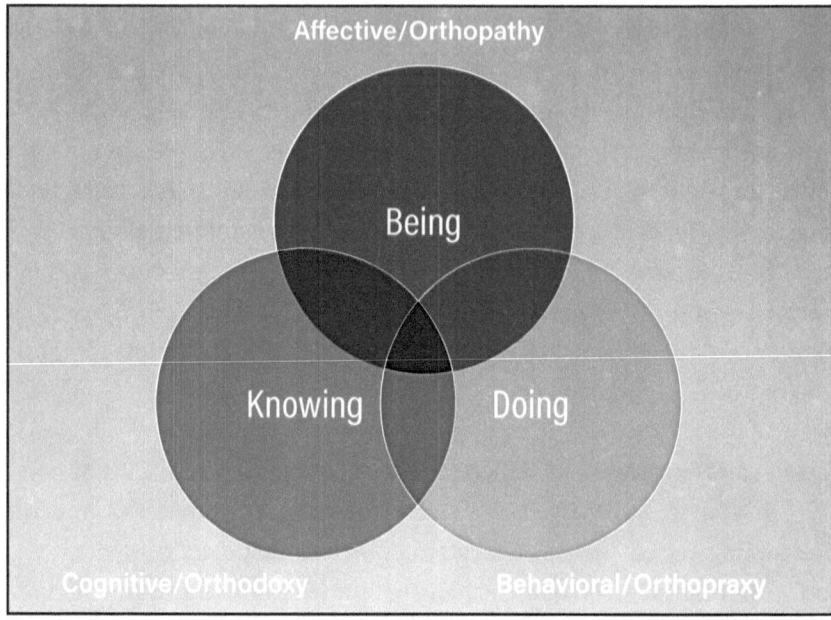

Figure 11.1. Knowing–Being–Doing Model[6]

---

[5] Jeff Barker, "The Power of Telling a Story," in *The Church of All Ages: Generations Worshiping Together*, ed. Howard Vanderwell (Herndon, VA: Alban Institute, 2008), 102.

[6] Visual created by Valerie Grissom, based off a graphic given to me by Holly Catterton Allen. See Benjamin S. Bloom and David R. Krathwohl, *Taxonomy of Educational Objectives: The Classification of Educational Goals*, handbook 1, *Cognitive Domain* (New York: Longmans, Green, 1956); David R. Krathwohl, Benjamin S. Bloom, and Bertram B. Masia, *Taxonomy of Educational Objectives*, book 2, *Affective Domain* (New York: David McKay Company, 1964); Anita Harrow, *A Taxonomy of Psychomotor Domain: A Guide for Developing Behavioral Objectives* (New York: David McKay, 1972); Greg Carlson, "Transformational Teaching," in *Christian Education: A Guide to Foundations of Ministry*, ed. Freddy Cardoza (Grand Rapids: Baker Academic, 2019), 132–43. Regarding the development of this graphic, Allen states: "The three domains of learning (cognitive, affective, and the psychomotor) are generally attributed to Benjamin Bloom, drawing from his original work with David Krathwohl, though others contributed as well. This first book in 1956 focused closely on the cognitive domain, describing most famously what came to be known as Bloom's Taxonomy of Educational Objectives. Later, Krathwohl, Bloom, and Bertram Masia developed further work on the affective domain (1964), along with its own taxonomy, and Anita Harrow wrote her work regarding the psychomotor domain (and its taxonomy) in 1972. (Others developed the affective domain as well.) In educational psychology, these domains are typically referred to as cognitive, affective, and behavioral domains. In Christian education, these three terms are used as well as knowing, being, and doing (see more in Carlson)."

Throughout history, the triune God has been revealed to us through story and has invited God's people to *participate* in this story. And God continues to invite us to participate in this story as we practice *being* the body of Christ. We, as God's people, are part of God's unfolding story—God's Church—God's new creation, *being* redeemed, God's kingdom come, right here, right now. We are called to *be* the body of Christ. We are placed "all together" in community through the gift of the Spirit to *become* Christ's body, *participating* in the unfolding story of God.

In my past, I used to think Scripture was merely something to help me grow or mature in my faith. I looked to the Bible as a great book to *know* and to *do* what it says. As a worship pastor, when I, myself, started *participating* in intergenerational Scripture presentation in worship,[7] I realized God was forming me by my communal participation in God's story. Spiritual formation does not happen just in the *knowing* and the *doing* but in the *being* of participating in Christian community—participating in God's story together.

In a similar way, I used to see story sharing as something outside the lanes of Scripture and more as a way to build community. I separated our everyday life stories from the pages of Scripture. As I began participating in mutual, intergenerational story sharing, I realized this practice enabled us to connect our stories to God's story. Suddenly, all our stories became interwoven in God's story through participation, or intergenerational *being*, in Christian community. As we continue to link these stories together with one another, they draw us into God's story and link us to all the stories of our faith. When we do this, the flat puzzle picture I talked about becomes a glorious picture of our God, through the body of Christ—a multidimensional, cosmic picture—as we experience *being* part of the rich picture of God's story. Our stories are intertwined, woven in a way that surpasses time, place, culture, diversity, ethnicity, and age. In Revelation 5, people from every "tribe and language and people and nation"—all the saints of every generation—all share together in cosmic

---

[7] Intergenerational Scripture presentation is another important *practice* of intergenerational being, which I talk more about in Valerie M. Grissom, "Spiritual Formation through Intergenerational Scripture Presentation," in *Engage All Generations: A Strategic Toolkit for Creating Intergenerational Faith Communities*, ed. Cory Seibel (Abilene, TX: Abilene Christian University Press, 2021), 101–10.

praise of God. This is what we talk about when we confess in the Apostles' Creed that "we believe in the holy catholic Church, the communion of saints"![8] This little glimpse into heavenly worship reminds us that *being* the body of Christ is to *be* in participation of God's cosmic story—a story that includes the sharing of stories throughout time and space and place. What a beautiful puzzle picture! The practice of intergenerational story sharing is training us to *participate* in the cosmic, inclusive, never-ending, relational, redeeming story of God for all of eternity. All the while, our sharing, in participation, glorifies God by painting the most beautiful, cosmic, divine puzzle picture ever! We *participate* in the *being* by sharing—sharing in the story of God—the story of us.

As my son aptly pointed out, *being* intergenerational means *being* the body of Christ. In the process of *being*, we are spiritually formed. When we practice intergenerational story sharing, we are practicing *being* the body of Christ. Intergenerational story sharing enables everyone to participate in the *being* by intentionally valuing and honoring each story and enabling all ages to participate in the communal story of God.

In my own practice of intergenerational story sharing, both as a leader and as a participant, I began my own list of *whys* of intergenerational story sharing:

> **Why Story?**
> God is continually revealed through story.
> God's story is intergenerational and intercultural.
> Story is a universal language.
> Story makes connections.
> Story crosses cultures.
> Story builds individual and communal identity.
> Stories provide shared experience.

---

[8] The Apostles' Creed, in *Book of Confessions: The Constitution of the Presbyterian Church (U.S.A.)* (Louisville: Presbyterian Distribution Services, 2016), 7. Early church theologians who authored the Apostles' Creed believed God was forming a holy, or "set apart," Church that encompassed all time and place ("catholic" means "throughout all time and place" here, not an institution), and that, because God is forming the Church, we are given the gift of communion with the saints (all believers of all time). Thus, our *communion* with one another is a reality, not something we build on our own.

> Stories are easy to remember.
> Stories draw people in.
> Stories usually involve the heart and faith.
> Stories heal.
> Stories build empathy.
> Stories encourage authenticity and vulnerability.
> Stories help us remember God's story.
> The story of God is the story of us.
> We are called to participate in the story of God.

I encourage you, as you practice intergenerational story sharing, to listen and reflect regarding how God is forming you and your community, and then add to this list of *whys*. Keeping these *whys* at the forefront will help you communicate to others *why* intergenerational story sharing is so important. At the same time, knowing the *why* informs your *how*, which we will discuss next.

The How: Valuing God's Gift of Community through Mutual Sharing

In the practice of intergenerational story sharing, we are spiritually formed by *how* we receive and share in one another's stories. The *how* becomes crucial in our pursuit of intergenerational *being*. My piano teacher used to say to me over and over: "*Practice does not make perfect. Perfect practice makes perfect.*" I do not believe she meant I needed to practice perfectly, but rather, I needed to pay attention to *how* I practiced. In the same way, if we are seeking to be spiritually formed by including everyone in mutual, intergenerational sharing, we must attend to *how* our community practices story sharing.

Essentially, our intergenerational *being* is God's intention for Christian community. Valuing diversity prepares us to participate—to *be*—in community with the triune God, who is our supreme model for mutual sharing in diversity—Father (Creator), Son, and Holy Spirit—three unique, diverse persons, practicing Christian community in equality, unity (not uniformity!), diversity, mutuality, and reciprocity, but above all, sharing in love.[9] Notice how the gift of the Spirit is what empowers us, as Christ's body, to participate in mutual sharing. In Acts 2, the early church shared "all together" as a community of faith, and that was facilitated by the Holy Spirit.[10] We must never forget, in our story sharing, that the Spirit gathers us "all together" to share our diverse stories in community. Practicing intergenerational *being*, at its very core, is spiritually formative because it teaches us to *be* the body of Christ—to participate in the community of the triune God—where we mutually share in the gift of God's diverse community.

Practicing intergenerational story sharing means receiving each story in a spirit of *mutuality and reciprocity* while valuing God's gift of diversity in community. God calls us throughout Scripture to mutually share with

---

[9] See Mike McCrary, "An Intergenerational Mission for God's Church," *Encounter: Journal for Pentecostal Ministry* 11 (Summer 2014): 1. Unlike multigenerational ministry, intergenerational ministry prioritizes this "mutual sharing," working to cross boundaries, and connecting people through a common family of faith. "Inter" in intergenerational implies reciprocal, interconnected relationships. God's Spirit places us in communion with God and one another, enabling us to participate in "mutual sharing" with "one another." Also see Luis G. Pedraja, *Jesus Is My Uncle: Christology from a Hispanic Perspective* (Nashville: Abingdon Press, 1999), 107–8. Not only is relationality seen in the Trinity, but Jesus, in the Incarnation, fully divine and fully human, modeled deep sharing. According to Pedraja, God's love was exhibited in the Incarnation, where God was fully present through Jesus, who is the foundation for all loving relationships in Christian community (*barrio*). God's union with us "inaugurates" a new Christian community formed solely by God's love, and our relationships in Christian community give us glimpses of God's future intent of a heavenly community of God and humanity. Accordingly, Pedraja finds that the Tower of Babel, where community is built on "conformity and singularity," contrasts with Pentecost, where God forms a diverse community, where, despite their differences, people "shared in the life of God."

[10] Robert W. Wall, email, April 14, 2021. Wall says that the repetition of the Greek phrase *epi to autou*, or "all together," in Acts 1:15, 2:1, and 2:44 suggests an "unfolding story," in which the Spirit is "gathering and growing a community for worship, for fellowship, for sharing goods, for instruction." When I expressed my finding that "all together" might mean a "mutual sharing," Wall expounded on this idea: "the preposition *epi* followed by an accusative, *to autou*, underscores the movement toward something—an object or a purpose, an end. Being together or 'mutual sharing,' then, might be understood as a goal or holy end of Spirit filling in Acts." Throughout God's story is a pattern of "all together" *being*, where God gathers the people of God together, to share their diverse gifts, to live in relationship, in mutuality and reciprocity, living out Christian community "all together." In each case, the Spirit is bringing the church together to mutually share "all together." They are called to share physically and spiritually, across ages and cultures, celebrating diversity in unity. The early church embodies how the Spirit continually gathers us to *be* the body of Christ—"all together." Also see Clark H. Pinnock, *Flame of Love: A Theology of the Holy Spirit* (Downers Grove, IL: InterVarsity Press, 1996), 113–47. Pinnock describes how the Spirit empowers the body of Christ to live in Christian community.

"one another" in Christian community.[11] Tokenism, apathy, indifference, and outright ageism are all dangerous practices that kill intergenerational *being*; in contrast, mutual sharing enables us to value and honor intergenerational stories as gifts from God.

At this point, some might ask: *So now that I know the "why" and "how," HOW do I actually start facilitating intergenerational story sharing in my context?* When ministry leaders hear the word "story," we often envision time-consuming interviews, video sessions, and complicated plans that take way too much time and resources, making story sharing seem unattainable. On the contrary, I challenge leaders to start with four simple but foundational steps for intergenerational story sharing: *setting the table, verbalizing guidelines, teaching Eric Law's mutual invitation (below), and conducting short story-sharing exercises.* Of course, these initial steps are merely foundational and are meant to inspire leaders toward further experimentation, creativity, and variation in the practice of intergenerational story sharing.

Step One: Setting the Table

First, as facilitators of intergenerational story sharing, we need to be meticulous about *how* we **"set the table."** My mom was a wonderful Southern cook and hostess who was not only known for her delicious food but, even more, for her down-to-earth hospitality. Even though my mom's house was not the cleanest or the best-decorated, people loved to come and wanted to stay, not because of *what* she served but *how* she welcomed those she served. My mom did several things to "set the table," such as explaining her menus, providing spaces for children and parents, and setting the table intentionally so all people felt they had their own special place at the table. Similarly, as story-sharing facilitators, we serve as hosts and hostesses. As intergenerational *beings*, we must set the table in our communities to *welcome* and *honor* people and their stories. I have visited pristine homes where the food and house looked like pictures from magazines, but I felt unwelcome. Similarly, we can have all the right intentions but lack Christian hospitality. As intergenerational story facilitators, we welcome

---

[11] Holly Catterton Allen and Christine Lawton Ross, *Intergenerational Christian Formation: Bringing the Whole Church Together in Ministry, Community and Worship* (Downers Grove, IL: InterVarsity Press, 2012), 115. Allen and Ross describe the pattern they found of "one another"—mutuality and reciprocity in faith formation, all in Christian community (115).

all and teach our community to welcome all. Intergenerational *being* works to make each person feel seen, heard, and loved by God in community. We do this by setting the table.

How do we as leaders set the table for intergenerational story sharing? First, we must practice *intentionality*. A lack of intentionality can communicate apathy or, even worse, indifference, which goes against the very core of intergenerational *being*. Instead, *intentionality* fosters empathy to ask ourselves, before we meet together, *How will people in our space feel welcome?* Visualize individuals, if you can, that are coming. Ask yourself: *How can I intentionally make them feel seen, welcome, and heard?* Little things matter, from ambiance to how we introduce one another, and how we invite people. Does the atmosphere promote a sense of welcome for *all* people? Perhaps round tables and coffee or a circular configuration might be better than a lecture-style room with chairs and a podium. *Intentionality* in setting the table for mutual sharing will look different in each space, but it will be obvious to those who participate.

Step Two: Verbalizing Guidelines

One of the ways I have learned to set the table for intergenerational story sharing is by communicating **verbal guidelines** from the start. Often, I use **Eric Law's Respectful Communication Guidelines:**[12]

- **R** = take RESPONSIBILITY for what you say and feel without blaming others.
- **E** = use EMPATHETIC listening.
- **S** = be SENSITIVE to differences in communication styles.
- **P** = PONDER what you hear and feel before you speak.
- **E** = EXAMINE your own assumptions and perceptions.
- **C** = keep CONFIDENTIALITY.
- **T** = TRUST ambiguity because we are not here to debate who is right or wrong.

Sometimes, taking the time to communicate these R-E-S-P-E-C-T guidelines can seem time consuming, especially when you might only be story

---

[12] Mutual invitation process taken verbatim, adapted directly from Eric Law, Kaleidoscope Institute, Free Resources, https://www.kscopeinstitute.org/free-resources, accessed August 10, 2021.

sharing for a brief time. For many people, these guidelines seem obvious, but I am surprised at how often we all, myself included, need to be reminded of these guidelines. Just as preschoolers do not all come to preschool the first day and instantly know *how* to share and *be* one another's friends, we do not all know *how* to come together in Christian community and honor one another's stories. By verbalizing these R-E-S-P-E-C-T guidelines, we are not just setting up guardrails for safe, authentic communication, but we are teaching an intergenerational way of *being* in the body of Christ.

Along this line, right before we share intergenerationally, I winsomely present my own set of Story Sharing NO-Nos and Story Sharing YES!:

Story Sharing NO-Nos:
NO laughing at one's own story or another person's story.
NO sarcasm.
NO Interrupting Chickens![13]
NO relating of stories, giving advice, etc.
NO spiritualizing a story. All stories are sacred—no need to talk in a "churchy" way.
NO talking right after someone shares. (Give fifteen to twenty seconds after each person's sharing before inviting another person to share, and wait to comment on each other's stories until all have shared.)

Story Sharing YES!
YES! To listening with honor.
YES! To being fully present.
YES! To authenticity and vulnerability.
YES! To sharing with one another after everyone has shared.

Again, some of these guidelines seem humorous and obvious, but I cannot tell you how many times people struggle with these guidelines. Some of us are used to laughing at our own stories or using sarcasm in order to avoid vulnerability and authenticity. Some of us grew up in places where

---

[13] I typically talk about my kids' favorite story by David Ezra Stein, *Interrupting Chicken* (Somerville, MA: Candlewick Press, 2010), and humorously talk about not interrupting.

interrupting happened all the time. Some of us are apt to jump in before the dust of another person's story has even settled and say: "*I know just how you feel! This happened to me too . . .*" And the attention moves from the person sharing to the person who has unknowingly hijacked that person's story.

Again, I know all these verbal guidelines seem like a mouthful to communicate, but remember, we are training our people for more than just a story-sharing exercise; we are training people in the *how* of intergenerational *being*, where we mutually share with one another, welcoming and valuing each story as a gift from God. Take time to write down your guidelines and intentionally set your table for intergenerational story sharing. By stating these guidelines upfront every time, we make it a safe, authentic space in which all people will feel empowered to share. When I forget to set the table with the R-E-S-P-E-C-T guidelines, I often have people unknowingly disrespect another person's story, or worse, people struggle to share honestly and authentically because they are unsure about how safe the table space we are sharing really is. Again, verbal guidelines are vital for mutual sharing.

Step Three: Teach Sharing by Mutual Invitation

Often, when we, as leaders, facilitate gatherings, we tend to include and welcome people the way we would want to be welcomed or included.[14] Unfortunately, not all people feel **included or invited to openly share** in the same way. For instance, in more communal, nonindividual cultures, people will not speak up when we say: *"Okay, who wants to go first?"* or *"Who has something they would like to share?"* We have seen this play out over and over during the pandemic, when we were thrown into breakout discussion rooms on Zoom. Often, only a couple of people dominate the

---

[14] Here, I speak for myself as a White leader who often leads in multiethnic spaces. I, along with many of my White colleagues, often forget that we lead from a place of privilege, as the majority. Often, we assume everyone else desires a casual welcome, where people will all feel welcome to speak up if they want. Practicing mutual invitation forces us to share our privilege, no matter our culture, with all the people in a gathering and to invite people from the margins to share in a place at the table with respect and honor.

conversation, while people of nonindividualistic cultures sit back and do not share. In this random, volunteer-style facilitation of sharing, nothing feels *intentional* about *how* we welcome and invite people to share!

Often, we tend to assume quiet people are shy; often, they are not. Regularly, people on the margins need not only to be given a seat at the table but be *invited* and *empowered* to share. For example, I recently attended a meeting where a young adult team member representing an ethnic minority sat silently through our two-hour meeting. She only spoke when asked a specific question. She did not contribute to our Bible study, discussion, or prayer. I am sure many in this meeting brushed this off, just thinking her shy or quiet-spoken. Because I knew her personally, I knew this was not the case. She had confided in me earlier that, in her culture, she would never speak to someone older without being spoken to first. She also explained to me how important it was for her to be given a position of power (a title) for her or anyone in her family to take leadership. In another ministry setting, when I announced her as the leader, she immediately took charge and led beautifully; here in this meeting, she did not feel welcome or invited to the table, so she did not contribute in mutual sharing.

When we speak of intergenerational *being*, we desire all to be welcomed and empowered to mutually share. Again, going back to the first step of setting the table, when you practice empathy, if you are unsure how to promote this kind of welcome and sharing, you should consider speaking with people you feel are on the margins *before* setting the table. Do not assume! Rather, practice *dialogue* and sincere *listening* so you know best how to welcome and invite individuals to share. *To be intergenerational is to be intercultural.* When we take the time to invite all cultures to share, we set up a space where people on the margins, no matter what age, ethnicity, sexual orientation, neurodiversity, socioeconomic status, or any other difference, might be welcome at our table for sharing. I challenge you as a leader to take time to observe *who* you may be missing in your settings. Whose voice is missing at the table? Who needs an invitation to the table? Pray, asking God to show you and those around you how you might include all ages and cultures in the life of your congregation.

For intergenerational story sharing, here is where I HIGHLY (notice my extreme emphasis here!) recommend using **Eric Law's Mutual Invitation Process:**[15]

- The leader[16] or a designated person will share first.[17]
- The person who has shared waits 15–20 seconds, lets the story "settle," and then he or she invites another by name to share.
- If you have something to say but are not ready yet, say "pass for now," and then invite someone else to share. You will be invited again later.
- If you don't want to say anything, simply say "pass" and proceed to invite another to share. IMPORTANT: *Create a culture where saying "pass" is okay!*
- We will do this until everyone has been invited to share.
- We invite you to listen to each person but not respond to someone's sharing immediately. Please, no crosstalk or side conversations. There will be time to respond and ask clarification questions after everyone has had an opportunity to share.

For me, Law's mutual invitation has revolutionized how I lead and teach. Because I work in a very multicultural setting, I learned to use mutual invitation in order to encourage and empower ethnic minorities to participate in story sharing. From that process, I realized how many other people in our spaces feel uncomfortable volunteering to share. For instance, mutual invitation enables youth and older generations, who are

---

[15] Mutual invitation is adapted directly from Eric Law, Kaleidoscope Institute, Free Resources, https://www.kscopeinstitute.org/free-resources, accessed August 10, 2021. In order to address more of the issues regarding White majority culture, cultural perceptions of power, and empowering people from more nonindividualist cultures, I highly recommend reading Eric H. F. Law, *The Wolf Shall Dwell with the Lamb: A Spirituality for Leadership in a Multicultural Community* (St. Louis: Chalice Press, 1993).

[16] As a leader, I often share first in my story-sharing exercises to model what will be done and hopefully put everyone at ease by displaying my own ability to be vulnerable and authentic as a leader.

[17] Kendy Easley, THEO 6742: Church Administration, Seattle Pacific Seminary, Fall Quarter, 2020. Easley taught me, when leading meetings, whether in person or on Zoom, to never leave that first person who shares to chance. She often says things like "*Whoever is wearing the most jewelry can share first,*" or "*Whoever has the most beverage at their desk can share first.*" I believe this is a powerful way, especially in Zoom discussion breakouts, to intentionally invite people to share at the table and create welcoming spaces.

usually reluctant to share, to participate because they feel that their sharing is wanted. Similarly, mutual invitation enables people to share who fear that they do not know enough or do not speak the right "church-ese." Mutual invitation also disassembles power dynamics, leaving it much more difficult for someone to monopolize a space with oversharing. Mutual invitation forces those who usually speak more to engage instead in more mindful listening. Mutual invitation values each gift at the table; no one is left out, and all are valued and respected.

Mutual sharing comes back to the idea of *intentionality* in setting the table. Do we intentionally seek to empower each person to share, or do we leave sharing up to casual chance? After conducting story sharing, as well as other intergenerational gatherings using mutual sharing, I cannot go back. I highly encourage you to bravely make this a part of your faith community as well.

Step Four: Facilitate a Brief Story-Sharing Event (30 Minutes)

Below is a procedure I use to facilitate brief sessions of intergenerational story sharing.[18] I want to emphasize that this is a framework, intended to be adapted for your circumstance and context. Typically, this exercise takes thirty minutes for an entire group to share but can be made shorter or longer to fit the context. I have used this story-sharing exercise in Bible studies, church dinners, concerts, online gatherings, team-building exercises, classrooms, workshops, music rehearsals, youth groups, Sunday school, and much more.

> **Important Preliminary Details:**
> - Provide 4 x 6 cards with instructions on one side (turned over until time to write) and blank or lined on the other side to write/draw. Provide pencils, crayons, and/or colored pencils,

---

[18] I first observed a similar story-sharing exercise that Jeff Barker led in our class, "DWS 702: The Renewal of Sunday Worship: Music and the Arts," The Robert Webber Institute of Worship, Jacksonville, FL, January Session, 2015. Barker has deeply influenced me regarding story sharing and how I view story sharing as participation in God's story. These exercise instructions reflect much of Barker's ideas and wording.

and larger paper for those who are artistic or young children who would rather draw their story.
- Provide tables (preferably round) for 5-8 people, preferably with a leader/facilitator at each table. A U-shape with rectangular tables works well for sharing "in the round" at meetings of 10-30 people.
- Very important: Instruct people to wait to write until everything is explained. People often tune out important guidelines and instructions if already writing. Also, if people write early, they tend to overthink, overshare, philosophize, or lack authenticity.

Question/Writing Prompt:
- Carefully read the question and instructions below:

Sample Question:
Describe a time you felt close to God.[19] Go back in your memory to a specific date, time of day, place, or event. Stand at that place and look and listen. Write down what you see and hear. Be specific. Pay attention also to what you were feeling and write that down. Avoid the temptation to summarize or draw conclusions. No need for "God-talk." Brief, incomplete sentences are okay. Just be the camera or the tape recorder and show us what's happening around you and inside you. Write two to four sentences. Please end your writing with:

1. Your first name
2. Year (approximately) OR XX years old (age when the story took place)

Extra instructions right before writing/drawing:
Children or those who enjoy the arts, feel free to draw your

---

[19] This first sentence can be altered or tailored to the event. For example, once we replaced that first sentence with: "Describe your favorite Christmas memory." Later, we used these stories for a rich Christmas scrapbook for our Christmas season at church.

story. If your parents are there, they can write words in for you. Feel free to write your story in your heart language[20] and translate later, if needed. If you finish early, please engage in a time of silent reflection until all are finished writing.

- Give everyone 5–7 minutes (not too long!). Watch to see when people are finishing. Ask everyone to remain quiet until all are done writing.

Please note: In each exercise, we use a different question or writing prompt unique for that group attending. The sample question above has worked many times but would not be appropriate in all settings. I encourage you to collaborate with others in your group to find a question that best suits your context. Here, it is important to choose a question that is inclusive of all who attend and easy to answer. I often test my question on several people from diverse cultures ahead of time to make sure it works well. Questions should not be too specific, open-ended, or vague. Helpful instructions include going to a specific date or place, rather than speaking in generalities. Limiting "God-talk" (or "church-eze") helps people who tend to need to philosophize or spiritualize an experience, rather than sharing authentically.

Sharing Our Stories:
After everyone is finished writing, have people put down their pens, and take the time to set the table and verbally establish guidelines (discussed earlier in this chapter):

- Eric Law's R-E-S-P-E-C-T guidelines.
- Story Sharing No-Nos and Story Sharing Yes!
- Teach the process of mutual invitation.

---

[20] The term "heart language" refers to the language a person would use to sing a lullaby to his or her child. In multicultural settings, using the words "heart language" avoids confusion when cultures have both a merchant (national) language and a local dialect.

- Important: Remind everyone to end their reading by saying (1) their first name and (2) the year or age when the story took place (e.g., Valerie, eight years old). Then, wait 15–20 seconds to let the story settle before inviting the next person to share. Wait until all have shared to comment on/discuss people's stories.
- Important to Model: Leaders should share their stories first. Then, invite the next person to share, using the rules of Law's mutual invitation. If you have several tables, invite each table leader/facilitator (designated ahead of time) to share first, and then invite the next person, and so on, until all have shared. Remember that modeling sharing as leaders establishes a pattern of authenticity and encourages others to share.
- When all are finished sharing stories, feel free to share and reflect with one another.
- Collect cards from those who wish to contribute to a story-sharing scrapbook or in other ways such as worship, church bulletins, etc.

Story-Sharing Scrapbook (Optional)
Below are samples from our **InterGenerate 2021 Story Workshop Scrapbook:**[21]

Rehoboth Beach, Delaware. Sunrise, July morning. First time at the ocean since my diagnosis of bipolar disorder. Sparkling jewels of sunlight on the waves. Horrible year, over at last. Such a joy to still be alive to see the sun rising on the water. Hope.
—Elise, 2006

---

[21] See the whole InterGenerate Story Scrapbook 2021: https://1drv.ms/b/s!AiP4d2BWIuA6juAoJ9Of759BL2wsow?e=BGk8Zd. For a better idea of how you might use church story scrapbooks, here are links to a few I have made: Calvin Church Story Scrapbook: https://1drv.ms/b/s!AiP4d2BWIuA6jtt6ofIjVNwoCFd43A?e=ob2WMR; Memories of Christmas Scrapbook: https://1drv.ms/b/s!AiP4d2BWIuA6jtwDRt8olaajo3VVgg?e=OfcryD.

Story Sharing as a Practice of Intergenerational "Being"

In the shade of an apple tree near the patio. Feeling the warmth of Dad's wisdom. Resting near his teddy-bear-like body. Asking important questions. Asking deep questions. Where is heaven? There is goodness everywhere. Good people everywhere even if you can't see them. Feeling reassured . . . feeling peaceful.
—Jim, 8 years old (1973)

I was in bed, in Australia, at my sister's house. I felt the tangible presence of God like the gentle but firm weight of two fingertips on my heart. It was dark and I felt warm, secure, and totally loved.
—Hannah, 2011

Splosh. Splosh. The sound of gas going into the gas tank. Then, I pulled the starter handle and the engine rumbled to life, and I sped off after I did three laps, I turned off the choke, and that's when I felt close to God. Thank you God for my dirt bike!
—Roryk, 9 years old

I'm in a field with people I don't know. I'm sad because, as a single mum, I have feelings of guilt and shame. When others leave, I am called by the workshop leaders. I show them a picture of my baby, James. They pray with me. I ask God to forgive me, even though I didn't really know I needed forgiving. He opened my heart and I gave my life to him.
—Alison, 1987

When I was in the C-A-L store, and I saw a little sebra he was very cute. I actually chose a little unicorn named Star. I think she was very cute. They had a BIG, WIDE selection. I felt close to God was because He made me pick here.
Margreta, 6 years old.

Star

—Margreta, 6 years old

> *An evening with friends, on a beach in Scotland during a beach mission. I am tired after a busy day, I can feel the spray on my face and hear the crash of the waves. We begin to sing, and something bigger comes close.*
> —Judy, 16 years old (1984)
>
> *Click-Clock-Clock-Clock. The click track starts as the song begins. It's church time. I get ready to play the drums as the intro starts. The first song, I feel tense, but by the second song these feelings wash over, and I begin to relax and lighten up. I finally feel like I was worshiping God. At the end of the second song the audience applauds. The third song goes smoothly, and we exit the stage.*
> —Bjorn, 14 years old

The Powerful Testimony of Story-Sharing Scrapbooks

These story samples above provide a great snapshot of the sharing that took place in just thirty minutes at our InterGenerate 2021 online workshop. Scrapbooks continue the story, leading to future story sharing and reflection. And the sharing continues as others read and share in these stories. For instance, my pastor keeps one of these scrapbooks we made years ago in his office to share with people new to the church to get a better sense of who we are as a church family. Many times, I have overheard deep faith conversations originate from people discussing these scrapbooks. And I often hear: *"I've known you for x number of years, and I never knew you did xyz!"* The first time I brought home cards from one of these events, my husband and I read them aloud in utter awe and amazement and with tears of joy, as we reveled at how God is at work in our faith community. What a great testimony to the power of story!

To Be or Not to Be?

In the famous *Hamlet* by William Shakespeare, Prince Hamlet famously asks: "To *be* or not to *be*, that is the question . . ."[22] As we continue to seek to *be* more intergenerational, we must practice our intergenerational *being*.

---

[22] William Shakespeare, *Hamlet*, Act III, Scene I, emphasis mine.

Intergenerational story sharing remains a vital practice for intergenerational *being*. In order to practice intergenerational *being* through story sharing, we must know our *why* and practice the *how*. When we learn to value God's gift of community through participation in God's story, through the mutual sharing of our own stories, we learn to move past the knowing and the doing to the *being*—*being* the body of Christ. "To *be* or not to *be*?" That is the question.

THEOLOGY IN PRACTICE: QUESTIONS TO CONSIDER

1. How is the practice of intergenerational story sharing a formational practice that helps people participate in the story of God?

2. How does intergenerational story sharing help us in the greater intergenerational practice of viewing each person and each story as a gift from God?

3. Identify the stories—the voices, ages, generations—missing in your context. What are deliberate ways, or next steps, that you could invite these people to share their stories?

4. How might you be more intentional in facilitating story sharing, or other kinds of sharing, using the process of mutual invitation in your gatherings?

5. Identify thirty-minute spots (or less or more) in your gatherings where you might be able to facilitate intergenerational story sharing. (Hint: dinners, rehearsals, Bible studies, Sunday school, youth groups, parties, retreats, leadership meetings, small groups, etc.)

6. How might you take this specific exercise and reimagine it or customize it for your context, while keeping the "how" of this intergenerational practice intact—setting the table, verbalizing guidelines, and using mutual invitation?

Section Four

STORIES OF INTERGENERATIONAL PRACTICE

"Everything we do is practice for something greater than where we currently are. Practice only makes for improvement."

—Les Brown, Motivational Speaker

CHAPTER 12

REINVENTING CHURCH WITH INTERGENERATIONAL CONNECTIONS
A Case Study

JIM MERHAUT

*"Change isn't just one thing, just one time,
just one big revelation.
Change occurs in stages, and phases,
which each add depth, color, character,
and create a multidimensional, multifaceted you."*

—Doe Zantamata

Several years ago, St. John's Episcopal Church in Youngstown, Ohio, recognized a need to bring together the generations in worship, but they had a long tradition of adult-focused worship that failed to connect effectively with younger generations. Before deciding how to address this issue, their pastor, Rev. Gayle Catinella, assembled a team of church members to study this lack of generational engagement in the fall of 2017. I was appointed to facilitate the team's work.

Church as we know it is passing away, and something new is emerging in its place. Two things are becoming more certain about future church experiences:

1. If churches are going to be true to their purpose of building a society of love and justice, they will have to be intentionally intergenerational. Loving and advocating for those who are different from us begins with intergenerational experiences.
2. If churches are going to grow, they will need to find ways to connect with and engage those who are not currently open to church participation and/or membership.

Both of the convictions above guided the work of St. John's worship reinvention team. I will explore St. John's story about worship reinvention, which includes three adult generations, one of which had no interest in belonging to a church. Their story can be instructive for any church that is working on reinventing itself with intergenerational connections.

What Is Reinvention?

Reinvention is an emerging field of study inspired by the work of organizational behavior scholar and reinvention guru Dr. Nadya Zhexembayeva.[1] Her five-part definition of reinvention follows:

1. A practice of embracing change by reimagining and remaking something so that it manifests new and improved attributes, qualities, and results
2. A systematic approach to thriving in chaos that includes ongoing anticipation, design, and implementation of change via continuous sense-making, anticipatory and emergent learning, and synthesis of cross boundary, cross-disciplinary, and cross functional knowledge
3. A way to foster sustainability of a system by dynamically harmonizing continuity and change
4. An immune system designed to ensure systematic health for individuals and organizations

---

[1] Nadya Zhexembayeva, *The Chief Reinvention Officer Handbook: How to Thrive in Chaos* (Canada: Idea Press Publishing, 2020), 2. Most of the reinvention insights expressed here are based on the work of Dr. Zhexembayeva, and I use her illustrations with permission.

5. A structured and deliberate effort to engage in healthy cycles of planned renewal, building on the past to ensure current and future viability

Reinventors approach change with joy and hope. They believe things can get better, and they find meaning in doing the work of change. Zhexembayeva identifies **three distinct pillars of reinvention:** *anticipating change, designing change, and implementing change.* No one individual can do all three well, so reinvention calls for a team effort. Additionally, reinvention teams include both *disrupters* and *stabilizers*, those who shake up the status quo and those who create a new status quo. Instead of promoting change for the sake of change, reinventors seek to build a better future by working the reinvention cycle in the present with a sharp focus on designing core values of the past in a way that connects those values to changing situations and changing target audiences. In reinvention thinking, change is not an occasional effort like strategic planning; rather, it is built into the organization as a daily practice in the same way that daily health and fitness practices help to keep your body immune from threats. By staying focused on the core values that have historically sustained it, a reinventing organization can maintain the most important part of its identity while developing new approaches to carry the organization successfully into the future. Figure 12.1 shows the common failures of organizations that become exclusively focused on the present or exclusively focused on the future with little attention to historic core values.

The ToTo Matrix

The ToTo Matrix (fig. 12.1), short for **To**day & **To**morrow, provides insights regarding dispositions, foci, aversions, and biases, which are symptomatic of decline due to an imbalanced organizational approach to current and future sustainability. The reinvention quadrant (upper-right-hand quadrant of the matrix), on the other hand, is descriptive of an organization that builds upon the past to create both present and future success. Four organizational dispositions are described in the ToTo Matrix that flesh out the various positions as you move along the two axes of today and tomorrow:

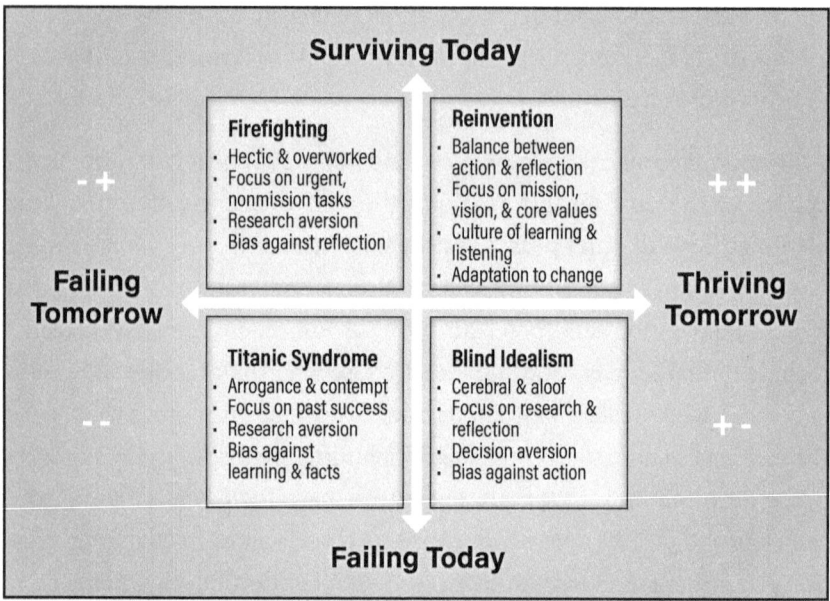

Figure 12.1. The ToTo Matrix

- *Firefighting*: Firefighting exhibits itself as hectic and overworked people who are busy and become exhausted by the pace of responding to one crisis after another. They have no time to reflect and plan for a better future. Slowing down is perceived as weakness. A firefighter's predominant thought process sees problems as relentless, which must be battled with all available resources. Each day's crisis consistently pulls the firefighter's organization away from focus on its mission and core values. The antidote to firefighting is to breathe and create space for learning and reflection.
- *Blind Idealism*: The disposition of a blind idealist is cerebral and aloof. Team conversations are interesting but seemingly endless. Team members conclude one topic by becoming distracted by another tantalizing topic, without drawing any clear conclusions or developing any action steps for the initial topic. Action is typically seen as premature and misguided. Attempts to reach perfection and consensus delay or entirely prevent forward movement on projects. Blind idealism's mantra is, "We need more data;

we need more research." An antidote to blind idealism involves distinguishing what is perfect from what is good enough.
- **Titanic Syndrome**: The tragic and very avoidable sinking of the great cruise ship the *Titanic* is the namesake of this quadrant. A Titanic Syndrome disposition is marked by arrogance and contempt. Team members operating within Titanic Syndrome believe their organization is too big, too powerful, too necessary, with too much history, and is too sacred to fail. Titanic Syndrome thinking breeds contempt for outsiders and competitors, with an underlying belief that "we and/or our ways are superior to others." Titanic Syndrome thinking manipulates, propping up current beliefs rather than seeing research as a source for learning and adapting. Here, facts that contradict accepted but unproven beliefs are considered lies. Little work is done to sharpen current performance or to plan for future improvements because the glory of the past is perceived as a sufficient storehouse for future success. An antidote for Titanic Syndrome thinking is a return to truth and a reliance on research and provable facts.
- **Reinvention**: In contrast to firefighting, blind idealism, and the Titanic Syndrome, as seen in the **repetitive reinvention cycle** (see fig. 12.2), reinvention is driven by a balance between *healthy chaos* and *normal stagnation*:

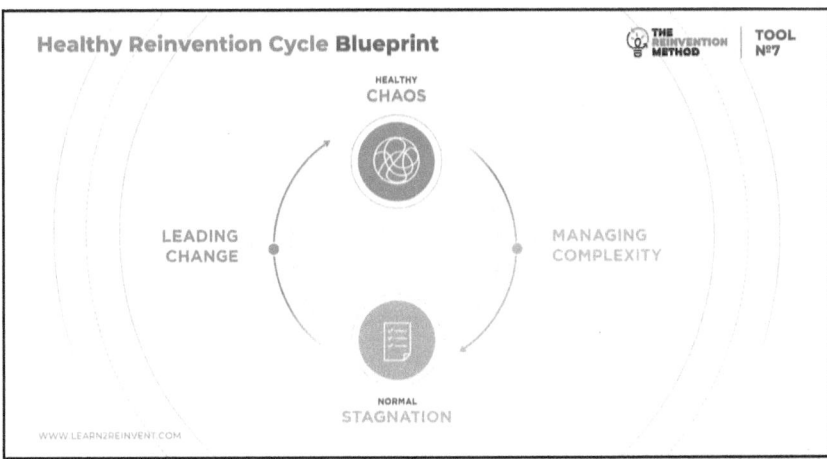

Figure 12.2. Repetitive Reinvention Cycle

- ***Healthy chaos***: Some leaders are **natural disrupters.** Disrupters see a better future and want to undo systems of today to make room for the wonderful vision they hold for tomorrow. When disrupters are functioning at their best, they bring healthy chaos to an organization. Disrupters challenge the status quo. Because disrupters are typically avid learners, they delight in observing emerging trends that might become new ways of solving puzzles that current systems in the organization cannot effectively address.
- ***Normal stagnation***: Some leaders are **natural stabilizers.** Stabilizers excel at building detailed structures and intricate systems that keep an organization running smoothly as it expresses its mission. When stabilizers function at their best, they bring normal stagnation to an organization that has recently changed. Stabilizers can take the vision of a disrupter and turn it into a well-managed project or program that has legs. Stabilizers turn ethereal visions into concrete realities that are the real-life expressions of the organization's mission.

Unfortunately, *natural disrupters* and *natural stabilizers* often see each other as enemies when, in truth, they are two essential sides to the same coin. Each one of them drives the reinvention cycle in a unique and indispensable way. Reinventing organizations strike a balance between disrupters and stabilizers as they work through the ***three pillars of reinvention.***

The Three Reinvention Pillars of Change

Anticipating change, *designing* change, and *implementing* change are the **three reinvention pillars** that influence the culture of an organization. As figure 12.3 indicates, creating the right mindset on a leadership team becomes an essential foundation for moving through the three pillars of change effectively.[2]

---

[2] For more about mindset work, see Carol Dweck, *Mindset: The New Psychology of Success* (New York: Ballantine Books, 2006); and Marilee Adams, *Change Your Questions, Change Your Life: 12 Powerful Tools for Leadership, Coaching, and Results*, 4th ed. (Oakland, CA: Berrett-Koehler, 2022).

Reinventing Church with Intergenerational Connections

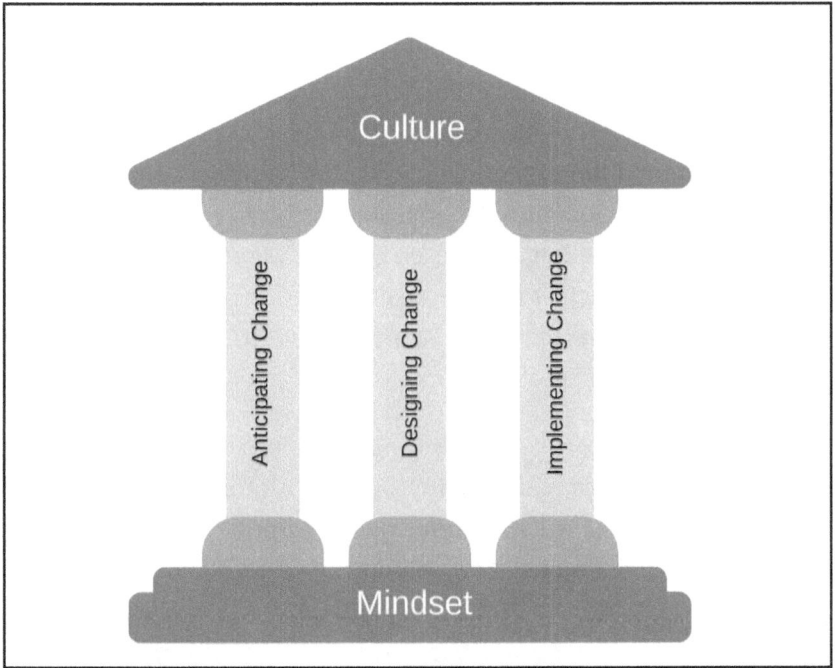

Figure 12.3. Three Pillars of Reinvention.

1. ***Anticipating change*** is the part of the process in which the leadership team listens and learns. It often includes research, surveys, focus groups, interviews, and more—all developed and employed as methods in order to assist in the team's discernment regarding what kind of change would be most beneficial for the organization. Anticipating change is work most often done by those who are natural disrupters. Leaders create healthy chaos when they do the work of anticipating change.
2. ***Designing change*** is the part of the process that includes experimentation. After the team has listened and learned, they are now ready to brainstorm ideas to address emerging needs. Brainstorming builds a menu of options that could work, but you cannot know if the ideas will work unless you test them. Pilots, experiments, and prototypes are all ways to try out an idea before you commit to it. Much can be learned in this essential part of the reinvention process.

3. ***Implementing change*** often includes what reinventors call a launch. Once a team has tested one or more ideas, they commit to move forward with a polished offering. Here, stabilizers really shine. Stabilizers often take a half-baked pilot or experiment and transform it into a fine-tuned machine. Stabilizers develop things like registration procedures, process outlines, and forms. Success of implementation depends on how a plethora of complex and intertwined details are managed. Implementation is not the time to focus on dreaming about the future; rather, it is time to do nose-to-the-grindstone work.

These three pillars—*anticipating*, *designing*, and *implementing change*—are all crucial parts of the reinvention process. With this understanding of reinvention in mind, I will now turn to the description of how the team at St. John's Church reinvented worship using the three pillars of reinvention

An Intergenerational Case Study: Anticipating Change

In reinvention theory, listening and learning are core movements of ***anticipating change***. To anticipate change, the team at St. John's spent time learning about intergenerational ministry theory and practice. They surveyed various ministry options at St. John's to determine which was in greatest need of intergenerational improvement. We decided to work on worship first. Given a strong commitment to traditional worship styles at St. John's, the team deemed it wise to create something outside of their current worship offerings. Developing something new also made more sense because of the team's desire to connect with younger generations who were not affiliated with a church. This target audience was clearly not interested in participating in current worship offerings.

Next, in order to anticipate change, the team shifted to qualitative research, a form of listening. They started with a simple social media survey to learn how unaffiliated Christians perceived Christian worship. Results were helpful but incomplete, and so the team decided to launch a series of focus groups in the fall of 2018 to learn more. Four focus groups originated—two that were for older adults, primarily Boomers, and two other groups for Millennials who were not affiliated with a church. These focus groups proved to be very successful, teaching us these key learnings:

- Older adults had mixed opinions of young adults—some positive and some negative. Our four focus groups revealed that the more time older adults spent with young adults, the more positive their opinions became regarding them; the same also rang true for young adults regarding their attitudes toward older adults.
- Some older adults related to younger adults exclusively from a position of power and expected young adults to conform to social norms that were valued by the older adults.
- Some younger adults were suspicious of the intentions of older adults who initiated conversations about faith and values. The younger adults seemed to think the older adults were less interested in mentoring them and more interested in manipulating them.
- Some older adults admired the energy, enthusiasm, and creativity of younger adults.
- Some younger adults admired the wisdom and kindness of older adults in their lives.
- Older adults generally expressed appreciation for worship that was offered, but other older adults saw a need for reform, especially with music.
- Young adults expressed little appreciation for Sunday worship services currently offered and suggested the following:
  - Rituals can be very meaningful, but rote repetition robs them of their power.
  - Worship needs to have a greater variety of experiences that include a multiple-intelligences approach—an approach that engages all the senses and styles of learning and includes full-body experiences. For example, young adults prefer not only to see and hear, but also to touch more and move more.
  - Sermons need to be more interactive and less of a monologue. Meaningful discussions in a structured, safe environment are a strong need for young adults. Most young adults do not want

to be told what to do or how to think, but they appreciate expert input on topics of discussion that matter to them.
- Many young adults desire variation and complexity in music, rather than just choosing between a traditional style and a praise band approach.
- Many young adults prefer not to limit sacred texts to the Bible only; they want to explore wisdom offered by all religions and even nonreligious sources.
- Intergenerational relationships are both challenging and enriching.
- Worship needs to be relevant to daily living.
- Church space is not the most desirable location for worship. Homes, outdoor spaces, and other places for small gatherings were mentioned as desirable.

Reflecting on and summarizing these key learnings from research concluded the *anticipating change* phase. Next, the team shifted its work toward the second pillar of reinvention: *designing change*.

Designing Change

Designing change begins with setting parameters for the work. If the team was going to design intergenerational worship for both church members and people who are unaffiliated with a church, they would have to be clear about several things:

- What is worship?
- Who will be invited?
- What will the ground rules be?
- How will we determine the focus and content?
- Where will we gather?

Answers to these questions emerged in team meetings between January and August of 2019. Our team eventually defined worship by describing seven key elements:

- A gathering of people who share values (for this group, the values were faith-based)

- A call to focus on a theme
- Expressions or prayers of gratitude and concern
- Storytelling and/or wisdom sharing
- Reflection time
- Music
- Leaving with a mission

All elements of worship would be included in each experiment, and there would be evaluations of each element following each experiment.

After securing grant funding for a full year of experimentation, the team invited six members of the congregation to participate. Members were a mix of Generation X and Baby Boomers. Their team also recruited six people who were unaffiliated with a church, all Millennials.

During an orientation meeting, we broke the ice between generations using a variety of nonthreatening storytelling experiences. Then we set ground rules for worship experiences and themes. We agreed to design each worship experience around one member's gift or passion; in turn, that person would serve as a worship planner along with one of the project leaders and one group member from another generation. Worship locations were inspired by theme. For example, one theme had a strong ecological focus, so a local park became the gathering place.

Experiments launched in the fall of 2019 and then abruptly halted in March of 2020, when the COVID-19 pandemic hit. Prior to the pandemic, the group conducted four worship experiments and a midyear evaluation with an outside facilitator. The midyear evaluation revealed that trust was high and friendships were forming across generations, but also that the group had been too timid about addressing spirituality explicitly. In response to these findings, the group decided to be more intentional about including God-language in further experiments. After a few months, in the summer of 2020, we began to worship online. Video conference experiences on Zoom were very successful, and several members were surprised at how meaningful online worship could be. Still, participants ultimately preferred in-person worship over Zoom worship.

They had two Zoom worship experiments themselves and then concluded the design year with two additional worship experiments with an outside consultant who assisted the group with an overall evaluation of the experiments, giving us some thought as to how this project could continue as an embedded ministry of St. John's Church. Working with a consultant, we noted several important learnings as we wrapped up the design phase. Our principal learnings follow:

- Valuing intergenerational relationships enriched all participants and were reported by group members as the highest of value during this experience.
- Fostering intergenerational relationships requires intentionality; they do not happen automatically.
- Articulating and affirming shared values facilitated group cohesion.
- Establishing rules for engagement helped the group build trust and facilitated open and honest sharing during structured conversations.
- Sharing meals and other experiences as integral to worship helped to build meaningful relationships among group members.
- Practicing intentional hospitality made members feel more at ease upon arrival at the worship experiences.
- Worshiping away from a church building, either in a home or another location, was preferred to worshiping in a church building.
- Connecting ritual actions to themes was meaningful. For example, participants moved in a processional with candles from the building entrance to the meal table to begin a worship experience on being light for others.
- Integrating worship themes into daily living was appreciated by group members.
- Including music, even though the group did not sing, functioned as a vital part of each worship experience.

All these learnings served as keys for successful implementation of a reinvented, intergenerational worship experience. At the end of our *design* phase, one young adult and one older adult decided not to continue with the group during the implementation phase. Both returned to more conventional church experiences.

Implementing Change

In this reinvention project, the *design* and **implementation** phases overlapped quite a bit. Worship experiments had elements of both design and implementation. As design experiences, they were experimental, unpolished, and adaptive; but they also had characteristics associated with implementation: detailed plans, communication systems, rules and guidelines, and goals.

After *anticipating, designing,* and *implementing change* using reinvention strategies, this implementation question still remains: *How do we situate this intergenerational worship experience within the larger context of St. John's worship ministries?* As we continue in this process, the group is currently deciding how to open the experiments so more people can be involved. Full implementation has not yet been realized, but the future is promising for the following reasons:

- The group remains committed to a regular worship gathering that carries forward the spirit of the experimental year.
- Outsiders have expressed interest in joining the group.
- All participants reported growth in their spiritual journeys as a result of their participation in the experimental year.

Conclusion

Worship reinvention at St. John's Church in Youngstown, Ohio, is an ongoing effort. St. John's remains committed to bridging generations through reinvented worship that is offered both to church members and to persons unaffiliated with a church. St. John's is unique in that it is not trying to create something internally and then attract people to it; rather, St. John's is trying to engage people first and then build a relevant worship experience based on the lives of the people involved.

I believe the principles of reinvented intergenerational worship that include unaffiliated persons as described in this chapter are applicable to other ministries too. Applying lessons we learned in this worship reinvention could assist other churches with reinvented worship, for learning, serving, or community-building ministries. Some important questions to consider, as intergenerational ministries move toward reinvention, might include:

- What is the value of entering into a reinvention process for our church?
- What kind of team do we need to build so we can accomplish all facets of reinvention: *anticipating change, designing change,* and *implementing change*?
- Who is our target audience for our reinvention?
- What do we currently know about the target audience and the ministry we seek to reinvent?
- What do we need to learn about the target audience, and what research tools will we use to learn it?
- What do we need to learn about the current state of innovations in the ministry area we seek to reinvent?
- Who are the thought leaders in the ministry area who can teach us?
- What is our timeline?
- What is our budget?
- What is our communication plan?

Wrestling with these questions will lead your team to reinvent in meaningful ways that could impact the identity of your church for decades to come. St. John's reinvention story is ongoing, but the seeds of promise are clear. Planting seeds for meaningful relationships across generations and between church members and those who seek God outside of churches promises to produce a grace-filled harvest.

THEOLOGY IN PRACTICE: QUESTIONS TO CONSIDER

1. How might the practice of reinvention become a formational process for you and your team that can help you implement new intergenerational practices in your context? How does this step-by-step process

differ from your current approach to change—especially in regard to intergenerational practice?

2. Identify an intergenerational aspect of your ministry that you and your team might want to "reinvent." Walk through the steps of anticipating change, designing change, and implementing change. Write down questions and discuss them with your team. How might firefighting, blind idealism, and Titanic Syndrome play into your context or into this reinvention project you are attempting?

3. Do you tend to be a natural disrupter or a natural stabilizer? Identify the natural disrupters and natural stabilizers in your context. How might you work to see these disrupters and stabilizers working together in "healthy chaos" rather than one side or the other as "enemies" to change? Even further, how might you embrace the strengths of these different approaches to help facilitate new intergenerational practices?

CHAPTER 13

CREATING SPACE TO "TASTE AND SEE" THE GOODNESS OF INTERGENERATIONAL MINISTRY

WES GALLAGHER

> *"On Saturday, he ate through one piece of chocolate cake, one ice-cream cone, one pickle, one slice of Swiss cheese, one slice of salami, one lollipop, one piece of cherry pie, one sausage, one cupcake, and one slice of watermelon. That night he had a stomach ache."*
>
> —Eric Carle, *The Very Hungry Caterpillar*

The psalmist writes, "Taste and see that the Lord is good" (Ps. 34:8 NIV). When I think of this verse, my mind goes back to the small rural town of Wartrace, Tennessee, population five hundred, where I was reared in the town's small, eighty-member Church of Christ. My parents and grandparents also attended this church, as well as parents and grandparents of many of my friends. Everyone knew each other. Even now, I still feel that every senior member in that church is a grandparent to me. Here, I experienced the "taste and see"—the sweetness of intergenerational relationships in my faith community. In contrast, my ministry setting for the past decade was a different experience. I served at Collegeside Church of Christ in Cookeville, Tennessee. This predominantly White, college-educated congregation is home to a large campus ministry with over one hundred participating college students from Tennessee Tech University, an active youth group, and a thriving children's ministry. These two congregations presented very different realities pertaining to engagement among different generations. In my small growing-up church experience, intergenerational relationships grew organically, while in my large church experience, I observed a tendency to program ministries based on separating people by age and stage.

As I approached a decade of serving in children's ministry with a goal of creating meaningful intergenerational experiences in this multigenerational congregation of more than five hundred members, two very significant issues surfaced. First, many members of our congregation had no interest in intergenerational ministry. For example, only a handful of our senior members considered sacrificing their weekly class time with peers to be involved in a class with other generations for six weeks. In the same way, many parents disliked attending functions that required they attend with their children; instead, these parents viewed children's church activities as a time for someone else to take care of their children so they could reconnect with God and other adults. Second, key church leaders failed to recognize the transformative power of intergenerational settings and did not participate in intergenerational events that I offered as a children's pastor. I realized these issues arose from people who had never experienced the "taste and see" of intergenerational ministry.

However, before you become despondent or consider throwing this book across the room, I wish to offer this encouragement: *intergenerational interactions—the "taste and see"—can move mountains!* For instance, children bring the largest smiles to our senior adults. And when parents observe their child's interaction at the table with older adults, they experience a fresh recognition of what it means to be the church. In the same way, I have observed how college students, living hours from their hometown and their own extended families, find it life-giving to spend an hour teaching our children on Wednesday nights. These young adults experienced growth, and our children are in love with these "big people" who have abundantly more energy and patience than their own parents. And though our senior saints do not usually brim with energy, our children bask in the attention given when seated at a table where they work together on a craft project or filling out a fun word game. All these observations reflect on how these "taste-and-see" intergenerational interactions have allowed for space in my ministry context for people to "taste and see" the goodness of the Lord.

Many of us find ourselves in communities of faith that place preeminent value on age- and stage-segregated ministry, yet we hear the call to create opportunities for all ages to "taste the goodness" of generations together. We dream of a fully integrated church in which older members organically mentor younger adults, and young adults gain experience with children before they are tasked with parenting their own. But the reality for many of us in congregations with long histories of adherence to age-segregated ministry models is that we must start with a different goal. *Before we can convert programming of an entire faith community, we must focus on creating a subculture of intergenerational bonds within our own ministry parameters.*

Perhaps you are a leader who is not able to institute a congregation-wide cultural shift. Working from the top down is impossible. But in your unique ministry space, you are allowed to work from the ground up. You can create intergenerational "taste-and-see" experiences that build a **subculture** (a smaller culture within the larger group) of intergenerational relationships within your faith community. Once this subculture is birthed and reaches a representative demographic of your congregation, subculture members will be in position to invite peers to "taste and see" the goodness of intergenerational ministry experiences. With this approach in mind, how might we build a subculture, laying the foundational "taste and see" groundwork that will lead to opportunities for nurturing future intergenerational relationships?

Utilizing my own experiences from a decade of work as a children's minister, I will share personal discoveries I made while building an intergenerational network within a large, established, multigenerational church. Rather than presenting a cookie-cutter approach, I hope to inspire intergenerational leaders in all pastoral roles to read the landscape of their own local church and begin to identify spaces, beginning with their own sphere of ministry, in which intergenerational opportunities can be inserted. I will share how I built an intergenerational subculture by developing a calendar of events as the children's minister for the sake of the whole church. The foundational steps of my journey, in which I sought to build an intergenerational subculture in my context, included *facilitating events that connected generations at the **table**, working to include children in **leading** corporate worship, providing opportunities for children to **serve and bless** other generations, and creating environments for generations to **learn together**.*

Connecting Generations at the Table

The birth of intergenerational relationships in our context happened in a room full of round *tables* with intentional programming. Our first event, "Munch," that we added to the children's ministry calendar was initially called "Monthly Munch with the Munchkins," but I quickly discovered several errors in this name. First, monthly was too often for this ministry for our church calendar. Second, the term "munchkins" was too constricting, giving people the impression that this event was only for young children and senior adults. Over time, our focus grew to include older children and teens more effectively, and parents realized they were among those ministering and being ministered to, as well. Themes for our Munch events have included magic tricks performed by kids, stories about favorite stuffed animals shared by seniors, and holiday themes. Ultimately, three holidays emerged as our standing dates for Munches: Grandparents Day, Martin Luther King Day, and Valentine's Day.

Munch always included food shared around the table, a picture book read by a senior adult to children gathered on the floor around a rocking chair, and some activity that engaged young and old together while seated at the table. Craft projects and word games such as Mad Libs were favorites. Trivia competitions constructed to include questions that required knowledge inherent to different generations allowed for great camaraderie as table competed against table. Questions and topics that created storytelling opportunities provided priceless experiences, where I overheard stories about one-room schoolhouses, segregation and the civil rights movement during people's teenage years, and various aspects of rearing children in different decades. Once generations were seated and engaged at the table, they were able to "taste and see" the sweetness of intergenerational fellowship and develop a hunger for more.

Including Children in Leading Worship

In addition to building a subculture of "taste and see" through intergenerational table experiences, I have found how important it is to include children as much as possible in **leading worship**. A weekly worship gathering in an auditorium of five hundred plus people is not the ideal time for interpersonal relationship growth; however, once meaningful intergenerational relationships have been established, opportunities to incorporate children into the assembly become much more meaningful. Milestone Sundays were a key time to celebrate and bless children as they grew; they served as an opportunity to remind the entire church body of the presence and importance of children within the church. Incidentally, the liturgy of these Sundays became crucial because it shaped our congregation's theology of children. So, as a children's pastor, I implore you to think critically and plan thoroughly regarding who speaks and what is spoken on these special days.

As the children's minister, I orchestrate two milestone Sundays each year. In January, we celebrate the babies born in the previous year. As a fellowship that practices adult baptism, we use this opportunity to celebrate our children and exhort our church to commit to the mission of their formation. We invite all infants, parents, and siblings to come before the church for a prayer of blessing and a renewal of the congregation's covenant to bring up these children in the love and admonition of the Lord.

The second milestone I plan is our back-to-school blessing each August. On this Sunday, we bless all students and teachers returning to school; but particularly, we invite new kindergarten students to come forward with their families for a prayer of blessing. After the worship gathering, we invite extended families of kindergarteners to attend a brunch. During the brunch, we spend time introducing families to one another and talking about the significance of the journey that the families, not just the children, are on together.

Beyond these milestone Sundays, we have found valuable ways to incorporate children into our Sunday morning worship gatherings. As ideas are formed related to the worship time, I strongly encourage collaborating with the worship leader and/or pastor weeks in advance. We found times when children could lead one of their favorite songs in that space. Similarly, groups of children have shared a memory verse. The key here is to know your context and creatively look for opportunities that allow children to be seen and heard in the whole-church gathering.

By including children in leading worship, new meaning is found in these moments for those who have *tasted* intergenerational fellowship and now actively *see* one another in their worship setting. These moments draw the hearts of the adults toward the children while communicating love, value, and acceptance to each child in the congregation. Including children in leading worship creates this "taste and see" subculture that builds bridges and pathways toward future intergenerational ministry.

Inviting Children to Serve and Bless

Worship gatherings give children an opportunity to be seen and appreciated; likewise, **service** gives children an opportunity to "taste and see" by **blessing** others. When I imagine Christmas at our church, I immediately think of caroling night. On the second Sunday night in December, appointments are made with senior saints to visit and carol at their home. Some hosts prepare refreshments; all anticipate the visit. For our senior saints, children coming to their door is an important sign that Christmas is coming.

In addition to Christmas caroling, we also paint and deliver pumpkins to the homes of seniors each October. The children love to create, and the seniors love to "ooh and aah" over those creations. At Thanksgiving, our congregation hosts a meal inviting the families that participate in our food pantry to attend. The children make special decorations to enhance the atmosphere. Older children serve drinks and desserts, while parents are encouraged to sit with their children beside a stranger to offer the gifts of hospitality and presence.

The giving and receiving of acts of service and blessing reminds parties of all ages of the *goodness* of fellowship in Christ. Adding simple cross generational touches of service throughout the year strengthens intergenerational bonds and magnifies the blessings of intergenerational ministry, allowing generations to "taste and see" the goodness of God through serving and blessing together. These moments serve as reminders of the love that binds generations together, building an intergenerational subculture, while fighting the inertia of age- and stage-based ministry.

Experiencing Learning Together

Finally, once we established a subculture of members who had tasted and seen the goodness of God in the context of intergenerational ministry, we progressed to development of ***short-term intergenerational class options***. Pulling children and adults out of the existing structure of classes organized by age and stage takes some planning, faith, and social capital. In my setting, weekly class time is of great importance to children and adults who look forward to the time together, not just in study but also in fellowship with their deepest spiritual life partners. Only adults who trusted my judgment and bought into my emphasis on intergenerational ministry would consider leaving their regular midweek class to try something new. The first attempt at a class of this kind is hugely significant. It needs to be a blessing to those who participate, or else the leader will lose social capital, and it will be a long time before she will convince anyone to try something new.

As the organizer of an intergenerational class, my first job was to do what I call "stacking the deck"—involving handpicking a diverse cross section of the generations from our church, bringing together people who are likely to enjoy an experience together. The way first-time participants talk to their peers about the new class is the greatest factor in whether those peers will ever consider such an opportunity in the future.

To date, I have successfully hosted two very different short-term intergenerational classes during our regular Wednesday night Bible class schedule. The first brought together fifteen participants, a third of which were ten- to twelve-year-olds, along with representatives from every decade of adulthood from twenties to seventies. In this group, we participated together in a unit using Jared Patrick Boyd's *Imaginative Prayer*.[1] I

---

[1] Jared Patrick Boyd, *Imaginative Prayer: A Yearlong Guide for Your Child's Spiritual Formation* (Downers Grove, IL: InterVarsity Press, 2017).

observed that all ages were more open to new experiences of contemplative prayer when introduced in an intergenerational setting. Also, all ages participated in discussion and expressed that they were surprised and blessed by interactions with other generations.[2]

More recently, I used the *WE: The Unshakeable Promise* curriculum in a midsized fellowship room, where we gathered at six round tables and engaged in lessons about God's covenants with us.[3] Each table purposefully included a mixture of ages, including ten- to twelve-year-olds, a few middle-aged adults, and several senior adults. Discussion questions provided an opportunity for each table to get comfortable with each other. Representatives from each age group participated in fun skits each week, which created hilarious moments. Each table completed a craft, and the whole group participated in discussion centered around a biblical text. When surveyed, all adults claimed to have learned as much or more than they would have in their regular class. For all participants, anticipation for each week's class was as high or higher than their regular age- and stage-segregated gatherings. I found that generations can learn together, but several years of fruitful intergenerational experiences were necessary to prepare church members to alter their weekly routine and invest themselves in such an opportunity. Here, again, building a subculture of people who have experienced the "taste and see" of intergenerational faith-building relationships is vital in order to build further bridges toward learning together.

Moving Forward

As advocates of intergenerational ministry, we are called to create opportunities for ages to come together—to "taste and see" the goodness of God, richly experienced in meaningful contexts with other generations. Organic bonds, whether in small churches or large churches, require intentionality. Sometimes it may seem easier for these bonds to happen when a church is

---

[2] For more description regarding our experience with intergenerational imaginative prayer, see Wes Gallagher, "Intergenerational Imagining," in *Engage All Generations: A Strategic Toolkit for Creating Intergenerational Faith Communities*, ed. Cory Seibel (Abilene, TX: Abilene Christian University Press, 2021), 121–29.

[3] Laura Keeley and Bonny Mulder Behnia, *WE: The Unshakeable Promise* (Grand Rapids: Faith Alive Resources, 2012).

not steeped in age-and-stage mentality. Even so, building a subculture of "taste and see" develops a foundation that enables future intergenerational ministry to continue and thrive.

The work of an intergenerationally minded minister, no matter the context, is to prayerfully and strategically initiate a plan of action to build a strong intergenerational subculture within the faith community. The foundational steps of my journey toward building this intergenerational subculture included *facilitating events that connected generations at the table*, working to include children in **leading worship**, *providing opportunities for children to* **serve and bless** *other generations, and creating environments for generations to* **learn together**. Congregational culture will not be totally transformed by one event, but each step—each "taste and see"—matters, so I encourage you to take the next step.

As the people of God, we are familiar with the tension that exists living in the kingdom that is both already and not yet. We know the gap between what is and what is to be. As leaders we envision the banquet table of Isaiah 25:6 filled with an abundance of rich foods and a diverse assortment of people of all ages. The next generation is not assimilated into the faith community by segregating them to a "children's table" but by including them at the banquet table. Maybe you are not the host of the primary table in your setting, but no matter what table you do host in your faith community, you have the opportunity to invite all ages to that table to "taste and see" the joy of intergenerational relationships. May the tables you set fruitfully nurture the growth of an intergenerational subculture in your faith community.

THEOLOGY IN PRACTICE: QUESTIONS TO CONSIDER

1. Are you in a ministry context where you do not have authority to make system-wide change? How might the initiation of subcultures experiencing intergenerational ministry help you in your context?

2. Identify subcultures in your context where you might initiate intergenerational experiences of "taste and see." Consider Gallagher's list of ideas and add to them. What might be a next step for you in creating an intergenerational subculture of practice?

3. Many of Gallagher's subcultures involved children because of his ministry role. Even if you are not a children's minister, how might you transfer Gallagher's ideas into other ministry areas and other generations of the church?

4. Perhaps you are the main leader in your context. How might the facilitation of intergenerational subcultures help you facilitate intergenerational practice in your setting? Even further, in what ways might you, as a leader or preacher, utilize the idea of "taste and see" to help people in your context experience intergenerational ministry?

CHAPTER 14

INTERGENERATIONAL WORSHIP EXPERIMENTS AT VIRGINIA SEMINARY

SARAH BENTLEY ALLRED

"It isn't hard, it's new. Practice makes it not new."

—Anonymous

In the fall of 2016, I was a new student at Virginia Theological Seminary in Alexandria, Virginia. For the first time, this residential seminary offered on-campus accommodations for students with spouses and/or children. In previous years, families lived off campus and were only physically present once or twice a month for community events. After a year of living into this new reality, the Chapel Department decided to move the weekly Community Eucharist service from Wednesday mornings to Thursday evenings at 5:15 so spouses and children could be present.

Community Eucharist typically included seminarians serving in a full range of worship leadership roles (acolytes, crucifer, lectors, etc.), a faculty sermon, a formal choir anthem, and Scripture readings in different languages when international visitors were present. All students and faculty members were expected to attend weekly. This service was originally prepared and intended for highly educated adults steeped in the Episcopal tradition. When the service moved to Thursday evenings, the date and time were the only anticipated changes. At the last minute, one of the Christian formation faculty members suggested that the Chapel Department include a rug with some materials for children off to one side as a way of welcoming and including families. In some contexts, this is called a "pray ground." We used the term "soft space."

You may already be able to guess what happened. The service did not really work for families. It took place at the end of the week after children had been in school or daycare all day long and before dinner. With different faculty members preaching each week, the service varied in length from an hour and fifteen minutes to nearly two hours. Almost no elements of the service were intended to engage children, and when the occasional preacher came over to the soft space to ask the children a question, children were so focused on coloring that they had to be prodded into interaction by their parents. Often, families left before the end of the service because their kids were hungry for dinner.

Likewise, the service did not really work for adults. Preachers, choir members, and congregants alike were distracted by the sounds the children made. These sounds were amplified by the chapel's stone floor and the fact that the children were grouped together in one area. While the materials were all quiet (colored pencils, board books, etc.), the playmates were not. By the end of the academic year, the attendance at this service had dropped down to a very few families and a very few single students.

When the academic year ended, our Chapel Department recognized that something needed to change. I was one of three students invited to reimagine what a service of Holy Eucharist *intentionally* prepared for the entire seminary community might look like. Over the summer, the other co-coordinators and I researched, dreamed, and gathered support. In September of 2018, we launched Thursday Night Live (TNL), an intergenerational Episcopal service of Holy Eucharist Rite II. Over the course of the 2018–19 academic year, we gently, imperfectly, *practiced* our way into a new style of worshiping together: *worship for all ages*. We encountered bumps and missteps along the way. And we also experienced so many sacred moments, moments of growth, connection, grace, and laughter.

Intergenerational Worship: Where to Start

Based on our experience with TNL, here are some recommendations for how to start a new intergenerational worship service or move an existing service toward being more intergenerational. Rather than trying to build a big machine from the start, try a few of these recommendations and iterate based on your experience. I suggest you start with intentional language and have a clear "why" *before* you move into developing and experimenting. At the end of this chapter, I will share a few specific learnings—not as a to-do list but for inspiration. Planning intergenerational worship can be very hard work, but it is also important work, and even small changes can lead to big transformation.

Intentional Language

One of the biggest challenges we encountered at the beginning of TNL had to do with **language**. Even though we communicated about the service using the term "intergenerational," people often referred to TNL as the "family service" or "the service for kids." Eventually, we began using the phrase "worship for all ages." This language significantly improved our ability to articulate the vision and purpose of TNL.

In addition to developing clear language, we also crafted a succinct definition of worship for all ages that helped guide our planning and communicate our goal: *worship that seeks to actively engage and equally value the gifts and needs of every generation.* This definition worked well for us for a few reasons. First, it was short and simple enough to memorize, which meant we could communicate clearly about TNL in conversation without pulling out our planning documents.

Second, this succinct definition captured many of the core values we identified. The phrase "seeks to" is both a nod to the value of presence over perfection and to our trust in God. Rather than being anxious and micromanaging the details of the service, we sought to prepare intentionally and then be as present in the moment as possible, trusting that God would show up even if someone forgot it was their turn to read a lesson or collect the offering.

Another core value that shows up in this definition is "active engagement." During the original Community Eucharist service, we often felt like passive observers of the liturgy, and yet, in our own experiences, participation and engagement were ways we connected with God and the body of Christ during worship. At TNL, we sought to pay close attention to the ways we could invite more engagement during every aspect of the service and be attentive to the ways in which people of different ages were invited to participate. The phrase "every generation" was a direct articulation of one of our highest values: intergenerationality.

Third, this definition states right up front that people of different ages have different gifts and needs. We worked hard to discuss these gifts and needs openly, identifying them as differences rather than calling them "good" or "bad." Sometimes, the needs of different generations were in tension. For example, older adults had a need to hear the sermon while toddlers had a need to "whisper" and move around during worship. We acknowledged these different needs together, as a community, and discussed ways to attend to both sets of needs. In this case, we offered the use of hearing devices to anyone who wanted to hear the sermon more clearly, and we also led a workshop for families on how to help children "get ready" for worship. During these workshops, we made it clear that it was normal for children to need to leave the sanctuary and "get ready" again during the service.

Clarify Your Why

In his 2009 TED Talk, Simon Sinek makes a powerful case for the value of **knowing your "why."**[1] Not only is it important to have clarity about your goal (for example, "to actively engage and equally value the gifts and needs of every generation in worship" is a clearly defined goal), but you also need to be able to clearly articulate *why* this goal matters. Another example comes from my colleague Jenna Campbell. This is how she articulates her why: "We are most fully the people of God when we are gathered—all

---

[1] Simon Sinek, "How Great Leaders Inspire Action," YouTube, TED Talks, September 28, 2009, https://www.youtube.com/watch?v=u4ZoJKF_VuA&t=4s.

ages—in worship together. We learn, worship, and build community best when we honor the perspective and gifts of all ages."[2]

Being clear on why intergenerational worship matters to you and your community allows you to communicate in a way that connects to people's hearts, not just their intellects. While some members of your community might be moved by research that outlines the benefits of intergenerational worship, others will catch the vision through hearing stories and articulations of why this ministry is important to someone personally.

For me, if I were to articulate my "why," I would say worship for all ages matters because it is an opportunity for the people of God to practice being the body of Christ together, to practice living into the counter-cultural values of the kingdom of God, and to be strengthened for being God's people in the world all week long. It matters that all generations are included because this is important, transformative work! The sooner we can form young people in this countercultural way of being in the world, the better. Furthermore, we cannot really be the body of Christ while relegating some members to a separate space or excluding them altogether due to any part of their identity (age, ability, sexuality, gender, race, socio-economic status, etc.). When I got clear about my "why," I became more invested in intergenerational worship and found myself naturally evangelizing others with ease and authenticity.

Next Steps: Experimentation and Development

After you have crafted intentional language to describe and define your worship gatherings and have worked to identify your "why," you are ready to begin *experimenting* with intergenerational worship in your context. As you continue in your experimentation, you will *develop* ideas unique to your worship community. Here are a few key ideas to help you and your team in the process of creating and planning intergenerational worship.

Draw Others In

Once you and other leaders have clarity of language and purpose, it's time to share the vision and build buy-in. This will most likely need to be a

---

[2] Used by permission from Jenna Campbell, chat discussion, Workshop, 2021.

multifaceted approach. You might engage people in a book study related to intergenerational worship, preach about inclusion of all ages, experiment with intergenerational ministry outside of worship, or meet with specific church leaders to gain their buy-in.

Start Small

You do not have to wait until you have a fully formed idea of what intergenerational worship will look like in your context before you begin experimenting. Even while you are working to build buy-in throughout the congregation, you can start making small shifts. For example, the adult choir and the children's choir might offer an anthem together during worship one week rather than separately, or you might begin inviting a more age-diverse group of people to serve during worship.

Reflect Together

One of the most transformative practices we implemented was intentional, regular opportunities for reflection. Each month, we invited the congregation to gather for a structured time of reflection. We asked three questions: *Where are you experiencing God in worship? What is distracting you from experiencing God in worship? What are your hopes and dreams for Thursday Night Live?* Here, we emphasized *listening* rather than problem solving. We listened to each other's experiences, where God was at work within individuals, and where the Spirit was leading us as a community. I know of another congregation practicing intergenerational worship that reflects for fifteen minutes right after worship using this simple question: *What did you notice?* We can practice reflection in a variety of ways, but the key is to do it regularly. In addition, we must create a reflective space that avoids a tendency to "fix" things, and invite everyone to participate in reflection.

Stay in Relationship

Most likely, people will oppose changes you make. Do your best to maintain the relationship, while keeping in mind that no person, no church, and no worship service can be all things to all people. Listen. Take feedback seriously with an open heart and mind. Your goal is not to convince or pacify anyone but to stay in relationship. When necessary, calmly restate your why.

Specific Learnings from Thursday Night Live

I am intentionally sharing *specific learnings* from TNL, including some nuts and bolts, last because worship for all ages does and should look different in every context. Rather than a checklist, the information below is intended to offer options, ideas, and inspiration.

Music

Our core learning related to music can be summarized as *"help everyone sing."* We prioritized short, familiar, accessible music over musical excellence, complexity, or beauty. In our context, we found that it worked best to have a balance between hymns and brief, repetitive-style pieces each week.[3] Our motto became "something for everyone, not everything for everyone." Each week we included some music that required the ability to read to fully participate and some short, repetitive songs that could be learned without the ability to read words or music.

Liturgy

In terms of liturgy, we prioritized familiarity, simplicity, and formation. We used the service of Holy Eucharist Rite II from the *Book of Common Prayer* because it was already familiar to most members of the congregation, and we wanted the language to become familiar for young children. We began the service with a brief welcome and formation moment each week. Here is an example: "You may have noticed the altar cloth is a different color than last week. We have entered a new season of the church year called Lent." We might add a few additional sentences about the meaning of Lent, the symbols of Lent, or the color of the season.

We kept the service length consistent from week to week at around forty-five minutes. A forty-five-minute service worked particularly well in our Thursday evening context because children were hungry by 6:00 p.m.,

---

[3] For more ideas for short and simple, but meaningful, worshipful songs, consider using music from the Taizé movement at https://www.taize.fr/en_rubrique12.html. Also, find music and resources at Music That Makes Community, https://www.musicthatmakescommunity.org/.

and families could walk right over to community dinner in the refectory in order to be home for bedtime by 7:00 p.m.

Preaching
In order to keep services to forty-five minutes, we had to keep the sermon short; our goal was eight minutes or less. In addition to length, we prioritized speaking to the whole room—from toddlers to octogenarians. As we experimented with intergenerational preaching, we learned to focus on one takeaway; we used stories, metaphors, and images to explore that focus from different angles. As with music, our preaching motto became "something for everyone, not everything for everyone."

Leadership
Through all our experiences facilitating TNL, we may have learned the most about leadership. As co-coordinators, we saw our role as *"be the vision, draw others in."* Not only did we dream the vision and communicate the vision, but we also tried to live out the vision, modeling that vision whenever possible. For example, one of our co-coordinators brought her two-year-old to worship and modeled leaving when he got too loud and returning at an appropriate time to help normalize this for other families. Also, in our learning, we quickly realized that drawing others in was very time consuming. Doing things ourselves, rather than collaborating and teaching, would be much easier. Ultimately, though, *sharing the work* led to a much more engaged, much less passive worship service.

Conclusion: Practice without Perfection

I have visited over a dozen churches practicing intergenerational worship across the United States. While we all possessed certain commonalities, the particulars of worship looked very different in each context. Take the preaching location, for example. In some contexts, the preacher stood at the pulpit. In some gatherings, the preacher stood in the aisle near the congregation. And in other churches, the preacher sat in a chair. In my experience, no one ideal, right, or perfect way exists for doing worship for all ages. We can only *practice*. In the churches that seemed the most intergenerational to me, the leaders were still iterating, learning, growing, and experimenting. On one hand, not having an exact outline or model to emulate might seem daunting; but on the other hand, I hope you feel liberated. You have freedom to experiment! And with the Holy Spirit's creativity, you are free to co-create something unique for your context. The possibilities are endless!

In my experiences of planning and facilitating intergenerational worship, I have seen firsthand that intergenerational worship can be very hard, time-consuming work. But I have also become deeply convinced of its transformative nature. Even small tweaks can lead to meaningful change. It all begins with a few small first steps.

> **THEOLOGY IN PRACTICE: QUESTIONS TO CONSIDER**

1. Where is your context in the practice of planning intergenerational worship? What things have gone well and what things need improvement?

2. Discuss the following question with those in your context who plan worship: *When it comes to intergenerational worship, what is your "why"?* If you do not have people who understand this "why," enlist people you might begin drawing together in your context to discuss this "why" further.

3. Write down one or two small steps toward intergenerational worship you might incorporate—to "practice" in your worship space.

4. Consider incorporating the new practice of "reflection" and communal listening in your worship planning, both individually and as a team. Use these questions that Allred suggested: *What did you notice? Where are you experiencing God in worship? What is distracting you from experiencing God in worship? What are your hopes and dreams for [your context]?*

5. Why would staying in relationship be the most important goal of intergenerational worship? How could the motto "something for everyone, not everything for everyone" help you when planning intergenerational worship in your context?

6. What specific learnings from Allred might help you in your context?
7. As an intergenerational leader, how might you use Allred's concepts of "be the vision, draw others in" and "sharing the work," especially when practicing intergenerational worship?

CHAPTER 15

BEING *FAMILIA*
Latino Intergenerational Connections—Honoring Our Generational and Cultural Treasures

ELIZABETH TAMEZ MÉNDEZ

"We crush [kill] all the caterpillars, then complain there are no butterflies."
—John Marsden, *The Dead of Night*

Our congregation was full of life! Week after week, families[1] gathered to worship. With about two hundred members at that time, all were highly involved in activities, programs, and meetings almost every day of the week—sometimes three times per day! We were united, active, and growing. Children and youth filled our congregation with energy!

---

[1] In this chapter *familia*, or "family," has a connotation of our extended family in Christ. We acknowledge the limitations the term "family" may have for some readers. In this piece, we uplift "family" as a reflection of the loving, inclusive, and empowering nature of the reconstituted family—Father, Son, Holy Spirit—and our role as children of God (Rom. 8:14–17; Eph. 2:19; Matt. 12:50), operating in solidarity, equality, mutuality, and agency. For more on this subject, see Zaida Maldonado Pérez, "The Trinity *Es* and *Son Familia*," in *Evangélicas: A Theological Survey from the Margins* (Eugene, OR: Cascade Books, 2013), 52–72.

Discovery: Honoring Our Latino[2] Treasures

As we grew, the trend became clear. Youth comprised a majority of our congregation, which is not uncommon in Latina churches.[3] In 2021, some 62.1 million Hispanic people were reported to reside in the United States,[4] and no other ethnic or racial group has a higher percentage of youth in its demographic composition.[5] In 2019, the Census Bureau reported that 58.2 percent of the Hispanic population is under thirty-four years old.[6] Latinos are the largest and the fastest-growing ethnic group of children; by 2050, more than one in three children in the United States will be Latino.[7] These demographic reports opened our eyes to the larger picture beyond our Baptist congregation in East Texas. *What is God calling us to do as we face this reality in our community?* Our new vision emerged: To make the most significant impact in our Latino community and the future of our church, our treasure of youth must be at the center of it all—and it takes all generations working together to build a *familia*!

Marc Freedman, CEO and Founder of CoGenerate.org, states: "The stakes couldn't be higher as we choose between two paths forward,

---

[2] Although the terms "Hispanic" and "Latino" have different meanings, they are used interchangeably in this piece to reflect both preferences. The U.S. Census Bureau uses the term "Hispanic" in its reports; others, such as the Pew Research Center, use the term "Latino." These terms do not connote race, and generally speaking, "Latino" refers to those in the United States with ancestry in Latin America; however, that excludes other Spanish-speaking countries like Spain and Equatorial Guinea. "Hispanic" refers to those in the United States with a Spanish-language ancestry and includes Spain but excludes non-Spanish-speaking countries in Latin America like Brazil and Suriname. Also, although we utilize the terms "Latino" and "Latina" for ease of readability, we acknowledge this terminology is limited in its connotation of inclusivity and could be expressed through variations of the term such as "Latino/a," "Latino@," "Latinx," "Latine," and "Hispanic-Latino."

[3] Throughout, the term "youth" denotes children, teens, and young adults.

[4] "Current Population Survey, Annual Social and Economic Supplement, 2021," U.S. Census Bureau, accessed March 22, 2023, https://www.census.gov/data/tables/2021/demo/hispanic-origin/2021-cps.html. Report does not include in count institutionalized population and those in armed forces living off post or with their families on post.

[5] For more on this topic, see Eileen Patten, "The Nation's Latino Population Is Defined by Its Youth," Pew Research Center, April 20, 2016, https://www.pewresearch.org/hispanic/2016/04/20/the-nations-latino-population-is-defined-by-its-youth/.

[6] "Current Population Survey, Annual Social and Economic Supplement, 2019," U.S. Census Bureau, accessed May 2021, https://www.census.gov/data/tables/2019/demo/hispanic-origin/2019-cps.html.

[7] David Murphey, Lina Guzman, Alicia Torres, "America's Hispanic Children: Gaining Ground, Looking Forward," Child Trends Hispanic Institute, September 24, 2014, accessed June 2021, https://www.childtrends.org/wp-content/uploads/2014/09/2014-38AmericaHispanicChildren.pdf.

prompted by the new demographic and the arrival of the profoundly multigenerational future—one characterized by scarcity, conflict and loneliness; the other by abundance, interdependence and connection."[8] We understood that our congregation had the opportunity and responsibility of seeking models to support our commitment to shift from adult-centric dynamics to fostering an environment with relationships and new ways of doing ministry that tapped into our cultural strengths—our **generational treasures**—while also bringing all generations together as one faith community, supporting one another as *familia* in Christ. Hence, we embarked on a search for answers. We began by asking ourselves questions: *What is God calling us to do in response? Does our current church structure serve us and reflect our cultural values and embody our way of life? Why should our congregation care to engage in the challenging and uncomfortable process of change?*

This is the story of our congregation's initial steps in the process of ***discovery, design, transition,*** and ***transformation*** from a multigenerational but age-segregated church to an intergenerational faith community where we all contribute and are interconnected as one *familia*.[9] We conceived a way of ministry that also addressed our cultural values and social needs. Our model for intergenerational change integrated developmental theories and theological frameworks that highlighted faith formation as a process to be passed from one generation to the next; and throughout, we sought to *develop and honor our Latino generational treasures: our children and elders.*

Design: Researching Developmental Theories and Theology

As with most challenges and explorations, we usually find more to it than meets the eye. We knew we wanted to invest in youth and bring all generations together, but where should we begin? We embarked on a research journey that led us to human developmental theories and theological

---

[8] Marc Freedman, *How to Live Forever: The Enduring Power of Connecting the Generations* (New York: Public Affairs, 2018), 14.

[9] Full framework published in Elizabeth Tamez Méndez, "Rethinking Latino Youth Ministry: Frameworks That Provide Roots and Wings for Our Youth," *Apuntes: Theological Reflections from the Hispanic-Latino Context* 37, no. 2 (2017): 42–91. Any portions of this chapter that have been previously published are republished with permission.

foundations for ***designing*** our work. These concepts served to help us understand *how* to engage with youth in a healthy and positive manner, and *why* it mattered. First, we considered two guiding concepts regarding developmental theories that helped shape what began as our youth outreach and would later become our intergenerational church structure. **Positive Youth Development Theory (PYD)** proposes the following: (1) youth development is holistic, and (2) contributing ecological contexts (i.e., healthy social contexts) support youth's healthy development.[10]

As part of this holistic approach in the developmental theories of PYD, we prioritized tending to the **six core needs** that are essential to engaging meaningfully with youth: *sense of security, deep connection, identity development, desire to learn, meaning in life, and spiritual growth.*[11] By design, healthy human development simultaneously addresses the body, mind, and spirit. If we are to contribute toward the spiritual growth of others, it requires a holistic approach that tends to all the other core needs of a person. Scripture points out that "Jesus grew in wisdom and stature, and in favor with God and men" (Luke 2:52).[12] Jesus's journey on earth was not only a spiritual one; Jesus ministered holistically. To prepare for this kind of holistic ministry, Jesus's development entailed growth in all other areas of his life, just like any other young person. In the same way, through our ministry efforts, we desired to find meaningful ways of tending to as many of the six core needs of our youth as possible.

Using these PYD theories and core concepts, we realized that, in order to create a deeper connection with youth, our congregation could create a social context—a *familia*—where our youth are nurtured and can

---

[10] Peter L. Benson, Peter C. Scales, Stephen F. Hamilton, and Arturo Sesma, "Positive Youth Development: Theory, Research, and Applications," in *Handbook of Child Psychology* (New York: John Wiley & Sons, 2006). This is my personal summary of concepts from this book.

[11] The six core needs are sense of security (psychological, emotional, support), deep connection (physical and social belonging), identity development (self, ethnic, sexual), desire to learn (cognitive), meaning in life (depth, purpose, direction, contribution, empowerment), and spiritual growth (transcendence, convictions, values). For more on this topic, see Michael J. Nakkula and Eric Toshalis, *Understanding Youth: Adolescent Development for Educators* (Cambridge, MA: Harvard Education Press, 2006).

[12] All Bible references in this chapter are from the New International Version (Grand Rapids: Zondervan, 1984).

experience healthy growth and thriving.[13] To do so, we learned that the following fundamental characteristics must be present in our interactions and opportunities through our activities and programs: (1) providing healthy and sustained adult-youth relationships, (2) creating opportunities for youth to actively engage with activities that strengthen their skills and competencies (leadership, teamwork, planning, public speaking), and (3) having a mutually beneficial relationship between the environment or social context (home, school, church) and the young person, where young people are making meaningful contributions and the social context is contributing to their well-being as well.[14] In other words:[15]

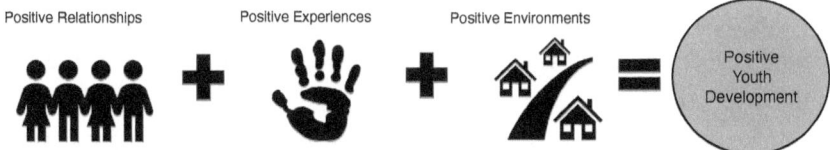

The more these ideal dynamics are fostered in our congregations, the more our congregations become supportive environments for young people to make meaningful, more profound, and lasting connections, supporting their spiritual development and engaging them in contributing to the congregation.[16] Scripture parallels these ideal dynamics. Ephesians 3:14–19 reveals that a person can only comprehend the length, width, height, and depth of God's love when one's roots draw from the love and relationships of a faith community, and our *familia* is by design intergenerational. Titus 2:1–15, along with other Scriptures, highlights the nature of faith-nurturing

---

[13] For more on connecting with the core needs of youth through congregational practices, see Elizabeth Tamez Méndez, "Reaching the Next Generation: Ministry to Culturally and Ethnically Diverse Youth and Young Adults," *Communitas: Journal of Education Beyond the Walls* 12 (2015): 12–18.

[14] William Damon, Jenni Menon, and Kendall Cotton Bronk, "The Development of Purpose During Adolescence," *Applied Developmental Science* 7 (2003): 119–28; Willis F. Overton, "A New Paradigm for Developmental Science: Relationism and Relational-Developmental Systems," *Applied Developmental Science* 17 (2013): 94–107.

[15] "Safe Youth, Safe Schools," Youth.gov, accessed June 2021, https://youth.gov/feature-article/safe-youth-safe-schools.

[16] For more on aspects of PYD in congregational life, see Elizabeth Tamez Méndez, "Leadership Development among Youth in Latino Congregations: The Relationship of Religious Participation to Social Service Involvement and Engagement in Leadership Tasks" (PhD diss., Andrews University, 2018).

relationships, as these are designed to cross generational lines where we encourage and teach one another what it means to embody our faith in Christ.

Next, not only do developmental theories inform our efforts to nurture deeper connections with youth and their healthy development, but biblical teachings also emphasize the vitality of intergenerational connections to reach these goals. Scripture provides a theological perspective outlining divine design—a **pattern of blessing**—where spiritual legacy is passed from one generation to another.[17] In Genesis 1:27–28, Adam and Eve, created in God's own image, are blessed and tasked by God to "be fruitful and increase in number," thereby multiplying God's image in each of us and passing down this legacy of blessing. Genesis 49:1–28 also recounts Jacob passing on the blessing and tasking his sons with what was to unfold for generations to come. Deuteronomy 4:9 and 6:6–7 instruct parents and grandparents that they have the God-given responsibility and blessing to pass on to the next generation the legacy of faith. In the same way, we are called to multiply "images of God." Divine blessing bestowed upon us enables us to fulfill this mission. The next generation (children and youth) flourishes because the preceding generation (adults and elders) releases the blessing of faith upon them; in turn, our faith is strengthened and matured as we share it. Our task is to intentionally create spaces for guiding youth in their faith formation holistically and intergenerationally, as adults understand their role in extending God's blessing to the next generation, and how it is only possible through the ties of close relationships (Deut. 6:6–7; Prov. 22:6; 2 Tim. 1:5).[18]

With these developmental theories and theological underpinnings in hand, we continued our design process of exploring, reflecting, and discerning how our ecclesial models might be transitioned to reflect the new knowledge acquired. Throughout our design process, all our initial steps of transition sought to bring generations together in order to build and strengthen our *familia*.

---

[17] The idea of "pattern of blessing" inspired by M. Sydney Park, Soong-Chan Rah, and Al Tizon, eds., *Honoring the Generations: Learning with Asian North American Congregations* (Valley Forge, PA: Judson Press, 2012).

[18] For more on childhood and theology, see Marcia J. Bunge, *The Child in Christian Thought: Religion, Marriage, and Family* (Grand Rapids: Eerdmans Publishing, 2001).

Transition: Strengthening Cultural Values and Intergenerational Pathways

Through reflection, we realized our ministry models did not align with what developmental theories were teaching us, and we had further work to do theologically, as well. In addition, our assessment showed that *our ministry practices were also not congruent with our cultural traditions and values.* To be fair, our congregation was simply following the ministry models we inherited from our denominational practices, primarily informed and influenced by the US majority culture and social structures, which tended to be more individualistic and age-segregated. To continue forming a **transition** toward a new design, we needed to include more dynamics that felt organic and culturally relevant to our congregation. This initial, transitional step entailed learning more about ourselves, our cultural values, and what mattered to our local faith community.

Generally speaking, our Latino community and cultural values in the United States are characterized by a collectivistic worldview and marked traits such as having deep faith, being fun-loving, taking pride in our heritage and traditions, being driven by determination to succeed in a system that's not ours, and passing down our culture through music, food, clothing, iconography, and *costumbres* (customs or ways of doing life). Among our most salient cultural values is that of familism. It involves dedication, commitment, closeness, and loyalty to family. Our families function as a collective intergenerational unit; thus, the family's needs are above the individual's. Everyone contributes to the well-being of the nuclear family, extended family, and family friends. The family's advice is sought for important decisions,[19] and the entire family is involved in raising and guiding the children—including *padrinos* (godparents or close family friends). At the core of *familia* is a sense of protection of familial honor, respect, pride, belonging, and cooperation. The family is relied upon for material, emotional, and spiritual support.[20] Spending time weekly with one's immediate and extended family is part of weekend rituals. Children are a

---

[19] Melissa A. Martinez, "(Re)considering the Role 'Familismo' Plays in Latina/o High School Students' College Choices," *The High School Journal* 97, no. 1 (2013): 21–40.

[20] Cecilia Ayón, Flavio F. Marsiglia, and Monica Bermudez-Parsai, "Latino Family Mental Health: Exploring the Role of Discrimination and Familismo," *Journal of Community Psychology* 38 (2010): 742–56.

source of pride and joy. Elders are respected as the foundation of wisdom and legacy. Both children and elders are deemed as treasures to be cared for and a source of honor for the family. Our sense of family connection is so strong that family members are still represented in family gatherings even after death. In brief, in Latino culture, family is not just an important aspect of life; rather, family is everything.

Because a majority of our congregation consisted of immigrant families who left their extended family network when they moved to the United States, our faith community became their new extended family. At church, we called each other *hermano* and *hermana* (brother and sister). Outside of church, families spent a lot of time together and were very involved in each other's lives. In contrast, they came to church only to be separated by age, stage of life, and gender-specific ministries. This was one of the main ways in which our cultural values and ways of life clashed with our ecclesial models.

We understood that if we were to reach our younger generations holistically and effectively, we had to make a cultural shift. We needed to create a healthy and rich ecological context with more adult-youth interactions and collaborations while simultaneously providing greater congruency with our cultural strengths and values; all the while we needed to provide organic transition. We realized our familial practices of intergenerational interdependence, when integrated into our church practices, could aid us in that transition. As a result, over the course of four years, our congregation engaged in a process of exploration and transition *en conjunto* (in togetherness). This exploration took different shapes, through sermons preached, intergenerational conversations on Wednesday nights over coffee and *pan dulce* (sweet bread or pastries), and many small experiments and test runs—all while juggling all other aspects of our congregation's needs and with only one person on staff.

Against the odds, we pressed onward in our pursuit of creating structures that would help us be *familia* in the church. One example of our beginning efforts involved changing our customary Sunday meals after morning worship service. These mealtimes were key in our congregation to build ties and strengthen a sense of connection; they were reflective of what would take place on the weekends if one were living near extended family in our countries of origin. At the same time, these mealtime dynamics also highlighted our cultural paradox: we highly value children but often tend to exclude them as equals in other aspects of life. Here, our practice diverged from the fundamental characteristics and relational dynamics that PDY theories promote for close adult-youth interactions and young people's sense of agency and contribution. Thus, we began with small steps. We encouraged everyone to sit in mixed-age groups that did not include immediate family members. During these meals, we provided prompts and props to spark conversations, to get to know each other in new ways, and to start building closer relationships among different generations outside of immediate family members.

At first, many found these cross age table experiences odd and sometimes uncomfortable. Some of it had to do with our cultural values in adult-children's relationships where obeisance dictates the protocols. Young people were not accustomed to speaking to adults and elders outside of their immediate family in a casual manner; they were used to listening as a sign of respect for parental authority and discipline and had a general sense that it was improper to express their opinions, feelings, and ideas to adults. Inversely, adults had a sense that children were to be "seen and not heard," that children played a secondary role, and that adults should receive preferential treatment—almost as if a person does not count until reaching adulthood.[21]

This tendency to measure children by adult standards became a hurdle to overcome. Many adults had not seen examples of instances where one could consider issues from children's perspectives; instead, adults were automatically presumed to be more knowledgeable. Over time, interest, openness, and trust were built, and we learned to navigate and overcome perceived hurdles. Our congregation became energized by the opportunity to get to know each other in a different light and environment. This opened the gateway to build upon and expand our efforts toward being *familia*.

As change was gradually embraced, and intergenerational relationships grew stronger and closer, we implemented more hands-on interventions.

---

[21] Enrique Pinedo and Harold Segura, *"Dejen que los Niños Vengan a Mí: Pistas Bíblico-Teológicas para el Ministerio con la Niñez y la Juventud"* (San José, Costa Rica: Movimiento Juntos con la Niñez y la Juventud, 2015).

For example, we began organizing ideation meetings where adults, children, and youth would get together in teams to express their opinions and discuss potential solutions to any needs our congregation identified. It took time to train some leaders in the congregation to host these group conversations. And not all attempts were successful. A paradigm shift is no easy feat! Not all leaders can let go of their ways of doing things or relating to others, especially when it comes to children and youth. As adults, we often view children and youth as recipients and spectators of church programs, and not co-creators. Even further, very few examples and models of such intergenerational conversation exist as points of reference.

In time, though, we arrived at a spot where these dynamics of intergenerational collaboration and youth agency no longer seemed foreign. A vision for a different model of ministry emerged where most efforts, projects, and ministries were organized intergenerationally. For example, adults no longer organized Vacation Bible School (VBS) alone and then invited children to come partake; instead, VBS became a project of the entire congregation. Some adults began mentoring youth who were interested in learning how to teach at VBS. Others organized teams where adults, youth, and children worked on preparations like creating posters and sorting materials for the event. Older youth helped with research and organized crafts and games that would interest the little ones. Some logistical aspects such as purchasing and preparing snacks were delegated to older teens as they worked alongside adults who were available to provide guidance as needed through scaffolding mentoring[22] until the task was complete. As we worked on these projects, our sense of *familia* and intergenerational interdependence grew.

Another pivotal effort of transition came by finding new ways to integrate our elders in the congregation through unique and more active roles that would impact the faith formation of youth. Typically, as part of our

---

[22] Scaffolding mentoring refers to a learning by watching-and-doing model—a type of mentoring where adults show children and youth how to do the task at hand, and then invite those children and youth to engage in the task on their own. At the same time, adults walk alongside them to help as needed during the learning curve. See Dana Mitra, Tiffanie Lewis, and Felicia Sanders, "Architects, Captains, and Dreamers: Creating Advisor Roles That Foster Youth-Adult Partnerships," *Journal of Educational Change* 14, no. 2 (2013): 177–201.

cultural practices, children spend a lot of time with their grandparents, and elders are the main source for passing on the family's traditions, culture, wisdom, and life experience to the next generation. Aging in our culture does not have a negative connotation. The older one is, the more respect one earns. Growing up away from extended family, many of our youth were missing these valuable, formative relationships. Why then were our elders in the congregation not connected to our youth? Through our efforts to engage elders in all aspects of congregational life through active roles and leadership, our elders gained a renewed sense of legacy and contribution; they became *abuelitos* (reverent, tender name for grandparents) for all the youth. To facilitate the relationship and faith-building efforts with our *abuelitos*, we encouraged elderly members to select a few young people they would personally pray for during the week, mail a card of encouragement to them from time to time, and intentionally ask about how their week was at school. As their relationships grew, youth enjoyed learning from elders as they heard their *testimonios* (recounting their journeys and God's faithfulness in their lives), as well as their migration stories and recollections of childhood in their countries of origin. Some elders began teaching our younger generations how to prepare traditional foods, and some of the youth would help our elders with chores, lawn care, or figuring out their cellphone settings. Through each step in these intergenerational interactions and efforts, our congregation became *familia,* and we knew we could count on each other.

Step by step, these patterns of intergenerational collaboration began extending to other efforts in our church, such as the worship ministry, mission trips, Sunday school teaching, and creative arts ministry.[23] Concurrently, we continued with age-specific activities such as Bible studies and occasional social events because time with peers is needed, too; however, our outlook had shifted to one of interconnectedness, collaboration, and spending time together at church as one extended *familia.*

---

[23] For more about our process, see "Enriching and Deepening Congregational Worship Life by Developing Young Leaders: Lessons from a Latino Congregation in Texas—The Roots and Wings Framework," in *Worship through Latinx Eyes: Interdisciplinary Perspectives on Public Worship Practices* (Cascade Books Publishing, forthcoming).

Transformation: Unfolding a Legacy

The process was not linear, and embracing change was extremely hard at times. We learned to practice forgiveness as we experienced trials and errors. Still, we knew the vision God had given us, and we listened to the promptings of the Holy Spirit along the way. ***Transformation*** is never an easy process. Conviction and faith kept us going, and we began seeing compelling results. We witnessed how, when we made the shift, everything else began falling into place. Our congregational ethos changed. Not only were we doing activities together, but we were also designing, serving, learning, and building together as *familia*. Only by all of us coming together could our small congregation (about 180 people at that time) have the capacity to become a rich ecological contributing context that honored and nurtured our generational treasures—those who gave heart and depth to all we did—our youth and elders.

As the work of building and being *familia* continues, the individual and collective transformation in the congregation keeps unfolding. We learn more and more about what it means to foster a model for intergenerational and culturally relevant ministry. Today, the youth have grown. Now, they are young adults forming their own families, and they are leaders in the church carrying on this work. They learned as a community, and now they are continuing as a community. Some are serving as pastors, treasurers, education coordinators, music leaders, and neighborhood liaisons. Recently, one of our elders, who is still our *abuelitos* prayer leader, had a big birthday party organized by the current youth of our congregation to celebrate her ninety-seventh birthday. In this case, the seeds planted seventeen years ago continue flourishing and multiplying as the *familia* grows.

Our congregation became the contributing ecological context where our youth and elders receive and experience an interconnected community of faith—where they find acceptance and respect; where they belong, are valued, and are received with open arms and are loved; where Scripture is taught and modeled; where they are known, heard, and empowered; and where they are always *familia*.

One of the beautiful aspects of ministry, which is equally challenging, is that it is very contextual, and it changes as the community itself changes. So, your ministry context may be very different from ours and you may not be able to integrate all these concepts. We pray, however, that this piece inspires you to continually seek a prosperous path forward filled with intergenerational abundance, interdependence, and connectedness. Perhaps your context might be different, but a starting point might be discovering and seeking to honor cultural and generational treasures.

THEOLOGY IN PRACTICE: QUESTIONS TO CONSIDER

1. How might your congregation find ways to interconnect and foster closer relationships between the generational treasures of elders and youth in your midst?

2. What unique cultural treasures in your context might provide pathways toward intergenerational ministry?

3. What cultural shifts might allow space for your faith community to discover, design, transition, and transform intergenerationally?

4. How might your congregation create more opportunities to build closer intergenerational relationships and be *familia*?

Section Five

SURVEY OF CURRENT INTERGENERATIONAL PRACTICES

*"Do it again.
Play it again.
Sing it again.
Read it again.
Write it again.
Sketch it again.
Rehearse it again.
Run it again.
Try it again.
Because again is practice, and practice is improvement."*

—Richelle E. Goodrich, author

CHAPTER 16

BENEFITS, CHALLENGES, AND RECOMMENDATIONS FOR INTERGENERATIONAL MINISTRY
Findings from Recent Congregational Research

HOLLY CATTERTON ALLEN

> *"Churches that are becoming more intentionally intergenerational in outlook and practice are moving toward a future that they cannot see; they are **becoming** something different."*
> —Holly Allen, Christine Lawton, Cory Seibel,
> *Intergenerational Christian Formation*

From 2010 to 2020, dozens of doctoral projects focusing on intergenerational ministry were completed. This chapter unpacks these fascinating projects, sharing details of their hopeful and encouraging findings.

For this work, I initially perused fifty doctoral projects, and ultimately have drawn information and insights from the findings of thirty-five of them. These doctoral works address pressing questions about the rationale and practices of intergenerational ministry in church settings. Taken together, they offer substantive responses to the following central questions:

- Why are churches seeking to become more intergenerational?
- What does it look like for churches to become more intentionally intergenerational in spiritually formative ways?
- What are the spiritual (and other) benefits of intergenerational approaches to Christian formation for *all* the generations; that is, for the whole church?
- What challenges might churches face when they begin to implement more intergenerational practices?
- What recommendations do these researchers offer to those coming along behind them?

These questions form the outline of this chapter.

For a closer look at each specific project, year of publication, and the granting institution, see table 16.1. In this chapter, all projects are referred to by the author's last name.

Table 16.1. Intergenerational Ministry and Practices Research Survey

Author	Title	Year/School
Azzopardi, Joseph	The Impact of Discipleship on Wellbeing in Intergenerational Congregations	2019 PhD Avondale
Burns-Marko, Robyn White	Intergenerational Ministry: Bringing the Generations Back Together	2017 Azusa Pacific
Coates, Jamie R.	Join the Band: Benefits of Engaging Intergenerational Volunteers in the Local Church Worship Ministry	2019 DWS Liberty
Cowell, Kirk R.	Facilitating Holistic Spiritual Formation at the Northside Church of Christ in Laredo, TX	2014 Abilene Christian
Dale, Craig Darryl	Strategically Increasing Inter-Generational Involvement among the Membership of Ivy Creek Baptist Church in Buford, Georgia	2015 Southern Baptist Theol. Sem.
Deames, Matthew	Inviting and Encouraging Racial, Cultural, Ethnic, and Generational Diversity within Ecclesial Community	2012 George Fox
Douglas, Scott	Intergenerational Discipleship for Leadership Development: A Mixed-Methods Study	2013 EdD Southern Baptist Theol. Sem.
Edwards, Matthew Robert	Under One Roof: Authentic Leadership as a Way of Retaining G2 Leaders in an Intergenerational Church	2016 George Fox

Eikenberry, David	Developing an Intentional and Transparent Intergenerational Ministry in a Small Congregation	2013 Trinity
Fallon, Seth	Developing a Strategy for Intergenerational Ministry at Mullen Memorial Baptist Church Through the Method of Multigenerational Story-Telling as Appreciative Inquiry	2019 Palmer Theol. Sem.
Fetterman, Amy	From Stories to Sisterhood: An Intergenerational Community of Women	2015 Drew
Green, Tassie	Training Church Leaders to Build Family Faith Through Creating Engaging, Intergenerational Worship Services	2015 Fuller Theol. Sem.
Houston, Alexander	How to Effectively Engage in Ministry with the Millennial Generation: Developing a Contextualized Intergenerational Church through Millennial Outreach	2015 Drew
Jamison, James	Preaching Prophetically to Foster Intergenerational Relationships in the Congregation	2019 Garrett-Evangelical Theol. Sem.
Kim, Jung Jun	Revive Us Again: Intergenerational Ministry as a Strategy for the Revitalization of Bongshin Church in Seoul, Korea	2017 Asbury Theol. Sem.
Lau, Tina Yuk-Yan	Mosaic Ministry: Challenges and Opportunities of Intergenerational Ministry among Chinese Churches	2017 PhD Trinity
Lee, Kyeoung Soo	The Reformation of the Household Church Worship: Finding Effective Ways of Leaving Spiritual Legacies to the Next Generation	2016 Drew
Linderman, Larry	The Relationship between Intergenerational Ministry Practices and Church Health	2016 PhD Southeastern Baptist Theol. Sem.
Lott, James Alan	The Intergenerational Worship Model: Youth-Specific Benefits	2020 DWS Liberty
Mason, Michael	A Qualitative Study Exploring the Implementation and Effects of Intergenerational Youth Ministry	2020 PhD Biola
McCoy, Lawrence Wilson, III	Forming the People of God: A Qualitative Study of the Formative Impact of Intergenerational Relationships through Dwelling in the Word	2016 Lipscomb
McCrary, Michael	Intentional Intergenerational Ministry Practices Discovered at Central Assembly of God in Springfield, Missouri	2014 Assemblies of God Theol. Sem.

Mitchell, Craig Duncan	(Re)forming Christian Education in Congregations as the Praxis of Growing Disciples for a Missional Church	2018 PhD Flinders
Norton, Allison	Passing on the Faith: A Mixed Methods Study of Intergenerational Religious Transmission in Transnational African Immigrant Congregations in the United States	2020 DIS Fuller Theol. Sem.
O'Donoghue, Denise H.	Critical Success Factors for Creating and Sustaining Intergenerational Women's Ministry: A Delphi Study	2013 EdD Southeastern Baptist Theol. Sem.
Schlesman, Shane Glen	The Passing Zone: Building an Intergenerational Leadership Team	2020 Assemblies of God Theol. Sem.
Snailum, Brenda	Integrating Intergenerational Ministry and Age Specific Youth Ministry in Evangelical Churches: Maximizing Influence for Adolescent Spiritual Development	2012 EdD Biola
Taylor, Faye Banks	Intergenerational Sharing in the African American Church: Re-establishing the Connection between the Elders and the Middle Generation	2010 Drew
Teague, Jonathan Andrew	Developing a Discipleship Model of Churches to Equip Millennials in the Southern Baptist Convention of Texas	2020 DEd.Min Southern Baptist Theol. Sem.
Turner, Robin	Children's Faith Formation as Mutually Transforming Opportunity: Leading Systemic Change	2019 George Fox
Wallace, Patricia S.	Gaining, Retaining, and Sustaining Young Adults: Developing Leaders for Generation to Generation	2020 College of Theology South University
Westmoreland, Janet Bahor	Identification of Barriers to Intergenerational Ministry by Older Women with Corresponding Success Strategies: A Mixed Method Approach	2019 EdD Southeastern Baptist Theol. Sem.
Whittaker, William	Exploring Characteristics of Choral Ministry within Georgia Southern Baptist Churches Committed to Intergenerational Ministry	2015 DMA New Orleans Baptist Theol. Sem.
Wilkerson, Richard	Lifters and Gifters: Keeping Millennials and Boomers Together to Build the Church	2019 Southeastern Assemblies of God
Wilson, Kristin D.	Turning the Hearts of Mothers to Daughters and the Daughters to Mothers: Building Intergenerational Bridges to Discipleship	2019 Assemblies of God Theol. Sem.

* DMin awarded unless otherwise indicated

Overview of Doctoral Projects Completed from 2010 to 2020

The thirty-five doctoral degrees were earned from many seminaries or divinity schools. The authors represent a broad spectrum of Christian traditions, and their research projects took place in a variety of cultural, ethnic, and racial contexts.

Nine of the thirty-five projects were essentially conceptual; that is, they examined historical, biblical, theological, theoretical, and/or sociological understandings of intergenerational ministry. The other twenty-six doctoral projects were (primarily) empirical in nature; that is, the doctoral student—after describing the context, outlining the problem they were addressing, and surveying the relevant literature—conducted a qualitative study, typically within his or her congregation, distributing surveys, leading focus groups, and/or conducting interviews

- to discern congregants' attitudes and interest in participating in intergenerational practices, or
- to evaluate congregants' responses to various intergrade ministry activities the researcher had implemented.[1]

Seminary, Denominational, Cultural, and Racial Representation

The thirty-five doctoral degrees were earned from sixteen seminaries, divinity schools, or theological schools.[2] The doctoral projects explored intergenerational understandings and practices in twenty different denominations, representing the theological breadth of church traditions.[3] Regarding church size, attendance in these studies ranged from seventy-five to five thousand (pre-pandemic).

---

[1] A few of the doctoral students also incorporated quantitative measures such as online surveys with Likert Scale response options; also, a few students gathered data from multiple congregations, not solely their own congregation.

[2] The sixteen schools are listed in Table 16.1. The thirty-five doctoral degrees consisted of about two dozen Doctor of Ministry (DMin) projects along with several Doctor of Philosophy (PhD), Doctor of Education (EdD), Doctor of Musical Arts (DMA), Doctor of Worship Studies (DWS), and Doctor of Intercultural Studies (DIS) dissertations and theses.

[3] African Methodist Episcopal (AME), American Baptist Church, Assemblies of God, Chinese Churches, Christian Church, Churches of Christ, Church of God in Christ, Church of Pentecost USA, Community Church, Covenant Presbyterian, Evangelical Friends Church, Evangelical Lutheran Church of America (ELCA), Korean Methodist Church, Korean Protestant Church, Presbyterian (EPC), Presbyterian Church USA, Seventh-day Adventist, Southern Baptist Church, United Methodist Church, Uniting Church of Australia.

Among the empirical projects, some of the researchers specified that their studies were conducted in predominantly Caucasian congregations, stating this concept in a variety of ways. Eikenberry, for example, describes his congregation as "predominantly white." Cowell states that "a majority of church members are white, with several Latino members, and a few African-American members." Dale and Mason used the phrase "ethnically and culturally diverse" (though the reader might infer the congregation is majority Caucasian). Some empirical projects did not describe the congregation or the participants in terms of race or ethnicity.

The research for eleven of the thirty-five projects was conducted in specifically African American, Korean, Chinese, or Australian contexts. Four of the projects took place in African American churches in South Carolina (Jamison), New York (Taylor), Florida (Wallace), and Illinois (Wilson). Norton reported data gathered in Ghanaian-led immigrant churches in the Mid-Atlantic, New England, and Western United States. Houston conducted his intergenerational research while serving as the first African American pastor at an ethnically and racially diverse congregation.

Two of the thirty-five research projects (Kim and Lee) focused attention on the challenges of intergenerational ministry in Korean churches. Lau considered key factors affecting intergenerational ministry in Chinese churches in Hong Kong, Taiwan, and the United States. And finally, Azzopardi and Mitchell wrote in the Australian context, with some of Mitchell's data being collected in Aboriginal church settings.

Purpose: Why Were These Churches Seeking to Become More Intergenerational?

Each doctoral student stated the rationale for their research, essentially addressing why they chose to pursue some aspect of intergenerational ministry. The researchers described their ultimate purpose in a plethora of ways, including the following:

- Azzopardi: to discern how a person's well-being is impacted by one's social and spiritual involvement in an intergenerational congregation.
- Cowell: to facilitate holistic spiritual formation.

- O'Donoghue: to discover patterns and themes found in sustainable intergenerational women's ministries.
- Dale: to strategically increase intergenerational involvement of the adult members of the church.
- Lau: to identify crucial factors that affect implementing intergenerational ministry among Chinese churches.
- Green: to "experience God's presence and power together in fresh, tangible ways that build faith, help one another grow toward faith maturity, and live as God's sent ones who serve in their neighborhoods, overflowing with God's love for God's world."[4]

About half of the doctoral students expressed their purposes in the broad, rich, and textured ways illustrated above.

My first surprise of this meta-analysis was that the stated purposes of *the other half of the empirical doctoral projects were related specifically to the waning of Christianity in their contexts*. This concern was expressed in two ways:

- the worry that the church is not passing on faith to the next generation, and/or
- the recognition that the researcher's congregation is aging or even dying.

The first concern was articulated in a variety of ways. For example, Kim's greatest anxiety regarding the church he leads in Korea is that "the succession of faith from one generation to the next is not taking place effectively."[5] He believes intergenerational strategies will help parents (and others) train the children of the church. Eikenberry, a lead pastor in Illinois, says parents and others are alarmed at the high dropout rate among young people in the church, and he suggests that "intentional, transparent intergenerational ministry may help address this concern."[6]

Fallon, pastor of a small Baptist church in Ohio, expresses the second concern, stating that decline in church attendance and the aging of the

---

[4] Green, "Training Church Leaders to Build Family Faith," abstract.
[5] Kim, "Revive Us Again," 14.
[6] Eikenberry, "Developing an Intentional and Transparent Intergenerational Ministry," 31–32.

congregation where he ministers "has created a critical state of survival."[7] Taylor notes that smaller African American churches like the church where she ministers "are increasingly in danger of closing their doors."[8] And Houston, the preaching minister of a Presbyterian church in New Jersey, says it this way: "Sustainability and viability of the local church is at stake due to the decreasing affiliation of the millennial generation within the mainline church."[9]

When I noticed that many of the doctoral projects were undertaken because the congregation was declining, I was initially disappointed. My concern was that becoming more intergenerational was being seen as a utilitarian fix to "save the church"—not primarily as a spiritually formative practice to grow the people of God. I will unpack this concern more fully later in the chapter.

In whatever way they crafted their purpose statements, these doctoral researchers shared their hopes and beliefs that becoming more intergenerational would bless their churches, would foster cross generational relationships, would be spiritually formative, and would—perhaps—even grow their churches numerically.

Intergenerational Practices: What Does It Look Like for Churches to Become More Intentionally Intergenerational in Spiritually Formative Ways?

The twenty-six empirical doctoral projects described various intergenerational practices, processes, or events that had been explored or implemented by the researchers. These experiences included telling stories in age-integrated settings, creating interage small groups, constructing a cross age VBS, facilitating cross generational Bible studies, crafting sermons that intentionally appeal to all generations, inviting younger generations onto committees, hiring ministers that represent at least three generations, purposefully nurturing relationships between middle and older adults, implementing fully intergenerational service opportunities

---

[7] Fallon, "Developing a Strategy for Intergenerational Ministry," 44.
[8] Taylor, "Intergenerational Sharing in the African American Church," 3.
[9] Houston, "How to Effectively Engage in Ministry with the Millennial Generation," 1.

(such as welcoming and feeding homeless families), integrating more traditional hymns into predominantly contemporary worship settings, and welcoming more diverse instruments such as guitars or drums into more traditional worship settings. Though many of the empirical projects concentrated closely on just one specific intergenerational practice, several researchers used two or more approaches, seeking to cultivate a more holistic intergenerational culture in the congregations they served.

Typically, the doctoral theses focused either on (1) the *process* of implementing a particular intergenerational practice or several intergenerational practices in a church, or (2) *how* intergenerational ministry impacts a particular generation or population.[10] Table 16.2 displays an overview of doctoral projects that explored one or more intergenerational practices either empirically or conceptually.

Table 16.2. Implementing Particular Intergenerational Practices in Churches

Multiple intergenerational practices aimed toward general congregational growth	Burns-Marko, Eikenberry, Kim, Lau, McCoy, McCrary
Intergenerational leadership	Douglas, Edwards*, Schlesman
Intergenerational preaching	Jamison*
Intergenerational worship	Coates*, Green*, Lee, Lott, Whittaker
Intergenerational Christian education	Cowell, Mitchell
Intergenerational ministry and congregational well-being or health	Azzopardi, Linderman

* conceptual projects

Table 16.3 exhibits those doctoral projects that focused on intergenerationality and its impact on a specific generation or population either empirically or conceptually.

---

[10] Thirty-three of the thirty-five projects I perused fit into the categories that emerged; one conceptual thesis did not focus on a particular practice or a particular population or generation, but was nonetheless instructive and insightful for this meta-analysis. This project is Matthew Deames's "Inviting and Encouraging Racial, Cultural, Ethnic, and Generational Diversity." This project offered insights regarding the interrelatedness of racial, cultural, ethnic, and generational diversity from historical, biblical, and sociological perspectives that can inform ecclesial practice. The other project that did not fit the categories that emerged was an empirical thesis: Norton's "Passing on the Faith," mentioned earlier. Norton gathered data regarding how faith was being passed on to the next generation in four immigrant Ghanaian congregations.

Table 16.3. The Impact of Intergenerational Practices on a Specific Generation or Population

Children	Turner*
Youth	Mason, Snailum*
Millennials	Houston, Teague*, Wallace
Older adult generations	Dale, Fallon, Taylor, Wilkerson
Women	Fetterman, O'Donoghue, Westmoreland, Wilson

* conceptual projects

What is particularly significant about some of the studies in table 16.3 is that they examine how intergenerational experiences impact generations beyond youth and Millennials. Major studies conducted by Christian Smith,[11] Kara Powell,[12] and David Kinnaman[13] over the past twenty years have established the importance of intergenerational connections and relationships for *teenagers* and *emerging adults*. Some of the doctoral projects in this meta-analysis focused on other generations—children, young adults, middle adults, and older adults.

---

[11] Christian Smith with Melinda Denton, *Soul Searching: The Religious and Spiritual Lives of American Teenagers* (Oxford: Oxford University Press, 2005). Smith directed the National Study of Youth and Religion (NSYR), a research project that was conducted with thirteen- to seventeen-year-olds between 2001 and 2005. The second wave of the research was conducted in 2007 and 2008 with many of the first-wave participants (then eighteen to twenty-three years old). The findings from that research were reported in Christian Smith with Patricia Snell, *Souls in Transition: The Religious and Spiritual Lives of Emerging Adults* (Oxford: Oxford University Press, 2009).

[12] Kara E. Powell, Brad M. Griffin, and Cheryl A. Crawford, *Sticky Faith: Youth Worker Edition: Practical Ideas to Nurture Long-Term Faith in Teenagers* (Grand Rapids: Zondervan, 2011); Kara Powell, Jake Mulder, and Brad Griffin, *Growing Young: Six Essential Strategies to Help Young People Discover and Love Your Church* (Grand Rapids: Baker Books, 2016). *Growing Young* is based on the results of the Churches Engaging Young People (CEYP) project by the Fuller Youth Institute.

[13] David Kinnaman with Aly Hawkins, *You Lost Me: Why Young Christians Are Leaving Church . . . and Rethinking Faith* (Grand Rapids: Baker Books, 2011), 203–5; *You Lost Me* is drawn from eighteen studies conducted by the Barna Group primarily between 2005–2010. David Kinnaman and Mark Matlock, *Faith for Exiles: Five Ways for a New Generation to Follow Jesus in Digital Babylon* (Grand Rapids: Baker Books, 2019); *Five Ways* draws from findings in the Barna study *Gen Z: The Culture, Beliefs and Motivations Shaping the Next Generation* (Ventura, CA: Barna Group, 2018).

Findings: What Are the Spiritual (and Other) Benefits of Intergenerational Approaches to Christian Formation?

This section shares ministry insights and findings from two or three doctoral projects in each of the following categories:

- intergenerational practices for congregational benefits in general,
- intergenerational leadership,
- intergenerational worship,
- intergenerational focus on adults, and
- intergenerational focus on women.[14]

Overall, these researchers found that mutual and reciprocal intergenerational practices fostered a deep sense of belonging, cultivated robust spiritual development, improved relationships across the generations, promoted the gifts of everyone, and rejuvenated congregations.

Intergenerational Practices for Whole Congregations

Many empirical projects concentrated closely on just one or two specific intergenerational practices. For example, Burns-Marko formed an intergenerational handbell choir that eventually included participants aged six to sixty-six, and Cowell taught an all-age Sunday school class for seven weeks.[15]

Other doctoral students, however, employed a more full-immersion approach, implementing opportunities for intergenerational service, learning, and fellowship, as well as intergenerational worship. Eikenberry first preached a series of eight sermons on biblical and theological underpinnings of intergenerationality, generational realities, and intergenerational principles. Then, over the several months of his doctoral work, Eikenberry

- invited and facilitated participation of all ages in worship,
- planned fellowship events that encouraged relationship-building across generations,
- educated the congregation about the uniqueness of each generation,

---

[14] I chose to unpack these specific topics primarily because at least three doctoral projects focused on the topic.
[15] Cowell, "Facilitating Holistic Spiritual Formation."

- equipped families to disciple children and youth,
- worked together with all ages to create a worthy outreach event, and
- involved all generations in leadership and planning.[16]

After completing his project, Eikenberry conducted an evaluation and summarized his findings, saying the various intergenerational experiences allowed the congregants "to reflect the nature of the church as one body, release the gifts of all the people in the church, appreciate our differences, support the family, pass on the faith to the next generation, and reach out to a fractured world in need of Christ and the family of believers."[17]

Other doctoral students who implemented a variety of intergenerational practices also reported positive outcomes. For example, McCoy summarized his findings, saying, "The project proved to be an effective means of cultivating a formative intergenerational experience. Participants reported experiencing robust faith development, deeper understandings of church community, and improved relationships with other generational cohorts."[18] And Kim concluded his dissertation with these encouraging words: "Bongshin Church [in Korea] has been rejuvenated through the implementation of intergenerational ministry."[19]

Intergenerational Leadership

The cumulative findings of three doctoral projects (Douglas, Edwards, Schlesman) make a strong case for the idea that intergenerational leadership teams are a valuable asset in building thriving churches that can reach all the generations of a congregation. In his doctoral project, Edwards draws on ideas from authentic leadership theory (a theory emphasizing power sharing and reciprocity). Edwards first establishes the importance of intergenerational leadership for building an intergenerational church, observing that "a church with generationally homogeneous leadership is more likely to be homogeneous itself."[20] Then he notes that

---

[16] Eikenberry, "Developing an Intentional and Transparent Intergenerational Ministry," 47.
[17] Eikenberry, "Developing an Intentional and Transparent Intergenerational Ministry," 73–74.
[18] McCoy, "Forming the People of God," iv.
[19] Kim, "Revive Us Again," 156.
[20] Edwards, "Under One Roof," 12.

cross generational leadership often leads to cross generational conflict with power struggles between the G1 (older) leader and followers, and the G2 (younger) leader and followers. Edwards concludes his work stating that, in healthy intergenerational churches, authentic leadership looks like both G1 and G2 adults being aware of their gifts and weaknesses and being willing to listen to the stories of others. It means empowering one another, especially in the areas of worship style, the Sunday morning platform, and the decision-making board.[21] And he sagely adds, "Since G1 adults typically have more power, this may require more effort on their part."[22]

Intergenerational Worship

Five doctoral students chose to explore how churches might lean more intentionally into intergenerational worship (Coates, Green, Lee, Lott, Whittaker). Though these doctoral projects examined intergenerational worship in five different ways and in various denominational contexts, several common themes were expressed:

- intergenerational worship fosters a sense of belonging;
- it nurtures spiritual connections and cross generational relationships;
- it transmits faith across the generations; and
- it values all generations and all gifts.

Perhaps the most important theme shared—in multiple ways—was that worshiping intergenerationally permeates the wider ministry of the church and ultimately shapes the entire culture of the church.[23]

Lee stated that the purpose of his doctoral project was to help Deep Springs Korean Methodist Church find "effective ways of leaving spiritual legacies to the next generation through reforming the current household church worship."[24] As Lee perceived the problem, the church's current worship practices were created by the older generation without

---

[21] Edwards, "Under One Roof," 159–60.
[22] Edwards, "Under One Roof," 160.
[23] See also Ray Crawford's study in a United Methodist Church in Oklahoma, "For All Generations: The Experience and Expression of Intergenerational Worship" (DMin thesis, Drew University, 2007).
[24] Lee, "The Reformation of the Household Church Worship," 3.

consideration for the younger generations who are less fluent in Korean. Lee said this approach "prevented the second generation from participating in the worship and from receiving spiritual legacies of the first generation."[25] To address this problem, Lee and the church's Lay Advisory Committee added some contemporary Christian music to the traditional hymns and distributed words of the songs in both languages. In addition to the (shortened) sermon in Korean, they also included a "brief testimony of a layperson and a time of sharing participants' stories of faith in their own language."[26] Lee movingly summarized the benefits of the church's worship adjustments, saying that these changes "gave both generations opportunities to take care of each other's souls, to resolve the intergenerational conflicts, and notably, for the first generation to leave spiritual legacies effectively to the next generation."[27]

Lott's thesis focused on the benefits of intergenerational worship, especially for youth. He distributed surveys to youth (ages 13–19) who were actively involved in churches that "conformed to an intergenerational worship paradigm,"[28] and young adults (ages 20–35) who, as youth, worshiped with such churches. Ultimately, seventy-five participants from ten churches completed the survey.

The surveys indicated that both the youth and the young adults recognized key benefits of intergenerational worship, including opportunities to develop meaningful cross generational relationships, worshiping with their families, intentional training in worship leadership, and connection with the entire church body. One key finding noted that the majority of the young adults (65 percent) agreed or strongly agreed that they would be less likely to regularly attend church now as a young adult if they "had not attended a church which practiced intergenerational worship as a youth."[29]

Intergenerational Focus on Adult Generations

Several DMin projects (Dale, Fallon, Taylor, Wilkerson) offered key insights on the importance of fostering intergenerational relationships

---

[25] Lee, "The Reformation of the Household Church Worship," 3.
[26] Lee, "The Reformation of the Household Church Worship," abstract.
[27] Lee, "The Reformation of the Household Church Worship," abstract.
[28] Lott, "The Intergenerational Worship Model," 95.
[29] Lott, "The Intergenerational Worship Model," 111.

among the middle and older adults in the congregation.[30] The authors of these projects noted that for churches to thrive, adult generations need opportunities to get to know each other and serve together, and the church leaders (typically persons over forty-five or fifty) must be willing to welcome the next generations into leadership.

Taylor notes that in the small AME church in New York where she ministers, the older generation is "tired, overwhelmed, [and] not really sharing the ministry load" while the "middle generation [middlers] between the elders and the youth is not poised to carry on the work."[31] Taylor's project entailed creating a series of intentional activities to bring together the elders and the middlers in the church to promote working together and building relationships to facilitate the eventual transition of leadership.

Taylor reported very positive findings. She saw evidence that the intergenerational activities she facilitated led to "sustained relationships, the stability of the church, and leadership transition."[32] Fallon, who leads a small church in Ohio, also created opportunities for the adult generations of the church to meet and work together; he reported that these intergenerational experiences effectively "brought seasoned and younger adults together to serve in ministry, which has created new life for the church" and ultimately yielded actual numerical growth.[33]

Intergenerational Focus on Women

Four intergenerational research projects (Fetterman, O'Donoghue, Westmoreland, Wilson) studied how women's ministry leaders can establish and sustain healthy ministries that serve all generations of women in a congregation. Though the projects took different approaches, the findings of the four projects were similar. All noted the importance of generational awareness for intergenerational women's ministries to flourish. For example, Wilson says that "young and old alike need to understand each other's

---

[30] Three other DMin projects focused specifically on the Millennial generation (Houston, Teague, Wallace). The four projects in this subsection did not focus on Millennials per se; they concentrated on younger middle, middle, and older adults rather than the youngest adults, who were primarily Millennials at the time the data for these projects was gathered.
[31] Taylor, "Intergenerational Sharing in the African American Church," 8.
[32] Taylor, "Intergenerational Sharing in the African American Church," 70.
[33] Fallon, "Developing a Strategy for Intergenerational Ministry," 97.

worldviews to help overcome conflicts that can occur between generations."[34] All four also found that successful women's ministries make sure all generations are represented and have equal voices on the leadership teams. They also noted that for intergenerational women's ministries to flourish, the whole church needs to value intergenerationality; according to O'Donoghue, "church leadership also must demonstrate that each generation is valued, celebrated, and necessary."[35]

Fetterman conducted her research with a Presbyterian Church (PCUSA) in Virginia, while Wilson worked with a Pentecostal Church of God in Christ in Illinois. Fetterman and Wilson led all-age gatherings of women with intergenerational activities that included telling their stories, baking bread, listening to speakers from each generation, renovating a house, and retelling biblical stories of cross age female relationships (e.g., Sarah and Hagar, Naomi and Ruth, and Mary and Elizabeth). Fetterman stated that her purpose was to promote cross generational relationships that encouraged each woman to participate in God's work in the world.[36] Wilson's purpose was to build "strong intergenerational relationships between young, middle-aged, and older leaders in order to develop and disciple future leaders for service."[37] The women who participated in the gatherings completed evaluations of the events, and both Fetterman and Wilson concluded their research projects stating that the evaluations indicated their goals had been reached.

Challenges: What Challenges Might Churches Face When They Begin to Implement More Intergenerational Practices?

The researchers who created cross age experiences in their congregations described several challenges they encountered. One theme that appeared in several theses was that the authors found it *difficult to lead toward intergenerationality if they were the lone advocate*. Related to this theme was that

---

[34] Wilson, "Turning the Hearts of Mothers," 126.
[35] O'Donoghue, "Critical Success Factors," 162.
[36] Fetterman, "From Stories to Sisterhood," abstract.
[37] Wilson, "Turning the Hearts of Mothers," 4.

having the senior pastor on board with an intergenerational philosophy was crucial to the success of their project.

On the other hand, some also commented that simply having the senior pastor on board—though necessary—was not sufficient. For a congregation to become more intentionally intergenerational in outlook and practice, *buy-in across the congregation is needed*. Top-down leadership and guidance is important, even crucial, but *winningly inviting congregants into a new paradigm is integral to successfully moving toward more all-age approaches*.

And finally, though all the researchers reported strong positive outcomes for their projects, they also recognized that successfully completing a yearlong intergenerational project did not transform their congregation into one that embraced intergenerationality in full. They acknowledged that *becoming more holistically intergenerational would be an ongoing, continuous process, and that this kind of deep change takes time and patience* along with the recognition that some congregants may not want to integrate the ages, and that ultimately, some may leave.

Recommendations: What Recommendations Do the Researchers Offer to Those Coming Along behind Them?

Along with their challenges, the researchers also offered very specific and practical suggestions to encourage those who desire to bring the generations back together. They suggested that first steps should include *seeking buy-in from congregational ministry leaders and staff first*, noting that congregants need to be hearing the same message from all the ministry staff. After general consensus among the ministry staff has been reached, the researchers suggested *teaching and preaching about the strong biblical and theological support for leaning into more age-integrated practices*, building a strong rationale for such a paradigm change. As congregational interest builds, the authors recommended identifying "early adopters"—those who jump on board quickly—and asking these intergenerational advocates, young and old, to *form a team committed to pursuing intergenerational approaches*, thereby avoiding the "lone advocate" difficulty mentioned above.

A prudent and sensible theme emphasized by several researchers was that churches should pursue a *both/and* rather than an *either/or* outlook; that is, churches should offer both age-integrated and age-specific opportunities. Jettisoning well-loved age-specific programs would disrupt the church, frustrate many congregants, and needlessly set some against more age-integrated approaches. Both approaches can be powerful, and both are biblical.

And finally, most of these now-seasoned intergenerationalists advocated that as church leaders begin to embrace more intergenerational approaches, they should start small with one or two intergenerational events or experiences that highlight the blessings and benefits of growing together spiritually, keeping in mind that the undertaking will be a several-year process requiring deep, adaptive change.

Big Picture Takeaways

Beyond the specific challenges and recommendations shared in the research findings, three surprising insights emerged as I worked through these thirty-five doctoral projects:

Intergenerational Ministry as a Church Growth Tool?

The first surprise (alluded to earlier) is that several of the researchers stated straightforwardly that the reason they were conducting this particular research was that their church was declining or dying, and they hoped that becoming more intergenerational would help revive it.

It distresses me that intergenerational ministry might be seen as a church growth tool. I have observed churches over the past several decades adopt dozens of new approaches, new programs, new methods in order to rescue their declining churches. To me, these attempts raise a red flag that we are trusting in ourselves rather than in God. I see becoming more intentionally intergenerational as embracing God's call to spiritual maturity, recognizing the deep biblical understanding of spiritual formation as a lifelong, *communal* process.[38] On the other hand, I must acknowledge

---

[38] Of course, as we grow in spiritual maturity, one consequence can be numerical growth—yet throughout history, faithfulness has not always yielded larger churches.

that each of the authors who hoped intergenerational ministry would grow their church became deeply committed to the intergenerational enterprise, ultimately becoming convinced of its importance and worth. Thus, their original concern (flawed, perhaps, as it was) prompted them to enter the intergenerational world with all its blessings and benefits; so I must finally conclude with Burns-Marko's practical wisdom gleaned from her research when she says, "there is nothing wrong with using the desperation . . . of a church to introduce intergenerational ministry."[39] Similarly, Fallon concluded in his research that "a crisis is sometimes necessary for change to take place."[40] And, finally, it must be noted that several of these researchers did indeed report actual numerical growth in their findings (e.g., Dale, Douglas, Fallon, Kim, Taylor).

Family Ministry or Intergenerational Ministry?

A second surprising insight arose from the discussions regarding family ministry and intergenerational ministry that appeared in some of the doctoral works. When I teach a family ministry course each spring at Lipscomb, we spend the first week looking at various models of family ministry. Most family ministry descriptions focus primarily on parents and children of the church, and though this would technically be intergenerational, I always encourage seeing intergenerationality as broader than families with children. Therefore, I was pleased (and surprised) that some of the researchers came to this understanding as well. McCrary says, "Family ministry, a popular concept, often gets confused [with] intergenerational ministry; however, intergenerational ministry holds a broader perspective."[41] And Kim writes, "While family ministry aims to involve individual families in the church for the faith formation of school-aged children, intergenerational ministry considers a congregation as a whole to be a family of God."[42]

---

[39] Burns-Marko, "Intergenerational Ministry," 79.
[40] Fallon, "Developing a Strategy for Intergenerational Ministry," 44.
[41] McCrary, "Intentional Intergenerational Ministry Practices," 4.
[42] Kim, "Revive Us Again," 64.

Small Churches—A Disadvantage?

A third surprising insight came from those who had conducted their research in small churches. They each had begun their projects considering small churches to be a disadvantage in some way. As they began to create a variety of intergenerational experiences in their churches, their understanding about small churches changed. Kim says, "I do not perceive a small church to be incompetent and limited any more. Rather, its innate flexibility, adaptability, and possibility provide a fertile soil to grow the new paradigm of intergenerational ministry."[43]

And Eikenberry concludes his strong doctoral project with these moving and convincing words:

> The benefits of intergenerational ministry offer encouragement and hope for smaller congregations such as ours. We do not have the resources of larger churches to provide a program for many different target groups. But we can capitalize on the benefits of an intergenerational approach which allow us to reflect the nature of the church as one body, . . . and reach out to a fractured world in need of Christ and the family of believers.[44]

It was indeed refreshing to read the researchers' comments about the purposes of intergenerational ministry, their insights about family ministry and intergenerational ministry, and their new and hopeful understandings of the advantages of small churches when leading toward intergenerational change.

Conclusion

Clearly, these doctoral research projects offer valuable, tested insights for others venturing into intergenerationality. They share substantive support for the benefits of intergenerationality for cross generational relationships, and they report actual numerical growth, faith transmission across the

---

[43] Kim, "Revive Us Again," 185.
[44] Eikenberry, "Developing an Intentional and Transparent Intergenerational Ministry," 73–74.

generations, and congregational cohesion as well as Christian spiritual formation.

The doctoral students began their research projects with a keen interest in intergenerational ministry. After conducting their research, they concluded their projects as even stronger advocates of the intergenerational enterprise.

These "intergenerationalists" saw their congregations grow; they watched cross generational relationships emerge; they participated in all-age worship that employed the gifts of every generation; they observed intergenerational leadership teams form; they facilitated small groups of ten- to eighty-year-olds reading the Word together, listening for God's voice, and sharing what they were hearing. And very importantly, these doctoral students were firsthand witnesses to the power of intergenerational Christian experiences to spiritually form, bless, and encourage the whole body of Christ.

THEOLOGY IN PRACTICE: QUESTIONS TO CONSIDER

1. What intergenerational research projects in this study resonated with you? What intergenerational research projects do you wish to see on this list in the future?

2. Are there any findings from these research projects that could be applicable in your context?

3. Why is intergenerational research and practice more than a church growth tool? As an intergenerational leader, how might you be bumping up against this assumption within church leadership and participants that intergenerational ministry is a church growth tool, especially when implementing new intergenerational practices?

4. Consider who might be excluded in traditional family ministry. How might we move past traditional family ministry and work to reimagine intergenerational ministry that includes all ages and all people in the newly formed family, as children of God in Christ Jesus (Gal. 3:26–29)?

5. In your context, do you feel that you are at a disadvantage when it comes to practicing intergenerational faith formation? Just as these researchers discovered their small contexts provided "fertile ground" for intergenerational practice, what disadvantages might you reimagine as intergenerational advantages in your context?

CONCLUSION

A CHALLENGE AND INVITATION TO BECOME

VALERIE M. GRISSOM

> *"'How does one become a butterfly?' she asked pensively. You must want to fly so much that you are willing to give up being a caterpillar."*
>
> —Trina Paulus

As seen through the pages of this book, intergenerational leaders attest to the fact that intergenerational ministry is more than a passing church trend or a tool for church growth. Community, rooted in intergenerational Christian practice, forms us in the participation of learning what it means to be the people of God. As a ministry leader, I challenge you to incorporate more than just intergenerational ideas and concepts into your context. I challenge you to reimagine and implement intergenerational Christian practices that aid you and your community in the formation of being God's people—all that God has designed you to be.

Being intergenerational is more than just a way of making sure children or elders are in our space; being intergenerational is a way of life—a way of being God's people—a practice in our *becoming*. The metamorphic, transformational pattern of the butterfly reminds us that we are in process. We are *becoming* more and more like Christ. We are being transformed into a beautiful, new creation: "Behold, all things have *become* new" (2 Cor. 5:17 NKJV—emphasis mine). But we cannot lose sight of our identity. Just as the caterpillar is indeed a butterfly, we are the people of God, destined to reflect all that God has designed us to be. Intergenerational Christian practice reminds us that *all* ages and *all* people are transformed together, in the likeness of Jesus, into the image of God.

Becoming: Voices of Intergenerational Christian Practice

In 2021, I interviewed fourteen intergenerational leaders from North America.[1] Our InterGenerate Team wished to listen to these intergenerational voices—to listen to where God is at work around us. As I interviewed these leaders, I realized that new intergenerational practices continue to spring up. All these intergenerational leaders testified to communities of hope, new emerging practices, and remarkable creativity in handling what some might deem to be immense challenges through the pandemic. As I listened to what God was doing among them, I came to some important realizations regarding intergenerational Christian practice as an intergenerational leader:

1. **Prioritize relationships.** Intergenerational pastor Christina Embree reminded me that "we can't go back to normal" because "our brains and our whole entire lives are fundamentally changed by this pandemic. I don't care if the person in front of you looks like the same person from two years ago. I promise you that they are not the same person."[2] As we emerge from the pandemic, building relationships must be at the forefront of all we do. When I asked all fourteen leaders, every leader emphasized relationships in some way. The consensus: it takes a lot of time and space to listen and rebuild these relationships. And we are not the same

---

[1] Valerie M. Grissom, "Voices of Intergenerational Ministry," fourteen interviews with Sarah Bentley Allred, Jenn Aspilla, Theresa Cho, Christina Embree, Sarah Han, Nancy Going, Danny Kwon, Elizabeth Tamez Méndez, Emily Peck, Doug Powe, Jason Brian Santos, Breen Marie Sipes, Cathy Souto, Amy Yu, October–December 2021.

[2] Christina Embree, "Voices of Intergenerational Ministry," Interview, December 6, 2021.

people, but we are continuing to *become* God's people together; so we must take time—lots of time—to listen and hear together how we have been changed and how God is continuing to work in us.

2. **Analyze rhythms of practice.** During the pandemic, we learned that we need to provide parents and households with rhythms of faith, or practices, that connect us with God and other generations. As we come back together for in-person gatherings, how might we incorporate rhythms of practice for both faith communities and households?

3. **Do not forget that being intergenerational is missional.** Several leaders reminded me that to be missional is to be intergenerational. Sarah Han says when we embrace all generations in the church, we are giving the world a "foretaste" of what the kingdom of God looks like.[3] How can we embody the kingdom of God if we do not value all the generations of God's kingdom? Even further, we cannot fully embody the gospel if we do not include all generations.

4. **Facilitate intergenerational discipleship.** It takes all the generations to practice Christian discipleship. Discipleship cannot be done in a generational vacuum. Just as we learned in the pandemic that "we are in this together," we realize that discipleship requires everyone and every age. Along this line, churches must equip and enable parents and household leaders to see how they are called to continue discipleship throughout the week at home, school, work, and play.

5. **Strive to see intergenerational gifts.** Intergenerational leaders must operate not from a mode of scarcity but by using what they have. They need to take stock of the gifts God has given them. Whether we only have two generations or five generations present, each generation, and all that each person has to offer our community, is a gift to be cherished. Even more, we must look to our culture, whether it be our location, our ethnicity, or our

---

[3] Sarah Han, "Voices of Intergenerational Ministry," Interview, November 24, 2021.

congregational history, and seek to find what gifts we have to cherish and honor. To see each person and every generation as a gift—that is at the heart of being intergenerational.

6. **Encourage curiosity and experimentation.** As intergenerational leaders, we must encourage an ethos where curiosity and experimentation are the norm. Not only does this help us *become* more open to how the Spirit is working in our midst, but it helps us learn to adapt to the ever-changing, somewhat messy, complicated efforts to build an intergenerational community. From charcuterie board nights[4] to grandparent-led Zoom story time[5] to community game night,[6] we must embrace curiosity as we engage with intergenerational experiments.

7. **Visualize a new intergenerational paradigm.** Intergenerational leaders must cast a vision—a new imagination (or reimagination)—for how we might *become* more intergenerational. Often, because we operate in paradigms that emphasize programming based on age and stage, we must learn to inspire new intergenerational imaginations for what could be in the future.

8. **Hold space for diversity and inclusion.** For intergenerational pastor Theresa Cho, part of being intergenerational means opening up space to allow for the inclusion and acceptance of different views regarding ethnicity, race, gender, sexuality, and much more.[7] Intergenerational relationships must allow space for us to live in the tensions that come from all generations practicing faith together.

9. **Empower more generations to lead and participate.** Many of these intergenerational leaders challenged current

---

[4] Christina Embree, "Voices of Intergenerational Ministry," Interview, December 6, 2021. Embree described a night where she and other generations got together to make charcuterie creations for a church event.

[5] Breen Sipes, "Voices of Intergenerational Ministry," Interview, November 29, 2021. Sipes described how her grandparents made a weekly Zoom time during the pandemic with her daughters where they read to their grandchildren, and their grandchildren read to them.

[6] Jason Brian Santos, "Voices of Intergenerational Ministry," Interview, December 2, 2021. Santos began a game night that started with him and his son and expanded past their church and into their community.

[7] Theresa Cho, "Voices of Intergenerational Ministry," Interview, December 9, 2021.

intergenerational leadership to reconsider how we might incorporate leadership and participation from *all* generations. Rather than merely addressing keychain leadership[8] (in which older generations need to hand over the keys of leadership to younger generations, which is definitely an appropriate first step), many of these intergenerational leaders spoke strongly regarding addressing systemic structures in their institutions that hindered younger and older generations from leading and participating in communities of faith together. Jenn Aspilla, who works with and teaches many Generation Z students in her seminary, believes this kind of including and empowering might mean changing how the church actually uses technology and media to include better ways of participation.[9] Similarly, Cho wondered how we might analyze our ministry in a new way to see the "fingerprints" of different generations in our practices and histories of ministry.[10] Additionally, Embree studies how churches might have a system for addressing the equal representation of generations in leadership in ministry structures. All these efforts express a need for us, as intergenerational leaders, to empower *all* generations to lead and participate.

10. **Resist the urge to go back to the old normal.** So many of these leaders insisted with urgency: "We can't and should not go back to the way it was before!" Instead, several leaders emphasized leading with a nonanxious presence, and pausing, learning to only pick up the things that are life-giving to all generations. Practicing discernment, rather than leading in survival mode, *becomes* an important practice for intergenerational leaders as we move forward.

---

[8] See "Unlock Keychain Leadership," in Kara Powell, Jake Mulder, and Brad Griffin, *Growing Young: Six Essential Strategies to Help Young People Discover and Love Your Church* (Grand Rapids: Baker Books, 2016), 50–87. Here, the authors address how older leaders might put the keys of leadership in younger generations' hands.

[9] Jenn Aspilla, "Voices of Intergenerational Ministry," November 15, 2021. In this interview, I learned about upcoming technology for the church, including the Metaverse (virtual communication).

[10] Theresa Cho, "Voices of Intergenerational Ministry," Interview, December 9, 2021.

These intergenerational leaders reminded me that intergenerational Christian practice continues to re-create and evolve, that intergenerational transformation is alive and well, because God's people are alive and well! God continues to do "a new thing" (Isa. 43:19) in our intergenerational communities of practice. "Intergenerational" is not going away. It may look different, but "intergenerational" continues to flap its wings, practicing ascent, practicing flight.

Becoming: What We Are to Become

Just as the butterfly in my opening story did not wake up able to fly, in the same way, intergenerational ministry does not just happen. The caterpillar did not say, "Boom, I'm a butterfly!" But we, like the butterfly, are called "out of darkness"—out of the cocoon—and into God's "marvelous light" (1 Pet. 2:9 ESV). In our journey of *becoming*, we go through transitions, failures, transformations—all in many steps and with lots of practice. Not every movement is graceful. We experience flutters. We experience falls. We even have to spin through dark cocoon-like spaces before we can experience the beauty of *becoming*. But the goal is worth it. We are created to *become* God's people—to live out the fullness of being *all* of the church, with *all* ages participating in the practice of *becoming* the people of God.

Becoming: A Challenge and Invitation

> "Do not be conformed to this world, but be transformed [metamorphosis] by the renewing of your minds, so that you may discern what is the will of God—what is good and acceptable and perfect."
>
> —Romans 12:2 NRSV

As I mentioned before, we, the people of God, are called to be transformed, to go through the metamorphic-like transformation of intergenerational Christian practice, to *become* more like Christ, to *become* the people of God. Directly after Romans 12:2 (above), Paul calls people to be transformed through communal Christian practices, telling the Romans that "everyone" should not "think of yourself more highly than you ought to think" (v. 3). He provides further instruction for collective Christian practice in his faith community: "For as in one body we have many members, and not all the members have the same function, so we, who are many, are one body in Christ, and individually we are members one of another. We have gifts that differ according to the grace given to us . . ." (v. 4–6). And Paul's list of mutually shared Christian practices continues: love, rejoicing in hope, being patient in suffering, persevering in prayer, contributing to those in need, extending hospitality to strangers, blessing the ones who persecute you, grieving with those who grieve, forgiving instead of seeking vengeance (vv. 9–21). Here, I find Paul reimagining their Christian practice, taking on the metamorphic transformation of Christ—to *become* God's people.

Using this Romans 12 passage, consider the various generations and ages in your Christian community and extend these words to them. Imagine, if you were Paul, how might you extend these Christian practices to all ages of your faith community? God is calling me and you to reimagine and implement a community of Christian practice, just as Paul did—to participate in the transformative, metamorphic, formational work of *becoming* the people of God.

As leaders among the people of God, we are called to *become. Becoming* takes place through Christian practice. To be intergenerational is to be formed in relational practice—all ages shaped together to be the people of God. Today, I challenge you to *become*. Participate. Engage. Cultivate. Reimagine. Study. Research. Practice. Fail. Begin again. Continue in your calling to *become* God's people, participating in the formational work of intergenerational Christian practice.

Even though the stakes were high for the Romans, Paul called them into miraculous transformation through reimagined, mutually shared, communal Christian practices. In the same way, God is calling us, as leaders, to participate in and facilitate communal cross age Christian practices—to *become*, to be formed—to be God's people. How is God calling you to join in intergenerational Christian practice? Perhaps in your readings or discussions, the Spirit has nudged you in a certain direction. I encourage you; I challenge you to start flapping those wings, to begin the practice of flight. God is calling you—challenging you—to participate in intergenerational

Christian practice. You are uniquely positioned, gifted, and experienced to reimagine and implement new intergenerational Christian practice in your context. Will you join us in this important work? Will you participate in what God is doing, forming *all* generations—*all* ages—in the *becoming* of God's people?

SELECTED BIBLIOGRAPHY

Allen, Holly Catterton, ed. *InterGenerate: Transforming Churches through Intergenerational Ministry*. Abilene, TX: Abilene Christian University Press, 2018.

Allen, Holly Catterton, and Christine Lawton Ross. *Intergenerational Christian Formation: Bringing the Whole Church Together in Ministry, Community and Worship*. Downers Grove, IL: InterVarsity Press, 2012.

Allen, Holly Catterton, Christine Lawton, and Cory Seibel. *Intergenerational Christian Formation: Bringing the Whole Church Together in Ministry, Community and Worship*. 2nd ed. Downers Grove, IL: InterVarsity Press, 2023.

Barton, Ruth Haley. *Sacred Rhythms: Arranging Our Lives for Spiritual Transformation*. Downers Grove, IL: InterVarsity Press, 2006.

Bass, Dorothy C., ed. *Practicing Our Faith: A Way of Life for a Searching People*. The Practices of Faith Series. Minneapolis: Fortress Press, 2019.

Bolsinger, Tod. *Canoeing the Mountains: Christian Leadership in Uncharted Territory*. Downers Grove, IL: InterVarsity Press, 2015.

Bonhoeffer, Dietrich. *Life Together: The Classic Exploration of Christian Community*. New York: HarperOne, 1954.

Calhoun, Adele Ahlberg. *The Spiritual Disciplines Handbook, Practices that Transform Us*. Rev. and expanded ed. Downers Grove, IL: InterVarsity Press, 2015.

Copley, Lora A., and Elizabeth Vander Haagen. *Teach Us to Pray: Scripture-Centered Family Worship through the Year*. Grand Rapids: Calvin College Press, 2016.

DeSilva, David A. *Sacramental Life: Spiritual Formation through the Book of Common Prayer*. Downers Grove, IL: InterVarsity Press, 2008.

Faith Practices: Holy Habits That Help Us Love God and Our Neighbor, Listen to the Spirit, and Become More Like Jesus. Grand Rapids: Faith Alive Christian Resources, 2022.

The Faith Practices Project. https://www.crcna.org/FaithPracticesProject.

Fleming, David L. *Draw Me into Your Friendship: The Spiritual Exercises; A Literal Translation & a Contemporary Reading*. Chestnut Hill, MA: Jesuit Conference, 2016.

Ford, David F. *The Shape of Living: Spiritual Directions for Everyday Life*. Grand Rapids: Baker Books, 2004.

Grenz, Stanley J. *Theology for the Community of God*. Grand Rapids: Eerdmans, 1994.

Hawn, C. Michael. *One Bread, One Body: Exploring Cultural Diversity in Worship*. Herndon, VA: Alban Institute, 2003.

Hellerman, Joseph. *When the Church Was a Family: Recapturing Jesus' Vision for Authentic Christian Community*. Nashville: B & H Publishing, 2009.

Kallenberg, Brad J. *Live to Tell: Evangelism for a Postmodern Age*. Grand Rapids: Brazos Press, 2002.

Law, Eric H. F. *The Wolf Shall Dwell with the Lamb: A Spirituality for Leadership in a Multicultural Community*. St. Louis: Chalice Press, 1993.

Newman, Barbara J., and Betty Grit. *Accessible Gospel, Inclusive Worship*. Wyoming, MI: All Belong (CLC Network), 2016.

Park, M. Sydney, Soong-Chan Rah, and Al Tizon. *Honoring the Generations: Learning with Asian North American Congregations*. Valley Forge, PA: Judson Press, 2012.

Pavlovitz, John. *A Bigger Table: Building Messy, Authentic, and Hopeful Spiritual Community*. Louisville, KY: Westminster John Knox Press, 2017.

Pohl, Christine D. *Living into Community: Cultivating Practices That Sustain Us*. Grand Rapids: Eerdmans, 2012.

Roberto, John. *Lifelong Faith: Formation for All Ages and Generations*. New York: Church Publishing Incorporated, 2022.

Seibel, Cory, ed. *Engage All Generations: A Strategic Toolkit for Creating Intergenerational Faith Communities*. Abilene, TX: Abilene Christian University Press, 2021.

Sinek, Simon. *Start with Why: How Great Leaders Inspire Everyone to Take Action*. New York: Penguin, 2009.

Sittser, Gerald L. *Resilient Faith: How the Early Christian "Third Way" Changed the World*. Grand Rapids: Brazos Press, 2019.

Smith, David I., and James K. A. Smith. *Teaching and Christian Practices: Reshaping Faith & Learning*. Grand Rapids: Eerdmans, 2011.

Smith, James K. A. *You Are What You Love: The Spiritual Power of Habit*. Grand Rapids: Brazos Press, 2016.
Turner, Rachel. *It Takes a Church to Raise a Parent: Creating a Culture Where Parenting for Faith Can Flourish*. Abingdon: Bible Reading Fellowship, 2018.
Warren, Tish Harrison. *Liturgy of the Ordinary: Sacred Practices in Everyday Life*. Downers Grove, IL: InterVarsity Press Books, 2016.
Webber, Robert E. *The Divine Embrace: Recovering the Passionate Spiritual Life*. Grand Rapids: Baker Books, 2006.
Westerhoff, John H. *Will Our Children Have Faith?* 3rd rev. ed. Harrisburg, PA: Morehouse Publishing, 2012.
Wirzba, Norman. *Living the Sabbath: Discovering the Rhythms of Rest and Delight*. Grand Rapids: Brazos Press, 2006.
Wright, Christopher J. H. *The Mission of God's People: A Biblical Theology of the Church's Mission*. Edited by Jonathan Lunde. Grand Rapids: Zondervan, 2010.

CONTRIBUTORS

Holly Catterton Allen, PhD, retired in 2021 from her position as Professor of Christian Ministries and Family Science at Lipscomb University in Nashville, Tennessee. In retirement, her areas of interest continue to be intergenerational ministry as well as children's spiritual formation. Dr. Allen's books include *Intergenerational Christian Formation: Bringing the Whole Church Together in Ministry, Community, and Worship*, 2nd edition (InterVarsity Press, 2023); *Forming Resilient Children: The Role of Spiritual Formation for Healthy Development* (InterVarsity Press, 2021); *InterGenerate: Transforming Churches through Intergenerational Ministry* (Abilene Christian University Press, 2018); and *Nurturing Children's Spirituality: Christian Perspectives and Best Practices* (Cascade, 2008). In 2015–21, she chaired two biennial, international, cross denominational conferences: InterGenerate Conference and the Children's Spirituality Summit.

Sarah Bentley Allred is a Senior Formation Associate for the Department of Lifelong Learning at Virginia Theological Seminary (VTS). Before joining Lifelong Learning, Sarah served as Director of Children and Youth Ministries for four years and then completed the MDiv program at VTS with a focus on Christian formation. She is passionate about children's spirituality, intergenerational worship, and small-church formation. She loves local coffee shops, board games, the beach, and exploring new places with her husband, Richard, their daughter, Eleanor, and their furry child, Grace.

Gareth Crispin, PhD, is a lecturer in Practical Theology at Cliff College, UK, where he is also Program Director for the BA in Mission and Ministry. He writes, publishes, and teaches across a wide range of subjects in Youth, Children and Families (YCF) ministry but has a particular focus on intergenerational ministry—his PhD thesis, from the University of Manchester, UK, was on impediments and encouragements to intergenerationality and family ministry. He serves on the Executive Board of the International Association for the Study of Youth Ministry and is Co-director of Generation, the Cliff College centre for the Study of YCF mission and ministry.

David M. Csinos is associate professor of practical theology at Atlantic School of Theology in Halifax, Nova Scotia. He is author and editor of many books, the most recent of which is *A Gospel for All Ages: Teaching and Preaching with the Whole Church* (Fortress Press, 2022). Dave is a sought-after speaker in the areas of children's and youth ministry, intergenerational faith formation, homiletics, culture, and ministry innovation. He holds a PhD from the University of St. Michael's College in Toronto.

Karen DeBoer is the Resource Developer for Faith Formation Ministries, for whom she curates and creates several ministry resources, including online toolkits (*The Intergenerational Church, Family Faith Formation*, and more), family resources (*Dwell at Home*), ministry blogs (*The Network*), a podcast (*Open to Wonder*), and intergenerational faith practice resources (*The Faith Practice Project*). She is the author of *Home Grown Handbook for Christian Parenting* and a contributing editor of *You're Invited: A Week of Devotions for Families on the Lord's Supper,* God's Big Story Cards, and *Jesse Tree: God's Big Advent Story*. She makes her home in Kitchener-Waterloo, Ontario.

Rev. Roberta J. Egli is the Executive Director of All Age Faith Formation, a 501c3 nonprofit organization that supports ecumenical congregations to start and then sustain an intergenerational worship experience. Since organizing in 2017, Messy Church has been the primary model used in equipping all-age faith formative experiences. The network of Messy Churches in the USA has grown to over 250 local churches from 20 Christian faith traditions in 47 states. She received her MDiv from Pacific School of Religion before her ordination in The United Methodist Church, where she served as a lead pastor prior to moving to her current role. Prior to her transition to pastoral leadership, she worked as an RN for twenty years in a variety of settings. She lives in Eugene, Oregon.

Wes Gallagher is currently pursuing a Doctorate of Ministry in Leadership and Spiritual Formation at Portland Seminary. He has ministered in Churches of Christ in Middle Tennessee for two decades, with most of that time devoted to child and family ministry. He earned a BS in secondary education from Tennessee Tech University and an MDiv from Lipscomb University, where he studied children's spirituality under Holy Allen. Wes lives in Cookeville, Tennessee, with his wife, Stephanie, and six children: Haylee, Cassie, Brayden, Bryson, Baron, and Kerrigan.

Valerie M. Grissom, MDiv, DWS (Doctor of Worship Studies), is a certified pastor in the Northwest Coast Presbytery, near Seattle, Washington. As a worship leader and pastor for over nineteen years in a variety of denominations and ecumenical settings, Valerie is passionate about worship renewal in the church. Valerie's research, writing, speaking, coaching, and mentoring focus on intergenerational and intercultural worship. Her personal mission statement underlies her intergenerational work: "to help every person feel seen, heard, and loved by God." Valerie and her husband, Ben, along with their four children, make their home on Whidbey Island and enjoy playing outdoors in the Pacific Northwest, spoiling their forty chickens, enjoying only the best coffee (Seattle coffee, of course!), camping, hiking, and going to the beach.

Rev. Elizabeth Tamez Méndez, PhD, is the founder and Executive Director of New Generation3 (NG3). Since 2005, NG3 has been dedicated to training leaders, conducting research, and providing consulting services in the United States and abroad. Through her work, Elizabeth merges her passion for seeing youth thrive and the lessons from her thirty years of global ministry experience. Her commitment to developing practical resources centers on bridging the world of academia with the needs of practitioners in multicultural settings. In NG3's upcoming book series *JUNTOS: Six Transformational Practices of Latino Churches and Youth*, through stories, research insights, and reflection questions, readers have a guided space to consider easy-to-integrate ministry and leadership practices that foster healthy intergenerational relationships in the church (JUNTOSseries.org).

Jim Merhaut, MSEd, PCC, is the Founder of Coaching to Connect, a coaching and consulting service focused on leadership development. Jim is certified as a leadership and life coach and as a reinvention practitioner. He is known internationally for his coaching, speaking, and expertise in lifelong faith formation. He holds an MS degree in Religious Education from Duquesne University. He has published and contributed to several books and other publications, including *Generations Together* and *Engage All Generations*. With decades of experience in intergenerational ministries and leadership development, Merhaut offers keynotes, retreats, and workshops on a variety of themes. He lives in Youngstown, Ohio.

Wilson McCoy, DMin, serves as a minister at the College Hills Church of Christ in Lebanon, Tennessee. Over the last twelve years with this church, some of his responsibilities have included working with young adults, preaching and teaching, adult formation, and small groups. Before College Hills, Wilson worked with churches in Tennessee, Texas, and Australia. His Doctorate of Ministry with Lipscomb University focused on intergenerational spiritual formation, and that work resulted in contributing a chapter to the book *Intergenerate: Transforming Churches through Intergenerational Ministry*. Wilson continues to write, speak, and consult with churches interested in intergenerational ministry. You can find out more and connect with Wilson at drwilsonmccoy.com.

Johannah Myers, DMin, is the Associate Director for Messy Church USA as well as the Director of Disciples Formation at Aldersgate United Methodist Church in Greenville, South Carolina. Her time at Duke Divinity School helped shape her call to disciple formation for all ages. She introduced Messy Church to her congregation in 2013, starting what has become a fabulously Messy journey into intergenerational ministry. In

2019, Johannah completed her Doctor of Ministry degree through Wesley Theological Seminary. Her doctoral project focused on intergenerational, hands-on faith formation in small groups using the foundational values of Messy Church as a rule of life.

Robert Pendergraft joined the University of Mary Hardin-Baylor faculty in the fall of 2016, where he currently serves as Associate Professor and James and Lena Hagan Chair of Church Music. An ordained Southern Baptist minister, Robert is passionate about getting the entire congregation actively participating in corporate worship. He carries out this passion weekly as the Associate Pastor of Music Ministries at First Baptist Church of Salado. Robert holds bachelor's and master's degrees in Music Education from Samford University in Birmingham, Alabama, and the Doctor of Philosophy degree in Church Music from Southwestern Baptist Theological Seminary. Robert was the recipient of an inaugural Teacher/Scholar Grant from the Calvin Institute for Christian Worship in 2019. He previously served as President of the Southern Baptist Church Music Conference and is on the Steering Committee for the Evangelical Theological Society of Biblical Worship Section.

Breen Marie Sipes is usually an ELCA pastor and is currently a full-time parent overseeing her children's education at an online STEM academy. She has been engaged in intergenerational experiments intuitively since 2005 and intentionally since 2015, and she is especially interested in the gift that introducing an intergenerational framework of ministry can be to small congregations. Breen is a founding member of the Nebraska Synod, ELCA Growing God's Generous Generations (4G) core team, which curates resources and provides support at the intersection of generosity and intergenerational ministry. Breen is also a leader with Music that Makes Community, seeing music and vulnerable shared leadership as a key pivot point for intergenerational interaction. She also curates Taking Worship Home, a website dedicated to providing resources to bring what happens in worship into our lives, and Feed My Faith, a website that furnishes faith formation resources for all ages and stages.

Linda Staats is a national speaker, workshop leader, curriculum writer, author, consultant, leadership coach, and Founder of HomeGrown Faith. With an MS degree in Human Development and the Family and minor degrees in Child Development and Gerontology, Linda brings a life span lens to ministry. Her passion and approach to all-age interaction is reflected in The Generosity Project, a resource that provides an intergenerational approach to discipleship and stewardship. Linda has held positions in the Evangelical Lutheran Church of America church-wide organization, served as Assistant to the Bishop for two regional ELCA offices, and coordinator for faith formation and household ministry in a large metropolitan congregation. She and her extended family represent six living generations.

Rachel Turner is the founder of Parenting for Faith and has worked in churches in the UK for over fifteen years as a Family Life Pastor, Children's Pastor, and a Youth Pastor. She continues to consult, speak at conferences, and run training days for church leaders, parents, and families around the world. Rachel is the author of nine books as well as the Parenting for Faith course. For more on the work of Parenting for Faith, go to www.parentingforfaith.org.

ACKNOWLEDGMENTS

I wish to express my gratitude to each contributor of this book. All your unique gifts, knowledge, experience, creativity, and energy regarding intergenerational practice have inspired me throughout this process. I am forever changed by experiencing your dedication to intergenerational ministry.

Thank you to the InterGenerate Team of the 2021 Conference, who supported this book and have contributed in many ways from its inception:

> Holly Catterton Allen
> Sharon Galgay Ketcham
> Wilson McCoy
> John Roberto
> Dawn Rundman
> Cory Seibel
> Linda E. Staats
> Lesli Van Milligen

Thank you to all the participants of our InterGenerate/Children's Spirituality Summit 2021 Conference. This book is a result of your collaborations, research, presentations, and practice as intergenerational ministry leaders around the world. I am so glad to be on this intergenerational journey with you.

Also, thank you to the publishing team at Abilene Christian University Press, especially Jason Fikes and Mary Hardegree, who have helped me so much in the process of getting this book to print.

I am also very grateful for the advice and mentorship of Holly Catterton Allen during this project. I appreciate her help in final proofreading and editing, as well.

Very importantly, I must express gratitude to my husband Ben and children Bjorn, Promise-Rose, Roryk, and Margreta, my cheerleaders, who have supported and encouraged me throughout the process of editing this book.

Above all, thank you to God who gives me strength and endurance to finish what I have been called to do. In the completion of this book, God gave me this verse, and I have used these words as I prayed over the contributors in our writing and editing of each page. Now, I pray for the readers of this book (for you!) that God would continue to bless you and strengthen you as you continue in your intergenerational calling:

> Every time you cross my mind, I break out in exclamations of thanks to God. Each exclamation is a trigger to prayer. I find myself praying for you with a glad heart. I am so pleased that you have continued on in this with us, believing and proclaiming God's Message, from the day you heard it right up to the present. There has never been the slightest doubt in my mind that the God who started this great work in you would keep at it and bring it to a flourishing finish on the very day Christ Jesus appears. (Phil. 1:3–6 *The Message*)

Soli Deo Gloria! All glory to God!

Valerie

InterGenerate

Transforming Churches through Intergenerational Ministry

ISBN 9781684261505

Edited by
Holly Catterton Allen

Christian leaders everywhere are asking, "How can we bring the generations back together." *InterGenerate* responds with new perspectives on generational theory, fresh biblical and theological insights, and practical steps for developing innovative practices in your ministries. The book is filled with a broad spectrum of voices—men and women ranging in age from millennials to boomers, representing multiple countries and over a dozen denominations.

"InterGenerate explores what church can be: an energetic, inclusive body of believers going about their mission from God. With honest stories about intergenerational practices—both the challenges and the encouraging outcomes—this book will help leaders shape communities that reflect the whole body of Christ working as one."

—**Rev. Dr. John Capper,** Director of Learning and Teaching, University of Divinity, Australia

1-877-816-4455 toll free
www.acupressbooks.com

Check out the other books in this series!

ENGAGE ALL GENERATIONS

A Strategic Toolkit for Creating Intergenerational Faith Communities

Edited by CORY SEIBEL

ISBN 978-1-68426-321-9

Everyone Can Learn, Worship, and Serve Together

Engage All Generations suggests how every church can build on its potential and become a more vibrant witness of God's Kingdom. Divided into three sections, the book focuses on key growth edges in the unfolding conversation about intergenerational ministry: "Learning and Growing Together," "Praying and Playing Together," and "Leading and Changing Together."

Practical, accessible, encouraging, and thought-provoking, this book provides the crucial next building block in our understanding of intergenerational ministry. It is sure to benefit congregations already fostering intergenerational approaches and those desiring to experiment with becoming intentionally intergenerational.

"*Engage All Generations* offers a menu ranging from philosophical and theological foundations to practical ideas and tools for ministry. It is an important addition to the conversation about intergenerational ministry. I will be returning to this table for nourishment again and again."

—**Dr. Tori Smit (DEdMin),** Regional Minister for Faith Formation, Synod of Central, Northeastern Ontario and Bermuda, The Presbyterian Church in Canada, Toronto

1-877-816-4455 toll free
www.acupressbooks.com

Dive further into engaging children in spirituality!

Children's Ministry and the Spiritual Child

Practical, Formation-Focused Ministry

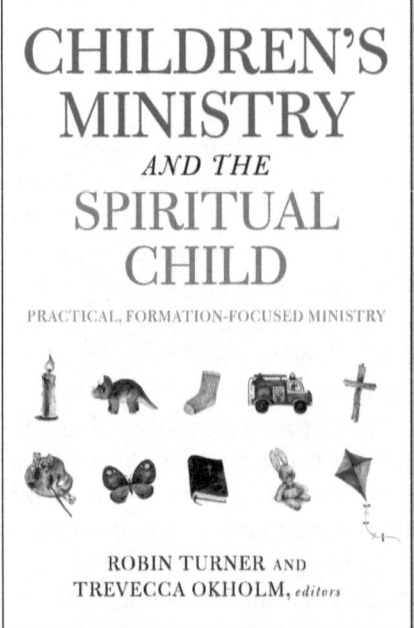

ISBN 978-1-68426-213-7

Edited by
ROBIN TURNER and TREVECCA OKHOLM

God Is at Work in the Lives of Children.

Most ministers are looking for inspiration but feel overwhelmed. *Children's Ministry and the Spiritual Child* offers practical tools with evidence-based research in an easy-to-read format, perfect for engaging and equipping passionate yet busy children's ministry leaders. Learn from the wisdom and research of some of the leading thinkers in the field of children's spirituality.

"*From a strong emphasis on receptive listening, cultivating internal motivation, and building developmental relationships to strategies for responding to difficult behaviors and trauma, each chapter offers connections with scripture and social science research.*"

—**Rev. Karen-Marie Yust,** Rowe Professor of Christian Education, Union Presbyterian Seminary, chair of the International Association for Children's Spirituality, author of *Real Kids, Real Faith*

1-877-816-4455 toll free
www.acupressbooks.com

www.ingramcontent.com/pod-product-compliance
Lightning Source LLC
Chambersburg PA
CBHW020519080526
44583CB00013B/666